Alice M. Fairhurst
Lisa L. Fairhurst

Effective Teaching
Effective Learning

Making the Personality Connection in Your Classroom

Davies-Black Publishing

Palo Alto, California

Published by Davies-Black, an imprint of Consulting Psychologists Press, Inc., 3803 E. Bayshore Road, Palo Alto, CA 94303; 1-800-624-1765.

Special discounts on bulk quantities of Davies-Black books are available to corporations, professional associations, and other organizations. For details, contact the Director of Book Sales at Davies-Black Publishing, an imprint of Consulting Psychologists Press, Inc., 3803 East Bayshore Road, Palo Alto, CA 94303; 415-691-9123; Fax 415-988-0673.

01 00 99 98 97   10 9 8 7 6 5 4 3 2
Printed in the United States of America

Cover illustration © Diana Ong/SuperStock

Library of Congress Cataloging-in-Publication Data
Fairhurst, Alice M.
    Effective teaching, effective learning : making the personality connection in your classroom / Alice M. Fairhurst and Lisa L. Fairhurst. — 1st ed.
        p.   cm.
    Inclues bibliographical references and index.
    ISBN 0-89106-078-2
    1. Teaching.   2. Learning, Psychology of.   3. Cognitive styles.
    4. Typology (Psychology)   I. Fairhurst, Lisa L.   II. Title
LB1027.F245   1995
371.3′28′2—dc20   95-8815
                                                                        CIP
FIRST EDITION
    First printing 1995

Dedicated to all
teachers who strive
to improve their
craft

Contents

Preface

We have written this book for you if you have ever asked yourself: How can I reach most of my students more of the time? Are there any simple ways of reaching students who are hard to teach? What makes an exceptional teacher exceptional? How can I increase the effectiveness of my teaching to create more effective learning in my classroom?

During our nearly thirty years of combined teaching experience, we have found that the related theories of temperament and personality type have provided us with the tools to find practical answers to these very questions.

In this book, we share the principles and applications that we have tested while teaching grades one through twelve and college-level students. Our experience has shown that these theories work with all students, including those who are ethnic minorities, disadvantaged, or immigrants. Since teaching requires constant communication between people, the assistance these theories have provided us in understanding different perspectives has proved invaluable. They also have helped us to identify which teaching techniques work most effectively with which students.

We decided to write this book to show how temperament and personality type theories can be applied to the field of education in a way that is accessible to teachers who may or may not be familiar with these theories. We believe that teachers can find the same level of success that we have experienced using them. We have both had teachers and parents ask us for advice on how to work with particular students. By identifying the temperament and personality type of such students, we have helped parents and teachers increase their effectiveness in working with them. These same people often tell us how amazed they are with the results they achieve.

We have designed this book to provide teachers with ideas they can use *now*. Unlike other books or classes that require teachers to completely rethink their educational methods, this book offers ideas that can be easily integrated with current teaching methods. Unlike many other teaching approaches, nearly all of the strategies we describe in this book require little time or money. By using this book, teachers will not need to change dramatically what they do naturally; rather, they will be able to add carefully chosen strategies to their repertoire, enabling them to increase their teaching impact.

By applying the principles of temperament and personality type theory, teachers can communicate with students in ways that will improve their ability to learn. The suggestions in this book for applying these theories are designed to help teachers discover what they can do to motivate hard-to-reach students and how to choose the most effective strategies for working with them.

It is not just teachers who can benefit from applying personality theories to education: School administrators can learn how to best encourage teachers to use a variety of teaching techniques in order to reach more students; counselors can help students and teachers focus on positive ways to improve communication and interaction; parents can better understand their children as students and help them maximize their learning potential; and students can understand their teachers more so that they can better communicate their needs to their teachers.

It is our hope that the information in this book will help everyone associated with education to achieve more effective teaching and more effective learning.

Acknowledgments

In passing on the knowledge of humankind, teachers have a great impact on the lives of others. There are many who have contributed to perspectives on human variation and learning. Those who have had a significant impact on our thinking have been David Keirsey, Marilyn Bates, Linda V. Berens, Katharine Briggs, Isabel Briggs Myers, and Mary McCaulley. Without the late Marilyn Bates, who encouraged Alice to take a master's in counseling under her direction and that of David Keirsey, this book would not have been written. Without Richard Fairhurst, who discovered Lisa, the connection between the coauthors of this book would never have occurred. We often do not know the ways in which we impact others.

Personal thanks go to Richard for his patience in editing and to the professionals at Davies-Black Publishing, a division of Consulting Psychologists Press. We have received support from members of the Association for Psychological Type, the International Type Users

Organization, the Center for the Application of Psychological Type, and Temperament Research Institute.

Our gratitude goes to teachers, writers, colleagues, friends, and relatives, upon whose wisdom and support we have drawn. We'd like to specifically acknowledge the contributions of Judie Apablaza, Betty Bainton, Janice L. Baldwin, Linda V. Berens, Mildred Bettingen, Becky and Roger Bissell, Mary Bowman-Kruhm, Sandra Brock, Sally A. Campbell, Pam Clute, David Dial, David Fairhurst, Richenda Fairhurst, Martha Ann Griesel, Lynn Hancock, Sandra Harvey, Denise Howard, Peter Malone, Sara Moore, Thomas F. Penderghast, Alice Raymond, Catherine Russell, Sandy Smith, Lola Taylor, and Linda Valenzuela.

PART ONE

Understanding the Role of Personality in Education

Teachers generally take a lot of pride in their craft. They enter the field of teaching because they want to positively influence students to be prepared to take their place in and contribute to society. They might express their objective in various ways, such as:

I help students become good citizens through gaining knowledge.

I want to see each student reach his or her own potential.

I want students to be skillful and to enjoy what they are doing.

I challenge students to search for the truth.

Sometimes the field of teaching proposes one "right" way to reach these objectives. Usually this "right" way reaches some students and not others, and teachers find themselves frustrated in their attempts to provide the best environment for all students. Then the pendulum swings, and a new "right" way is proposed. Usually, this method works for a different segment of the student population, while it neglects others.

Teachers have long realized that their students have different personality styles. For example, one student may be very outgoing and enjoy learning through discussion; another student may be quiet and prefer learning through solitary activities such as reading books. The objective of this book is to provide teachers with a method for observing their students' behavior and connecting that behavior with teaching techniques that are likely to work with particular students.

This section will discuss the benefits of learning about the connection between personality type theory and learning styles. Chapters two and three discuss two related personality theories: temperament and type. As each theory is presented, teachers will be shown classroom examples of student behavior exhibiting particular personality styles. These two theories will provide the necessary background that will enable teachers to apply personality theory and the benefits inherent in understanding differences in their own classrooms.

Chapter 1

Using Personality Theories to Teach and Understand Students

Those of us in education are too often seeking the one perfect method that we can use to teach every student in the classroom. Many different techniques have been tried only to be soon discarded. Reading, for example, has been especially affected by new waves of "the best way" to teach. In California in the 1940s, the most effective way to teach reading was thought to be through phonics. By the 1950s, teachers were encouraged to use the "look-say" method, which involved looking at how a word was shaped and then saying it aloud. The phonics method worked well for auditory learners, while the look-say method was geared toward learners who were good at identifying visual shapes. Some students had problems with one or both methods. Kinesthetic students learned best by manipulating objects such as 3-D letters.

In the 1960s, the "reading through writing" method became popular. With this technique, students drew pictures, then described the pictures to their teacher, who wrote the student's words at the bottom of the pictures. The students then learned to read their own words. This was fun for artistic and verbal students, but quite painful for the less artistic and verbally shy. All of these techniques, as well as others, have been recycled in waves and each touted from time to time as the "best" way to teach children to read.

The same problem has occurred in the field of mathematics. The pendulum swings back and forth from "back to the basics" to "new math." The back-to-basics method works well with students who learn math best when taught in a step-by-step fashion with plenty of examples and only little explanation of the underlying principles. The new math method is designed for students who want to understand the why of math. It asks students to make logical guesses and inferences about problem-solving methods so that they can discover the rules for themselves. Although this method is intended to encourage development of critical thinking skills, it can leave some students feeling incompetent. Likewise, students who do well with new math often find the back-to-basics approach boring and unclear.

Each of these reading or mathematics techniques was tried because it offered an effective teaching technique for at least some students. But none of the techniques worked for all students. The same is true for other educational waves: manipulatives, mastery learning, computer-based learning, contract learning, discovery learning, cooperative learning, touch math, humanities core curriculum, and so on. Instead of being caught up with the latest fad, isn't it time we started identifying which techniques work with which types of students? We need to change our focus to look at how we could combine the different teaching methods to effectively reach *all* students.

Why Use Personality Theories in Education?

The most useful tools we have found for determining which techniques work best with which students come from two related theories of human personality: temperament theory, and the theory of psychological type. Both theories have helped us better understand core student needs and select teaching strategies that reach more students more effectively.

Many teachers are familiar with other learning theories. One theory describes learners as auditory, visual, or kinesthetic. Howard Gardner (1983) describes learners as verbal/linguistic, logical/mathematical, spatial, musical, interpersonal, and intrapersonal.* These theories are valuable in helping teachers recognize and respond to differences in learning styles. However, like most available learning theories, these theories focus primarily on the student's learning process without taking into account the needs and skills of the teacher. Temperament and personality type theories allow teachers to evaluate themselves as well as their students in ways that lead to effective learning experiences that can help meet everyone's needs.

According to temperament and personality type theories, people learn and teach differently because they *are* different. By learning the necessary techniques, teachers will be able to recognize the strengths that their style brings to the teaching process and learn how to communicate with people who have other styles.

Learning about temperament and personality type will also help teachers appreciate themselves as teachers and better understand their students and identify their strengths. It is important that teachers understand that there is a wide range of acceptable behavior. Messages to students that they are not okay, just because they are different from the teacher's perception of what is "normal," can damage the student's self-esteem. Temperament and type theories can help teachers better tap into their own, as well as their students' strengths.

These two personality theories are compatible with just about every other educational theory and can be used in conjunction with them. Unlike many other systems of educational thought that require teachers to learn and implement a large quantity of new material before any part of the system can be effective, teachers can try out a single teaching strategy suggested in this book and benefit from its use. For instance, some students may experience difficulties with certain activities and may benefit from having some activities customized for them. By understanding

---

*In his book, *Frames of Mind: The Theory of Multiple Intelligences*, Gardner claims that Western education emphasizes verbal/linguistic and logical/mathematical intelligence and pays little attention to the others.

a student's preferred learning style, a teacher can more quickly identify an effective teaching technique for that student.

For example, one teacher who was tutoring a first grader in reading and writing asked the student to write a two-sentence story about a picture she had drawn. The student seemed paralyzed and unable to begin the assignment. By applying the principles of temperament and personality type, the teacher was able to realize that the student could not begin the assignment until she knew the "right" way to do it. The teacher then helped the student design a list of questions that she could ask herself, such as Who are the people in the picture? What are they doing? and What will they do next? The student then answered these questions in her story and was able to complete her assignment.

Most teachers regularly attend classes and read books designed to help them improve their craft. They have a sense that they can reach their students better, so they often begin to use new techniques at random in the hope of becoming more effective teachers. The temperament and type theories explained in this book can help teachers fine-tune their approaches to teaching. First, they can recognize the key characteristics that affect how a student or group of students learn. Second, teachers can identify the techniques that are most likely to reach those students. Finally, teachers can choose the techniques that they personally feel most comfortable using. By adding a few carefully chosen activities, teachers can provide positive reinforcement to students' own learning styles. As students receive positive reinforcement, they learn more and become more cooperative and positively engaged in the learning process.

What Is in This Book?

Part 1, Understanding the Role of Personality in Education, provides a foundation of information on temperament and type. Four basic temperaments and sixteen personality styles, or types, are explained in simple, easy-to-understand language.

Part 2, Teachers, Teaching Philosophy, and Teaching Style, will help teachers identify their teaching styles as well as the styles of other educators in their school. It explains the strengths each style brings to teaching with each. This section also offers many helpful ideas about the stresses each style commonly experiences as well as potential solutions for those stressors.

Part 3, Students and Learning Style, describes the behaviors that characterize each type of student and helps teachers to understand their motivational needs. It offers insights on how teachers can increase the cooperation of and minimize the conflict with each type of student. The descriptions of each learning style include discussions of attendant discipline, academic, and personal issues that can arise, along with suggested solutions. When reading these descriptions, it would be helpful to identify real students who appear to match or resemble each of the descriptions.

Part 4, Making the Personality Connection, identifies the teaching techniques and methods that work best with particular learning styles of students. It includes descriptions of many classroom strategies and how different types of students, based on their preferred learning style, are likely to respond to them. It also will help teachers match each type of student with the kinds of teaching materials—books, homework, tests, games, and computer programs—most likely to motivate them to learn. The final chapter of the book describes how teachers can use this book to better evaluate their effectiveness with all types of students and to help individual students.

The material in this book describing the relationship of temperament and personality type theory to education is based primarily on experience and anecdotal evidence. Whenever research on these topics is available, it is cited. And although more research is currently being done, as yet there has been no systematic study of the implications of temperament and personality type in education. Until a definitive model is available, teachers can use the information and suggestions that are offered in this book about applying these theories to the educational process.

This book provides only the necessary information about the theoretical models that will enable teachers to apply a knowledge of temperament and type theory to teaching. For additional information on these theories, please refer to the references listed at the back of this book for some excellent resources. *Please Understand Me* by Keirsey and Bates (1988) about temperament theory and *Gifts Differing: Understanding*

(1988) about temperament theory and *Gifts Differing: Understanding Personality Type* by Myers and Myers (1995) about type theory provide the best introductions to the two theories. Materials such as these will enable teachers to delve further into the concepts of temperament and type.

In the next chapters, we will introduce temperament and personality type theory and explain how both can be applied to the field of education.

Chapter 2

The Four Temperaments

Temperament theory provides a useful lens through which teacher and student styles can be viewed. Temperament theory has its roots in *constitutional psychology*, which traces back to early Greece. Constitutional psychology is based on observable human features and behavior. It is holistic in nature and views people as functioning, integrated systems.

According to temperament theory, people are born with a basic template that determines what aspects they are likely to develop. In the world of physiology, a person may have green eyes and brown hair. In the world of personality theory, a person is likely to develop a particular temperament. As Keirsey and Bates (1984) put it, "One's temperament is that which places a signature or thumbprint on each of one's actions, making it recognizably one's own."

Four styles of commonly observed human behavior have been noted since the time of Hippocrates, who, in about 450 B.C., referred to the four styles of human behavior as Melancholic, Sanguine, Choleric, and Phlegmatic. In the sixteenth century, Paracelsus, the Swiss physician and chemist, described four natures whose behavior and health was affected by four "humors"—Gnome/Earth, Salamander/Fire, Nymph/Water, and Sylph/Air. The eighteenth century German philosopher Immanuel Kant as well as the Russian physiologist Ivan Pavlov discussed four temperaments. In the early part of this century, the German psychologist Ernst Kretchmer (1925) identified the four styles Depressive, Hypomanic, Hyperaesthetic, and Anaesthetic. Four of the value types of Edward Spranger (1928), German psychologist—economic, aesthetic, religious, and theoretic—parallel these themes. More recently, psychologists David Keirsey and Marilyn Bates (1984) referred to them as Epimethean, Dionysian, Appolonian, and Promethean. Later, Keirsey changed the terms to Guardian, Artisan, Idealist, and Rational.[1]

Each of these four temperaments is driven by four different core need sets and is naturally adept at particular skills. These core needs and skills are summarized in table 1. These needs and skills are key definitions to each of the four temperaments, which will be described extensively throughout this book. In the temperament framework, the emphasis is on themes or core values of the type and its associated behaviors. Instead of only one channel for self-esteem and one mode of self-actualization, temperament theory describes four. These four temperaments take on the names originally coined by Keirsey—Guardian, Artisan, Idealist, and Rational.

To self-actualize, Guardians seek membership and belonging as well as responsibility and duty. Artisans increase self-esteem through freedom to act; they thrive on excitement and variation. Idealists seek continuous personal growth and search for a life of meaning and significance. Through willpower and mastery, Rationals build self-esteem by expanding their knowledge and gaining competence.

In the United States, Guardians are the most prevalent in the population, followed by Artisans. Guardians focus on stability by using experience from the past, while Artisans focus on variety and flexibility by

---

[1]See appendix A: *Temperament Needs, Roles, and Archetypes.*

Table 1 Core Needs and Skills of the Four Temperaments		
Temperament	Core Needs	Skills
Guardian	Membership and belonging Responsibility and duty	Logistics and facilitation
Artisan	Freedom and action Excitation and variation	Tactics and performance
Idealist	Identity and self-actualization Meaning and significance	Guidance and advocacy
Rational	Knowledge and competence Willpower and mastery	Strategy and design

spontaneously experiencing the present. Idealists and Rationals usually account for the smallest proportion of the population. Idealists focus on unmet needs that can be realized within a foreseeable future, while Rationals focus on ultimate truths and discoveries that are timeless. Throughout this book, we will discuss the temperaments in the order of their predominance in the general population, that is, in the order of Guardians, Artisans, Idealists, and Rationals.

To observe these four temperaments in action, let's visit a high school classroom where students are learning to use computers. Donald makes sure he understands all of the assignments and meets the teacher's standards. When a classmate is unsure of what is required, Donald is a good source of information and usually provides some practical tips on how to do the assignment. Donald often seeks out roles of responsibility; in fact, he plans to run for a school office next year. Donald's actions are most like the Guardian temperament.

Elena is often very experimental when she uses computers. She completes her assignments, but not always in the same step-by-step way in which the teacher has explained the process. Elena has lots of fun exploring different avenues and discovering what she can make the computer do. Sometimes she has to make a final rush to complete the assignment on time, but she says she enjoys the excitement. She ensures that she does well in her classes so that she can stay on the school basketball team. Elena's behavior is most like the Artisan temperament.

Reggie prefers assignments that allow him to express his individuality. He particularly enjoys learning shortcuts in word processing because it helps him in his work for the school newspaper. On the newspaper, his specialty is human interest stories that focus on students helping others. He has also submitted work to poetry and short story writing contests sponsored by the local college. Reggie has been selected from the school choir to be in the prestigious Madrigal Singers. Reggie's behavior is most like the Idealist temperament.

Yoko, like Elena, usually explores what the computer is capable of doing. While Elena enjoys her experimental adventures on computers, Yoko seems driven to understand what a particular software program is able to do and how to make it work best for her. Students seek Yoko out when they need to learn how to do something new on the computer. She is particularly good at researching user's manuals and discovering more efficient ways to use computers. She has applied her computer knowledge in her science classes and wants to become an engineer. Yoko's behavior is most like the Rational temperament.

Each student described here relates to their class differently. Each is driven by a distinct set of values and needs, and each exhibits different skills. Having seen a real-world example of how the temperaments are played out, let's take a closer look at the four temperaments.

The temperament descriptions that follow discuss, for each temperament, core needs and favorite words, general characteristics, typical careers, famous people representative of that temperament, and strengths and weaknesses. A couple of cautions are in order before we begin discussing temperament styles. First, keep in mind that no one style is limited to the careers we list for each here. The career examples given are merely devices to help readers form mental pictures of what might be typical for a given temperament. Second, the famous people listed are meant only to help illustrate the temperament; the public personas of these people function as an example only.

The Guardians

Guardians concern themselves with protecting and preserving society's standards and well-being. Their core needs are membership, belonging, responsibility, and duty. Words that describe Guardians include accountability, tradition, serving, and "shoulds." Guardians typically look to the past ("We've always done it this way before") and want security and stability. They are usually very reliable, but they can be fatalistic. For Guardians, "To serve is to be."

Guardians want to belong, but the belonging needs to be earned. They want to be the providers and caretakers and feel guilty when they are not contributing to their own or others' welfare. They dislike being dependent, not so much because they want independence but because they want to serve and be useful.

Guardians strongly support hierarchical structures and recognize the value of authority figures. As the stabilizers of society, they usually obey authority and expect others to do the same. Guardians believe that there should be rules to govern authority, and they are especially sensitive to doing what they think is appropriate.

Guardians like tradition and enjoy traditional celebrations and ceremonies. If no traditions exist, Guardians will often establish and maintain them. They may be suspicious of change. Although they recognize change as inevitable and even desirable, they will often resist change that means losing heritage.

A typical Guardian perception is that everything that can go wrong, will go wrong. Striving to be prepared for every contingency, they often make lists and use them to plan for effective actions.

Guardians are the backbone of society. They work hard for the goals of their organization, their families, and the groups to which they belong. They find it hard to refuse extra work—often with the idea that "If I don't do it, who will?"—and may sometimes feel harassed, overworked, and underappreciated.

While Guardians are often cautious and conservative, they may be found among rebels and risk takers, particularly if they belong to a group in which such behavior is valued. They can also be successful entrepreneurs, learning essential information and making a move when conditions are right.

Guardians make up about 38 percent of the U.S. population.[2] They are strongly represented at the elementary level, comprising 50 percent of these teachers (Myers and McCaulley, 1985). About 40 percent of high school teachers are Guardians, while 30 to 35 percent of college and university teachers are.

Typical occupations for Guardians include accountant, banker, clerk, customer service representative, financial planner, lawyer, manager, religious leader, nurse, police officer, secretary, social worker, soldier, supervisor, or teacher. Some famous probable Guardians include Tom Bradley, George and Barbara Bush, Henry Ford, Barry Goldwater, Orel Hershiser, General George MacClellan (from the American Civil War), Jack Nicklaus, Nancy Reagan, Nolan Ryan, Harry Truman, and George Washington.

Guardians tend to be reliable, stable, trustworthy, hardworking, self-motivated, goal oriented, and obedient. They like to follow through on things, care for the physical needs of others, and maintain meaningful traditions. Sometimes they can be rigid, worrisome, quick to judge, and resistant to change. They may attempt to remake people in their own image.

What would the world be like without Guardians? It would be chaotic, unorganized, anarchic—potentially, a real mess. There would be no clear standards for anything and many things would not be completed.

The Artisans

Artisans possess such high energy and skill for adapting that they are often referred to as the "can do" people. Their core needs are freedom, action, excitement, and variation. Words that describe Artisans include spontaneity, strength, grace, boldness, and impulsiveness. Artisans tend to live in the present. They are good negotiators and tacticians. For Artisans, "To do is to be."

---

[2]Percentages listed for temperaments in this chapter are taken from Keirsey and Bates, *Please Understand Me: Character and Temperament Types* (5th ed., Del Mar, Calif.: Prometheus Nemesis, 1984). Teacher percentages are derived from Myers and McCaulley (1985), *Manual: A Guide to the Development and Use of the Myers-Briggs Type Indicator.*

Artisans live in the here-and-now. For them, the past is irrelevant, and the future is not here yet. They want to be free to act on their impulses. Action for its own sake excites them. Artisans tend to be enthusiastic, unpredictable, generous, exciting, optimistic, cheerful, and fun.

Usually clearheaded in a crisis, their responses are quick, practical, and decisive. If their first effort does not work, they quickly try something else without suffering a loss of ego. Artisans get a sense of accomplishment from doing something that will work or that makes something happen. They may fail to follow through with their actions once the crisis is over. Because they are good at coping with crises, they often do not invest much energy in preventing them.

Artisans will practice something for hours, days, even years on end because of their compulsion for perfection in action. They must *do*. Artisans are consummate tool users. Tools, which can be in a variety of forms for both playing and working, become extensions of themselves. Tools may be such things as musical instruments, an automobile with a stick shift, or even a gift for words. They are compelled to master tools.

Artisans are often iconoclasts. They will refuse to do something simply because it was always done that way before. They are usually pragmatic, focusing on results rather than cooperation or convention. Unlike Guardians, Artisans do not respect authority for authority's sake. They respect authority only if the authority figure can prove his or her ability to act and if the actions have a pragmatic result.

Artisans may become bored with routine. They often need a change of pace and enjoy both relaxation time and high adventure. They enjoy putting out fires and may start some themselves if none exist. However, Artisans can choose routine if it offers them a high enough payoff. Their favored payoffs include fun, freedom, action, and excitement.

Artisans are typically egalitarian. They view themselves as equal to everyone and everyone else as being equal to them, although as supervisors they can sometimes demand total compliance. They are fiercely loyal and will often defend the people they care about at all costs. However, they are the most likely of all the temperaments to leave relationships or patterns of living if they find them too confining.

Artisans typically may put up with more unpleasant things for longer periods than other temperaments because, as Keirsey and Bates (1984) explain, "they live in the present. They do not doubt their ability to endure because they are not conscious of the passage of time. Artisans simply keep on going, far beyond the limits for other types."

Artisans make up about 38 percent of the U.S. population. Not commonly employed as teachers, they comprise less than 15 percent of elementary teachers and about 7 percent of high school, college, and university teachers.

Typical occupations for Artisans include artist, athlete, beautician, construction worker, customer service representative, dancer, entrepreneur, firefighter, police officer, sales manager, stockbroker, surgeon, trainer, trial lawyer, and truck driver. Keirsey and Bates (1984) found that Artisans are the temperament most likely to be in the public eye. Some famous probable Artisans include Mohammed Ali, Cher, Ernest Hemingway, Magic Johnson, Jackie Joyner-Kersee, John F. Kennedy, Joe Montana, Martina Navratilova, Arnold Palmer, Dolly Parton, General George F. Patton, Pablo Picasso, Elvis Presley, Teddy Roosevelt, Babe Ruth, Lee Trevino, Fernando Valenzuela, John Wayne, and Chuck Yeager.

Artisans tend to be flexible, tolerant, adaptable, bold, skilled at entertaining and crisis management, and zealous. They characteristically show a lack of fear or worry, and have an ability to assess situations quickly. Their potential weaknesses include rebelliousness, lack of organization, a failure to envision consequences, unpredictability, and procrastination.

What would the world be like without Artisans? It would be boring, drudgery—all work and no play. Artisans provide the high-level energy and troubleshooting perspective that is needed to expedite projects and get results.

The Idealists

Idealists strive to help themselves and others reach their full potential. Their core needs are identity, self-actualization, meaningfulness, and significance. Words that describe Idealists include becoming, authenticity, catalyst, facilitating, and romantic. They value meaningful relationships and look to the future. For Idealists, "To be is to do."

Idealists like to search for identity and meaning in life. Idealists can spend their whole lives seeking answers to the ultimate questions in life.

Whereas Rationals want to explain how the world works in scientific terms, Idealists want to explain how it works in personal, spiritual terms. Their life goal is to *become*. Idealists seek to grow, to reach their own potential, and to become completely who they truly are.

Idealists also see the potential in other people and want to help them reach it. Idealist parents are likely to say that they most enjoy their children when the children are doing things that are typical for their own personality styles.

At their best, Idealists are full of empathy, caring, warmth, and harmony. They are crusaders for the people and ideas they care about. They support the underdog. They are extremely insightful and can almost seem to read others' minds. Effective communicators, they love to inspire people and make them feel valued. They are good at seeing the possibilities in others and drawing out the potential of others.

At their worst, Idealists can be toxic in their communications. They often know exactly what to say to most hurt a person. They can make others feel guilty, and they may become self-centered in their quest to know themselves.

Idealists can also be quite charming. Idealist students learn early how to charm their way out of trouble. Their charm may function partly as a defense mechanism because criticism can paralyze them. They usually take criticism very personally.

Idealists are often seen as creative because they like to express their unique identity. They are also able to integrate things that seem to be entirely different. They look for universals and are gifted at using metaphors to bridge different perspectives.

Idealists want to be authentic and to have integrity. They want to be themselves and not feel obligated to play a given role. When Idealists do play a role, they often lose themselves in the part.

Because of their caring, Idealists can sometimes seem wishy-washy to others. However, most Idealists have values that they are unwilling to violate. When they have moral certainty behind them, they can be very firm in their beliefs.

Idealists make up about 12 percent of the U.S. population. They are well represented as teachers at all grade levels, ranging from over 25 percent at the elementary level to between 30 and 35 percent at the high school, college, and university levels.

Typical occupations for Idealists include actor, counselor, health professional, journalist, marketing professional, religious leader, photographer, psychologist, researcher, salesperson, teacher, and writer. Some famous probable Idealists include Mahatma Ghandi, Jim Henson, Joan of Arc, Martin Luther King Jr., Michael Landon, John Lithgow, Carl Rogers, Mister Rogers, Eleanor Roosevelt, Charles Schultz, Albert Schweitzer, Vin Scully, Meryl Streep, and Kristi Yamaguchi.

Idealists tend to be sympathetic, empathic, inspiring, creative, authentic, encouraging, and enthusiastic. They are often able to see possibilities in others and be tuned in to others, and they tend to have a strong regard for interpersonal relationships. Sometimes they can also play favorites or be overly helpful, inconsistent in administering discipline, too slow to make judgments, or emotionally vulnerable.

What would the world be like without Idealists? There would be little hope. Idealists provide a vision of what is possible in ourselves and others and lead the way in fulfilling that vision.

The Rationals

Rationals pursue knowledge for its own sake, often becoming experts in their fields. Their core needs are demonstrations of knowledge, competence, willpower, and mastery. Words that describe Rationals include logical, reasoning, abstract, and intellectual. Rationals desire precision, especially in thought and language. They have an unusual sense of time. They have an ongoing drive to comprehend things. For Rationals, "To know is to be."

Perceiving themselves and having others perceive them as competent is a core need for Rationals. They have an insatiable desire to acquire knowledge and to demonstrate their intellect. Rationals long to be able to master the universe by completely explaining it. They may spend much of their time formulating theories. Rationals are not interested in learning facts as much as they are in learning systems and frameworks. They enjoy making logical and analytical judgments.

Once Rationals embrace a theory, it becomes extremely difficult for them to reject it or any part of it. If a part of a theory is disproved, Rationals then often question the whole theory and must engage in a thorough reassessment until a cohesive framework is reestablished.

Rationals tend to be ruthlessly self-critical. For them, today's exceptional performance often becomes tomorrow's poor performance. Even playtime is used by Rationals as a time to improve skills. They are driven to perfection. Rationals may sometimes even refuse to participate in an activity in which they do not believe they can excel.

Rationals tend to be very careful and precise in their use of language. They also enjoy puns and other forms of wordplay. They can be difficult to understand if they become more concerned with saying something correctly and elegantly than in communicating clearly. Rationals also dislike repeating themselves and stating what they think is obvious, which may not always be obvious to others.

Rationals respect authority figures who have proven their competence. They can seem arrogant in their belief of their own knowledge. Their expectations of others can vary: On the one hand, they may expect little out of others, since others may have difficulty understanding their abstract ideas; on the other hand, they may expect other people to live up to their own high standards.

Rationals have a remarkable ability to see connections between things that are not evident to others. They can often retain an incredible number of facts in their minds and manipulate them to find relationships between them. They like to think in terms of systems, which helps them determine how each piece of data relates to the whole. They tend to be excellent long-term planners and can often accurately predict the effects of specific actions. Many inventors and scientists are Rationals.

Rationals make up about 12 percent of the U.S. population. In the field of education, Rationals compromise only 10 percent of elementary teachers, about 15 percent of high school teachers, and over 30 percent of college and university teachers.

Typical occupations for Rationals include computer programmer, doctor, engineer, entrepreneur, lawyer, manager, philosopher, politician, professor, researcher, scientist, systems analyst, and writer. Some famous probable Rationals include Arthur Ashe, George Washington Carver, Marie Curie, Leonardo Da Vinci, Thomas Edison, Albert Einstein, Dwight Eisenhower, Jane Goodall, Steven Hawking, Thomas Jefferson, George Lucas, General Colin Powell, Ayn Rand, Carl Sagan, Pete Sampras, and Stephen Spielberg.

Rationals are often competent, intelligent, intellectual, clear-sighted, logical, skilled at reasoning, thorough, and scientifically creative. They can also be proud, lack regard for others' feelings, expect too much out of others, fail to deal with the here-and-now, or be sarcastic.

What would the world be like without Rationals? It would be nasty, brutish, and short lived. Rationals have discovered most of the medical and technical inventions that help increase our life span and keep us more comfortable.

Understanding Temperament

Temperaments provide us with a way of looking at normal human behavior through four different lenses. Many people will try on the behavior of more than one temperament during the course of their lifetimes, but, for most of us, one style dominates throughout our lives.

The more teachers understand the wide range of commonly occurring behavior in students, the more they will be able to appreciate this range of human behavior. An understanding of temperament theory better prepares teachers to help each individual student develop in a healthy manner.

Teachers can use themselves as their first subject for understanding temperament by reading through the temperament descriptions contained in this chapter and determining which ones seem to most accurately describe them. If you are

- A Guardian, and if this theory makes sense to you, you are probably taking notes or wishing you were. You probably already have several questions formulated along the lines of, "So how will this help me deal with Bobby?"

- An Artisan, you want some action. Theories may leave you cold if they do not have any impact. You are probably scanning the descriptions to see what the payoffs would be if you used this theory.

- An Idealist, you have probably already taken the theory and gone forward with it. You are miles down the road with sketchy ideas about how you can use it to improve your relationships with particular students.

- A Rational, you have seen several logical implications to this theory. You are probably fascinated with the ideas behind it or are considering the implications of this theory in relation to your present system of viewing the world.

Now that you have an introductory understanding of temperament, we will explain the other theory that will help you work with your students, personality type theory.

Chapter 3

The Personality
Type Preferences

One way of looking at individual differences in personality is temperament theory; another way has come from the school of *psychological type,* or personality type theory. Swiss psychiatrist Carl Jung (1875–1961) hypothesized dynamic internal processes to explain normal human behavior. According to Jung, a person's attitude or readiness to act in a certain way is demonstrated by one of two preferences: Extraversion, which focuses on the external world, or Introversion, which focuses on the internal world. He also identified four dynamic psychological *functions:* Sensing or Intuition, and Thinking or Feeling. In perceiving the world, a person uses either Sensing by looking at the concrete, real world, or Intuition by looking at the world of possibilities, the not-yet-created world. In making judgments about what is perceived, a person uses either Thinking, an objective or logic-based criteria, or Feeling, a subjective or values-based criteria. Again, these contribute to the make up of a person's psychological preferences or personality type.

American Katharine Briggs (1875–1968) began studying personality theory in order to develop characters for her writings. In 1923, she discovered Jung's work. Some years later, her daughter, Isabel Briggs Myers (1897–1980), became inspired to help in the war effort of World War II by designing a psychological instrument that would help fit workers to specific jobs. Building upon the previous work of Jung and Briggs, and adding her own Judging and Perceiving scales to the instrument in order to determine if a person had a stronger attraction toward one of the perceiving functions (Sensing and Intuition) or one of the judging functions (Thinking and Feeling), Myers developed the first version of the *Myers-Briggs Type Indicator*® (MBTI®) personality inventory.

Today the MBTI inventory is one of the best known psychological instruments in the world and has been translated into many languages. It is used in many fields, such as career counseling, couples counseling, and organizational team building as well as in education. The inventory must be administered by a counselor or other professional trained in its use and interpretation. Another instrument, the *Murphy-Meisgeier Type Indicator for Children* (MMTIC), is designed for determining the personality type preferences of children ages six to twelve.

Now let us look more closely at the four pairs of preferences. The first is Extraversion–Introversion (E–I). We all have some extraverted features and some introverted features, but most of us have a *preference* for one or the other and we feel more comfortable doing one of the two. The second pair of preferences is Sensing–Intuition (S–N). The third set is Thinking–Feeling (T–F), and the fourth is Judging–Perceiving (J–P). Preferring one side of the dimension does not mean a rejection of the other. For example, let's say you have a choice between strawberry and apple pie. You may prefer strawberry pie, so you will usually choose it; however, you can and will occasionally choose apple pie. Table 2 defines the preferences and summarizes what distinguishes them.

Obviously, people act differently. But while we are all unique, it is still possible and beneficial to group types of behavior. Some people enjoy being the center of attention, while others prefer to experience life more from the sidelines. This demonstrates the Extraversion–Introversion dimension. Some people are very observant of another's physical appearance, while others are much more aware of the person's moods and/or thoughts. This demonstrates the Sensing–Intuition dimension. The following sections describe each of these dimensions in detail.

Table 2 The Preferences Briefly Defined	
Source of Energy	
Extraversion (E)	Introversion (I)
External stimulus	Internal stimulus
What Is Observed	
Sensing (S)	Intuition (N)
Concrete reality	World of possibilities
Evaluation Style	
Thinking (T)	Feeling (F)
Objectivity	Personal values
True/false	Good/bad
Energy Direction and Flow	
Judging (J)	Perceiving (P)
Coming to a conclusion	Taking in informaton

When trying to convince someone else to do something, some people present clear, logical arguments, while others appeal to the person's values and emotions. This is an example of the Thinking–Feeling dimension. Some people want things decided, while others prefer keeping options open. This illustrates the Judging–Perceiving dimension.

You can get an idea of your own preferences by examining the definitions in the following four tables. Is one of the paired preferences more like your normal behavior? You may feel that you can identify with both. Remember that each pair of preferences describes the range of normal human behavior. Ask yourself which you do more frequently and more comfortably and which is most like you. You may recognize preferences that are not your own, but which are more typical of a friend or co-worker.

Extraversion–Introversion (E–I)

The Extraversion–Introversion dimension focuses on whether an individual is most energized by the external world or the internal world.

Table 3   Characteristics of Extraverted and Introverted Types

Extraverted Types (E)	Introverted Types (I)
Are expansive and less impassioned	Are intense and passionate
Are generally easy to get to know	Are generally more difficult to get to know
Like meeting new people; are friendly	Have to exert effort to meet new people and may try to avoid having to do so; are reserved
Have many close friends	Have a few close friends
Would rather figure things out *while* they are talking	Would rather figure things out *before* they talk about them
Often enjoy background noise, such as the TV or radio	Prefer peace and quiet
Are more likely to know what is going on around them than what is going on inside them	Are more likely to know what is going on inside them than what is going on around them
Often do not mind interruptions	Like stating their thoughts or feelings without interruption
May think that those preferring Introversion are standoffish or cold	May think that those preferring Extraversion are shallow
Often are considered good talkers	Often are considered good listeners

Individuals who prefer Extraversion become energized when they are with others, while people who prefer Introversion become energized when they are alone. Approximately 75 percent of the U.S. population prefers Extraversion and 25 percent prefers Introversion.[1] Slightly more than half of elementary teachers prefer Extraversion, while slightly more than half prefer Introversion at the college level.[2] Some of the common characteristics of people exhibiting each of these preferences are listed in table 3.

[1] General U.S. population percentages for the preferences listed in this chapter are taken from Keirsey and Bates (1984), *Please Understand Me.*
[2] Teacher percentages listed for the preferences in this chapter are derived from Myers and McCaulley (1985), *Manual: A Guide to the Development and Use of the Myers-Briggs Type Indicator.*

Table 4   Characteristics of Sensing and Intuitive Types

Sensing Types (S)	Intuitive Types (N)
Are practical and realistic	Are imaginative dreamers
Prefer facts	Prefer theory and abstraction
Seek enjoyment and experience	Seek inspiration and insight
Are often pleasure lovers and consumers, and contented in general	Are often initiators, inventors, and promoters, and restless in general
Like to live in the real world	Like to live in the world of possibilities
Would rather do than think	Would rather think than do
Focus on practical, concrete problems	Focus on complicated, abstract problems
See the details and may ignore the big picture	See the big picture but may not notice the details
Want specifics	Want a general outline
Tend to be literal in their use of words	Love puns and word games
May think that those preferring Intuition are impractical	May think that those preferring Sensing lack vision
Believe "if it ain't broke, don't fix it"	Believe anything can be improved
Focus on the present or the past	Focus on the future or the eternal

Sensing–Intuition (S–N)

Sensing focuses on the world that *is*—the world of facts experienced by the five senses—and Intuition focuses on the world of possibilities. Approximately 75 percent of the U.S. population prefers Sensing and 25 percent prefers Intuition. About 60 percent of elementary teachers prefer Sensing, while about 60 percent of college teachers prefer Intuition. High school teachers are evenly divided on this preference. Some of the common characteristics of people exhibiting each of these preferences are listed in table 4.

Thinking–Feeling (T–F)

The Thinking–Feeling dimension relates to the processes by which we make judgments. Both preferences are rational. The main difference between the two is that the Thinking preference focuses on making judgments based on objective standards, while the Feeling preference focuses on making judgments based on personal values. This is the only one of the four preferences that demonstrates some sex-based differences. Overall, 50 percent of the U.S. population prefers Thinking and 50 percent prefers Feeling. While 60 to 75 percent of men prefer Thinking, 60 to 75 percent of women prefer Feeling. Almost 70 percent of elementary teachers and 60 percent of high school teachers prefer Feeling; college and university teachers are evenly divided on this preference. Some of the common characteristics of people exhibiting each of these preferences are listed in table 5.

Judging–Perceiving (J–P)

The Judging preference focuses on making judgments or arriving at conclusions. The Perceiving preference focuses on continually scanning and adapting to the environment. Approximately 50 percent of the U.S. population prefers Judging and 50 percent prefers Perceiving. Between 65 and 70 percent of teachers at all levels prefer Judging. The main difference on this dimension is that Judging focuses on goals and achieving results, while Perceiving focuses on processes and continuing experiences. Some of the common characteristics of people exhibiting each of these preferences are listed in table 6.

Preferences as They Appear in Students

Elizabeth Murphy (1991), cocreater of the MMTIC and longtime educator, refers to the Extraversion–Introversion and Judging–Perceiving scales as attitudes that are characteristic of daily *living* skills. The daily living skills describe the way a person chooses to interact with the world. These preferences become apparent from an early age and do not appear to

Table 5 Characteristics of Thinking and Feeling Types	
Thinking Types (T)	**Feeling Types (F)**
Like words such as principles, policy, firmness, justice, standards, and analysis	Like words such as intimacy, mercy, humane, harmony, good or bad, sympathy, and devotion
Respond most easily to people's thoughts	Respond most easily to people's values
Want to apply objective principles	Want to apply personal values— their own and others
Value objectivity above sentiment	Value sentiment above objectivity
Will usually be truthful	Will usually be tactful
Are analytically oriented	Are people oriented
Are good at assessing the logical consequences of things	Are good at assessing the human impact of things
Believe it is more important to be just than merciful	Believe it is more important to be merciful than just
Assess reality through a true/false lens	Assess reality through a good/bad lens
May think that those preferring Feeling take things too personally	May think that those preferring Thinking are insensitive
May argue both sides of an issue for mental stimulation	Prefer to agree with those around them

change over time. Murphy also refers to the Sensing–Intuition and Thinking–Feeling scales as functions that are characteristic of learning skills. These are learning skills because they explain how people prefer to take in information about the world and process it. Unlike the living skills, the learning skills seem to develop over a person's lifetime. We will discuss each of these in detail below to illustrate their key points of contrast.

Table 6 Characteristics of Judging and Perceiving Types	
Judging Types (J)	Perceiving Types (P)
Plan ahead	Adapt as they go
Are self-disciplined and purposeful	Are flexible, adaptable, and tolerant
Like things finished and settled	Like leaving options open
Thrive on order	Thrive on spontaneity
Usually get things done early by planning ahead and working steadily	Usually get things done late, depending on last-minute spurts of energy to meet deadlines
Define and work within limits	Ignore or work against limits
Want closure	Want more information
May be too hasty in making decisions	May fail to make needed decisions
Are time and deadline oriented	Think there is plenty of time
Dislike surprises	Like surprises
May think that those preferring Perceiving are too unplanned	May think that those preferring Judging are too rigid
Usually make effective choices among life's possibilities, but may not appreciate or make use of unplanned or unexpected happenings	Are usually masterful in their handling of the unplanned and unexpected, but may not make effective choices among life's possibilities

The Four Living Skills:
Extraversion–Introversion and Judging–Perceiving

The four living skills—Extraversion, Introversion, Judging, and Perceiving—are developed in most children by the time they enter school. Differences in these preferred living skills are frequently the source of conflict in our daily interactions with those who are close to us.

Fraternal twins Kevin and Keith, who have just entered kindergarten, behave very differently around strangers. Kevin is friendly and sociable, while Keith is reserved. He clings to his mother when she brings him to school, while Kevin runs straight toward his classmates. It is likely that Keith prefers Introversion and Kevin Extraversion. The Introverted child needs time to adjust to new stimulation and prefers to have more control over his or her environment. The Extraverted child likes more stimulation and prefers to explore new environments.

Latanya and Denicia are third-grade classmates. Latanya keeps her desk neat and clean and reminds the teacher when it is time to change activities. In contrast, Denicia drops things whenever she is through with them. Sometimes she goes so fast that her classmates can't keep up with her. At other times, it appears that she becomes lost in thought and nothing will hurry her up. She adds a lot of sparkle to the classroom. Latanya seems to prefer Judging, whereas Denicia more likely prefers Perceiving.

One fifth-grade teacher who understands personality type preferences uses this knowledge to help her students relate more effectively to her. Since she has a strong Judging preference, she has explained to her students about her need to have the classroom organized, neat, and clean. She talks about her own comfort zone and helps her students understand that their personal comfort zone may be different from hers. She reports that respecting and understanding comfort zones that are different from her own has helped her relate more positively to all of her students.

The Four Learning Skills: Sensing–Intuition and Thinking–Feeling

The four learning skills—Sensing, Intuition, Thinking, and Feeling—are emphasized in schools. There is more training that requires Sensing in the elementary and secondary grades and more training that requires Intuition at the college level. Sensing focuses on information about the real world gained through the senses, while Intuition focuses on the world of possibilities.

Let's look at a fifth-grade classroom to observe Sensing and Intuition in action. Joletta and Virginia have lived in the same neighborhood since they were toddlers. The girls have played together regularly, but they are beginning to drift apart. Both girls have a playful and joyous attitude. Joletta is very interested in what is going on and is full of facts about everything. She shows no interest in Virginia's fantasizing and wants to talk about things that are real *now*. Virginia asks the teacher such questions as, "Why do we do the math problem this way?" and "Why couldn't we do this?" She's always wondering about future events and wants to know what the teacher thinks about different possibilities. She has a lively imagination and uses it in creative writing.

Both girls are friendly and outgoing and likely prefer Extraversion. Both prefer to be spontaneous and leave their options open, and thus seem to prefer Perceiving. They are so alike in some ways, yet their differences are highly apparent to the teacher.

What are these differences the teacher perceives? Joletta seems to prefer Sensing: She is practical and concrete and is very aware of the present and the past. Virginia seems to prefer Intuition: She is fascinated by the world of possibilities, the world of the future. The two girls' ways of seeing the world are becoming increasingly different. This differing perception is beginning to influence their style of communication.

Now let's observe two other students in the same fifth-grade class. Thomas has a reputation for being "smart," and Joseph has a reputation for being "helpful." Both children are quiet and reserved, so they seem to prefer Introversion. They are also neat, orderly, and very conscientious about turning all of their papers in on time. These behaviors tend to suggest that both boys prefer Judging. Neither seems to prefer the world of possibilities and the future. Both are good with facts and details, so both seem to prefer Sensing. Yet they behave differently.

Thomas is very meticulous in his work. When he works out a process for doing his assignments, he sticks to it unless he is shown that a different way is more efficient. He can explain his procedures clearly and tell the reasons for doing them. His last teacher observed that he had an "orderly mind that cut like a razor."

Joseph is also a very bright student. But the teacher has noticed that Joseph's concentration on his work is interrupted when another child needs assistance. In fact, other children seem to seek him out to help solve their conflicts. Joseph also takes time to help the teacher.

Thomas seems to prefer Thinking: His behavior emphasizes the analysis and organization of Thinking. Joseph, in contrast, seems to prefer Feeling: His behavior emphasizes sensitivity to other people and a desire to resolve conflicts. Their teacher understands their differences and enjoys both boys' contributions to the classroom.

Understanding the Preferences

There is a wide range of commonly observed human behavior. Taking preferences into account is one way to help us understand these differences. Each preference is normal and useful in the world. In the early stages of learning about personality type, people often begin labeling others as "Ps" or "Js," for example. But people are not really Ps or Js; they simply prefer to use the Perceiving or Judging preference in most situations. Keep in mind that *all* people have Extraverted *and* Introverted, Sensing *and* Intuitive, Thinking *and* Feeling, Judging *and* Perceiving abilities.

On the other hand, translating your own behaviors and those of others into probable personality type preferences is a good way to learn about type. For example, people with different preferences probably reacted differently to the material presented in this chapter:

- Extraverted types may be wondering when they can discuss this material with someone. They may need to talk about the material in order to clarify their thoughts.

- Introverted types may want some quiet time to digest the information.

- Sensing types probably want practical applications. They may be thinking, "OK. Now how will this help me in the classroom?" They want to know *how* it works.

- Intuitive types have probably generated some insights that may open new possibilities for reaching students.

- Thinking types probably would like some facts and figures as evidence that this theory is true.

- Feeling types would probably like lots of anecdotal evidence to prove that this will help them and their students feel better about each other.

- Judging types have probably already decided what personality style they are and have probably decided what the types of several other people are, too. They probably have also made a decision about whether this material is useful or not.

- Perceiving types may be leaving their options open and wondering how they could play with this material, although they may have tentatively decided what their type or the type of someone else is.

The Sixteen Types

In the late 1950s, David Keirsey read descriptions of psychological types written by Isabel Briggs Myers. The sets of descriptions were remarkably similar to his own. He then described four variations of each of the four basic temperaments, yielding sixteen different types. The possible combinations of Myers' four sets of preferences also resulted in sixteen distinct personality types. Keirsey's Guardian variations correlated to Myers' types preferring Sensing and Judging (SJ), his Artisan variations with her types preferring Sensing and Perceiving (SP), his Idealist variations with her types preferring Intuition and Feeling (NF), and his Rational variations with her types preferring Intuition and Thinking (NT). Table 7 shows the relationship between the Keirseyan temperament variations and the sixteen personality types generated by Myers for teachers and students, providing a generalized map of the sixteen types that are key elements of this book.

Since both temperament theory and type theory have sixteen types, some people may wonder if there is any difference between them. The main differences are almost philosophical in nature. Temperament theory is static in assuming that a person's core needs remain constant throughout his or her lifetime. Temperament holds to synergy; the total equals more than the sum of the parts. In contrast, type theory is dynamic and describes the development of preferences throughout a person's lifetime. Type is defined by determining each of the four preferences individually.

Because of this difference in emphasis, temperament theory uses descriptive names for each of the sixteen types, while type theory identifies them through the possible preference combinations. For example, in type theory, if Carla prefers Extraversion (E), Sensing (S), Feeling (F), and Judging (J), she is identifying herself as an ESFJ; according to temperament theory, she would be the variation of Guardian described as a Caretaker. We use both conventions throughout this book to illustrate the sixteen different types.

Let's look further at the example of Carla, who identifies with the description of the Guardian teacher style of an ESFJ Caretaker. To

Table 7 Type and Temperament in Education

	NF Idealists				SJ Guardians			
Core Needs	Identity and Self-Actualization Meaning and Significance				Membership and Belonging Responsibility and Duty			
Major Skill	Guidance		Advocacy		Logistics		Facilitation	
	NFJ Mentor		*NFP Advocate*		*STJ Monitor*		*SFJ Provider*	
	ENFJ	INFJ	ENFP	INFP	ESTJ	ISTJ	ESFJ	ISFJ
Teacher	Mobilizer	Developer	Enthusiast	Questor	Administrator	Inspector	Caretaker	Protector
Student	Teacher	Writer	Booster	Dreamer	Stabilizer	Perfectionist	Harmonizer	Conserver

	NT Rationals				SP Artisans			
Core Needs	Knowledge and Competence Willpower and Mastery				Freedom and Action Excitation and Variation			
Major Skill	Strategy		Design		Tactics		Performance	
	NTJ Organizer		*NTP Inventor*		*STP Operator*		*SFP Performer*	
	ENTJ	INTJ	ENTP	INTP	ESTP	ISTP	ESFP	ISFP
Teacher	Director	Planner	Innovator	Definer	Promoter	Troubleshooter	Entertainer	Composer
Student	Commander	Scientist	Improvisor	Theorist	Negotiator	Tinkerer	Actor	Artist

paraphrase Isabel Briggs Myers, in some ways Carla is like all other ESFJs, like some other ESFJs, and like no other ESFJs. However, there are still many things about her that are true about most ESFJs. The descriptions in this book give common patterns for each of the sixteen types. No person will be exactly like any one of the types because each person is unique. Nevertheless, understanding patterns of behavior that are common for each type will help you understand and develop effective classroom strategies for students of other types.

The sixteen descriptions may provide you with insight into your own skills and motivations and those of your colleagues. You may read a student type description that helps you better understand a particular student. For instance, the description of the ESFP Performer student can help you perceive the student's desire for action, excitement, socialization, and attention. You can then seek ways of making the student's high energy an asset in the classroom. By using part 4 of this book to see what teaching techniques can be most useful in working with this type of student, you can increase the probability of carrying out effective teaching and effective learning in your classroom.

PART TWO

Teachers, Teaching Philosophy, and Teaching Style

There are many things teachers cannot control. One thing they can control is development of personal skills and teaching style. One source for the skill and style of teachers are the models they were exposed to as students. Another source is the instruction they received about "how to teach" in college. The style of the particular schools where they teach, the resources available to them, and the techniques encouraged by their principals or school districts are also influences. And one cannot dismiss the influence of a teacher's temperament or personality type preferences. When teachers are better able to analyze their own preferred teaching techniques and analyze the styles and needs of their students, the educational process is likely to become more successful for both students and teachers.

For example, most of the teachers in elementary, middle, and high school are SJ Guardians. The second most common style of teacher at these levels is NF Idealists. One could almost define the schools of preferred teaching styles that gain ascendancy and then wane by these two temperaments.

While SJ teachers are apt to focus on standardizing or "normalizing" the curriculum and moving the focus of study "back to the basics," NF teachers are more likely to concentrate on customizing or individualizing instruction and teaching from the perspective of individual students.

Both approaches have validity. On the one hand, the SJ emphasis on standardization brings needed structure to the classroom and curriculum. Based on state standards, each school district sets up a curriculum that is intended to provide students with the appropriate skills they will need to become productive citizens. SJs believe that a student's performance must be compared to such standards.

On the other hand, the NF emphasis on individualized instruction brings needed instructional flexibility to the academic experience; the individual student does need attention and not every teaching technique will work for every student. The NF is very conscious of the need for each child to have a positive school experience.

SJs tend to focus on performance, while NFs focus on individual acceptance. Both temperaments have a need to promote socialization and affiliation. The SJ affiliates with group standards; the NF affiliates with other individuals. These two groups are likely to debate over what standards and techniques will best help students become effective citizens and healthy individuals. SJs will complain if students are not grounded in traditional, proven knowledge that helps maintain societal stability. NFs will complain if students are not encouraged to grow into worthwhile individuals who can share their unique identity with others.

Without a balance, SJs can become so rigid in setting standards that some students of differing types will have difficulty succeeding. These students can then be labeled negatively. On the other hand, NFs can become so focused on individualizing instruction and affirming a student's worth that they fail to help enough students meet effective standards. NF teachers may also burn themselves out in their efforts to individualize instruction for their many students.

Let's not forget the impact of the other two styles of teachers. SP Artisan teachers think that learning should be fun and believe in seizing the moment, while NT Rational teachers emphasize the importance of students understanding processes and not just learning by rote and repetition.

Again, both approaches are valid. The SP approach to seize the moment, have fun, and get immediate impact or payoff can be very effective. Adult teaching theory focuses on the experiential method of teaching. Simulations teach actions and behaviors in real time.

The NT approach to understanding the why of things is equally important. The what or specific details can change rapidly in our fast-paced world, but knowing the why can help people modify processes and use the latest technology.

SPs tend to focus on the moment, while NTs focus more on the eternal. Both have a pragmatic bent and both are the most likely to question whether traditional standards are still effective in meeting current employment needs. SPs will be bothered if students are not adequately shown the how to of things and if there is no current application of the material. NTs will be bothered if the curriculum does not move beyond the surface so that students can prepare themselves for the future by understanding underlying theories.

Without a balance between traditional forms of learning and action, SPs can become so caught up in the action of the moment that they may fail to include some significant parts of the curriculum. Students may have problems compensating for this shortfall. SPs may also train students with experience that will remain current only for the very near future. At the same time, if NTs focus exclusively on the underpinnings of knowledge, ignoring practicum, they can create a knowledge base for students that is difficult to translate into reality. The benefits may be so distant that many students will not see them as relevant.

Effective education must balance standards, individual acceptance, the action of how to, and an understanding of the why behind things. If any of these essential pieces is missing, some of our students will fail to get what they need to become successful citizens.

The following four chapters will describe characteristics of each of the sixteen personality types as they appear in teachers. We will discuss their typical style of teaching and how they operate in a typical classroom. Chapters 4 and 5 will discuss Sensing teachers: the SJ Guardians and the

SP Artisans; chapters 6 and 7 will review the Intuitive teachers: the NF Idealists and the NT Rationals. The sixteen type descriptions include a discussion of the basic characteristics of each type, where each type is most frequently found in education, and what each type's preferred teaching techniques, strengths, potential weaknesses, and causes of stress are.

Chapter 4

Sensing–Judging Guardian Teachers

Sensing–Judging (SJ) Guardian teachers prefer to use tried-and-true methodology and often model their teaching style on traditional techniques they experienced as students. SJs tend to have excellent memories of experiences and are able to use these concrete memories to the benefit of themselves and their students. They are often more comfortable with techniques that contain explainable step-by-step procedures. When in a playful mode, they may be spontaneous, but when they get down to the business of work, they are more likely to prefer well-planned activities that have been proven through experience or endorsed by trusted authorities.

SJ teachers are able to learn new techniques as educational styles change; however, since they usually invest so much of themselves in developing their procedures, they need time to adapt to changes. They learn new procedures best when they are provided a model and are given the exact steps to follow. As they practice the procedure, they become more effective and comfortable with the style. SJ teachers don't tend to see themselves as highly experimental or inventive and generally prefer a more "practical" way of teaching. They often feel more comfortable when they are in control of the classroom with well-planned teaching methods.

Self-actualization for SJs comes from membership in a group, that is, from being considered a worthy member of a team. They tend to seek responsibility. By performing their duty as it is defined by the group, they become the keepers of the social "norm." They seek cooperation from others to meet agreed-upon standards. SJs are the stabilizers of organizations through which they create affiliations and a sense of belonging. With their beneficent stance, they help to preserve and protect the individual, the family, the institution, and the nation.

The language of SJs often contains the words "should" and "ought." Concerned with orthodox conventions, they are also conscious of comparatives. It is not uncommon to hear them talk about event A being "like" or "different from" event B. They can be very tied to the past, often referring to events from the past with great frequency and a high degree of detail and accuracy.

From a values standpoint, they are often perceived to have an economic posture. They are conscious of the cost of material goods, time, and effort. Many are unofficial historians of their schools and can recall exactly when specific school events occurred. They remember specific examples of techniques that worked successfully and do not see the point of retrying ones that didn't.

Sometimes SJ teachers are seen as pessimistic, since they sometimes seem to expect things to go wrong. From their viewpoint, they are merely being realistic, anticipating the reality that things do occasionally go awry in the real world. They tend to maintain rules and regulations, defer to hierarchical authority, and show concern for effective logistics.

SJs usually have a great deal of endurance; when they stop working, it is usually because they have completed all of their tasks or they are forced to stop from sheer exhaustion.

SJ teachers, while often of a serious demeanor, may show a lighthearted side by placing stars on assignments or writing upbeat comments on papers. They also like to celebrate completion through ceremonies such as school assemblies, classroom awards, and formal graduations.

SJ teachers are good at helping to meet basic needs. They make sure students have pencils, paper, books, and other supplies, or else they enforce penalties if students are to provide them and don't. Their classroom is often neat and uncluttered, maintained at a comfortable temperature, and relatively quiet and organized. SJ teachers are usually reliable—students know what to expect from them and feel secure. They tend to clearly communicate classroom standards for behavior and achievement. Students usually know exactly where they stand academically in relation to other students and are aware of the teacher's expectations. SJ teachers usually return work to students in a timely manner, and are good examples of self-discipline and organization. Administrators appreciate SJs because they create and adhere to lesson plans and because they are loyal and responsible representatives of the school. SJs may work tirelessly and take on too many commitments in their quest to serve their students and their community. Students often like SJ teachers because they are dependable and hardworking.

There are two major categories of SJ Guardian teachers: STJ Monitors and SFJ Providers, which are illustrated in table 8.

Table 8 SJ Guardian Teachers	
STJ Monitors	SFJ Providers
ESTJ Administrators	ESFJ Caretakers
ISTJ Inspectors	ISFJ Protectors

STJ Monitors

STJ Monitors are comfortable being direct and giving orders; it is easy for them to assume authority. For instance, they will say, "Open your books to page 102," rather than "Let's open our books to page 102"—a softer style more typical of an SFJ Provider. STJ Monitors are very task and time driven and give directions that facilitate the most efficient use of time and resources. They are the most likely of all the types to have daily routines that help them maintain order and achieve results.

ESTJ Administrators
Basic Characteristics

Adjectives that describe the typical ESTJ are decisive, direct, and matter-of-fact. ESTJs tend to be industrious and responsible. They like to use structure or routine to get things done efficiently. Even when a deadline doesn't exist, they often take charge and run events or tasks as if there were no time to waste.

Where They Are Found in Education

ESTJ teachers are found at all grade levels, but less often at the primary level, where students are more dependent and require more nurturing than older students. ESTJs can often be found teaching in trade, industrial, and technical fields; they may also be coaches or math teachers. They often become school administrators in elementary and secondary schools, colleges, and technical institutions. The sequence of teaching level that is typically preferred by ESTJs is adult education, high school, middle school, elementary school, community college, university, and preschool. ESTJs can be very good at helping students to use logical thinking in the real world to create concrete results.

Preferred Teaching Techniques

Since ESTJs find it easy to give oral directions, they often use teacher-led question-and-answer, lectures, and explanations of procedures. They may use audiovisuals to provide a reality background for their lectures. They also prefer using oral drills, memorization, and teacher-led discussions. For quiet time, they often give workbook assignments. Sometimes they use contracts with students, and they typically provide written course outlines.

Strengths

ESTJ teachers are often perceived by students and faculty as having many well-planned procedures. Many ESTJ teachers rise to positions of responsibility within their schools and may become school administrators. It should be noted that in the business world, this personality type is common for managers due to their ability to economically manage resources. As teachers, ESTJs are frequently the ones organizing field trips or other special school activities. Their logistical abilities help them to identify exactly what needs to be done and when it should be completed. They have the ability to make assignments and ensure that others carry them out. They are able to combine their abilities to set goals, make decisions, and give assignments so that things get done.

ESTJs like to organize daily time lines, lesson plans, activities, and procedures into step-by-step routines. They are likely to know precisely how much time is needed to complete an activity. If a daily schedule changes due to an emergency, they will often rearrange the set routine. ESTJs are usually able to tell others about their lists of priorities and the steps they have planned for the day to meet these priorities. They are excellent at enforcing rules, regulations, and standards of propriety.

Their routines and standards often lead to smoothly running classrooms. One ESTJ elementary teacher established a routine using student workgroups in practice centers. She trained her new teacher's aide to help students in the school's math center. One day, the teacher was suddenly called out of the class. When the aide expressed concern about being left in charge of the class, the teacher reassured her that the students knew what to do, then turned on a timer and left. The aide resumed helping the math students. When the timer went off, every student immediately moved to the next center and began to work again. The aide never had to say a word, she simply reset the timer and again worked with the math students. This process continued until the teacher returned an hour later.

ESTJ teachers tend to live by rules that result from their decisions about what are the "best way to do things," and they often expect their students to live by them, too. They do not like to change traditional rules unless they can be persuaded that there is a logical reason to do so. To be accepted, these logical reasons must be backed up by concrete facts. This preference for rules helps ensure that classrooms are organized, fair, and predictable. Students often report that ESTJ teachers are tough but fair.

ESTJ teachers provide a model of objective problem-solving skills for their students. When a problem arises, they are likely to remain calm and clearheaded. They are usually able to provide specific instructions to others concerning what to do and often also focus some attention on how to prevent the problem from recurring.

ESTJs tend to be results focused. They want to see that students have mastered or achieved specific objectives. They try to keep the schedule and objectives for the school year firmly in their minds, and will often go to great lengths to ensure that all of the material identified is covered. An experienced ESTJ teacher knows exactly what will be taught in his or her classroom every month of the school year. New material is more apt to be used if its use has been mandated from a source above the teacher or if the material is convincingly better than older material in helping students meet learning objectives.

ESTJs usually learn best through experience, not necessarily through lengthy explanations. Their own lectures are likely to include specific examples of real-life experiences, including their own. Practice that generates continual concrete achievement is a cornerstone of their teaching methods.

ESTJs are most likely to praise students who have accomplished concrete observable tasks, such as a set number of homework assignments. They tend to be very specific in their praise, leaving students clear about what they are doing well.

Potential Weaknesses

Since they judge themselves by how well they do things and how much they can accomplish, they can be quite critical of themselves when they fail to achieve their objectives. They may also judge their students with the same criteria, and they can be quite critical of others, including other staff members, whom they perceive as ineffective.

They may have problems with students who tend to sit and think—more often Introverted Intuitive students. This type of student is often less likely to produce a large number of concrete products that fit the measurement criteria for success that is preferred by the ESTJ teacher. It is important that ESTJs learn to perceive and appreciate the gifts of other types so they can give appropriate feedback.

ESTJs may lose patience with a student who is performing slowly. Sometimes they will themselves complete parts of a project that the student is capable of doing because they want to ensure completion of the project or adhere to a schedule. They may have an accurate internal time clock and assume that everyone else does, too. Students who either lack this ability to track time or have one that is contrary to their ESTJ teacher's may receive particularly negative feedback from their ESTJ teachers.

The student who "talks back" is often not appreciated in an ESTJ class-room. ESTJs tend to firmly believe in hierarchy—they want to be in control and have the authority and responsibility to be in control. The temperaments that have the most difficulty with this authoritarian manner are the SPs and NTs.

While ESTJs are usually very interactive with other people, they may need to practice listening to other people's points of view. They sometimes make judgments too quickly without getting all of the facts or without taking other people's feelings into consideration.

ESTJs are good at finding things that need correcting. Students can be sure they will not be left in the dark about the areas in which they need to improve. Since their praise may be reserved for students who achieve high results, they may give some students more negative feedback than others. ESTJs should make an effort to find something to praise about each of their students. Students who continually see positive feedback being given to others and not themselves may eventually give up or resort to negative behavior in order to get attention from the teacher. ESTJs often do not realize how they can sometimes unintentionally encourage negative classroom behavior. Improving their listening and praising skills will help ESTJ teachers in their efforts to correct this problem.

The decisiveness, quickness to action, and comfort with giving orders may cause some students to see ESTJ teachers as too abrupt, threatening, or controlling. It is perhaps a minority of students who will react this way, but it would help them to recognize that some students might feel threatened by such behavior. The simplest solution is to address their needs with positive feedback and attention.

Causes of Stress and Possible Solutions

Environmental and Systemic Stressors   When an environment such as the classroom or the school becomes less predictable, an ESTJ teacher is likely to feel stressed. Major changes in school district policy may leave ESTJs feeling frustrated or resentful. *Solution:* When ESTJs are actively involved in evaluating or creating the changes, their stress level begins to decrease. ESTJs do not want to solve problems that they do not perceive as real. To help ESTJs deal with change, those making the changes should present a convincing case that a problem exists and that the proposed solution will create an effective procedure for solving the problem.

When ESTJs Bring Stress to Others   ESTJs sometimes make snap decisions without hearing all the evidence from others. They often do their
best thinking while talking and may find it difficult to stop and find out
what the other person is saying. This problem can exist between themselves and students, peers, administrators, or partners. *Solution:* ESTJs
need to practice hearing and repeating other people's words and their
meanings. They will need to listen in a way that ensures that both the
speaker and the listener agree on what has been said. Paraphrasing other
people's comments is a useful skill for the ESTJ. Adding this element to
their conversation will greatly decrease interpersonal conflicts.

When ESTJs Are Stressed by Others   If ESTJs do not get signals from
others that their contributions are needed and appreciated, they may feel
stressed. If they receive feedback that they are disruptive or not an effective member of the group, they may even begin to develop health problems. *Solution:* There is no simple solution for this problem. First, ESTJs
must ensure that they are healthy by getting adequate rest, nutrition, and
exercise. Second, the relationship problem must be defined. What is it
that causes others to see the ESTJ as ineffective? Asking others for information and getting descriptions of the specific behavior that leads others
to see them as ineffective will be useful. Learning about the different styles
of people and their needs can help the ESTJ identify what the problem
might be. Third, ESTJs need to experiment to see if there is anything they
can do, say, or hear from others that will improve the relationship.

Personal Stressors   ESTJs can get themselves in trouble by overusing
their gifts. If they take on too much responsibility, they can exhaust themselves. If their current environment underuses their gifts and does not
leave them feeling responsible and needed, they will become stressed.
ESTJs need to be aware of the signals that they are stressed, such as chronic complaints about physical ailments or emotional outbursts. *Solution:*
ESTJs need to examine the balance between responsibility and duty, and
relaxation. They need to receive positive feedback on responsibility and
duty in some part of their lives. If a momentary setback is occurring at
work, they need to make an effort to increase their positive feedback
through other avenues such as at home, through their religious institutions, or their community. When ESTJs become too inundated with

responsibility, they need to learn to say no and find time to do an activity that they feel is personally rewarding and different from current daily routines. One ESTJ teacher experienced difficulty with her fifth-grade class. She found herself experiencing back pain by the end of each day due to excessive muscle tension. To relieve this tension, she took a pottery class. She enjoyed the fellowship at the class and let herself experiment and learn something new. She did not set exacting standards for her work but treated it as play. The experience was highly successful in helping her relax, lose muscle tension, and gain a more positive outlook.

Summary

ESTJs are often gifted organizers who can be decisive and focus on results. They often excel in positions of leadership. They provide their students with a stable environment, effective procedures, and useful rational problem-solving methods. Their classrooms tend to focus on the accomplishment of measurable results.

ISTJ Inspectors

Basic Characteristics

Adjectives that describe the typical ISTJ are dependable, reliable and steadfast. They often work in a very systematic, step-by-step fashion, and their work can be painstaking and thorough. They can usually be counted on to complete all agreed-upon tasks in their own serious and quiet way.

Where They Are Found in Education

Like ESTJs, ISTJ teachers are found at all grade levels, but less often at the primary level, where the issues of dependency and nurturing are of greater importance. They are often attracted to teaching in the trade, industrial, technical, engineering, and business fields. They may be mathematics teachers or coaches. Like ESTJs, they often become school administrators. The sequence of teaching level that is typically preferred by ISTJs is university, community college, high school, middle school, elementary school, adult education, and preschool. ISTJs often excel at designing logical processes to use in the outside world, which they then teach to their students.

Preferred Teaching Techniques

ISTJs usually prefer more quiet concentrated work than ESTJs, and they often assign pencil-and-paper drills, workbook assignments, and quiet desk work. They like to stress the importance of memorizing correct procedures and facts, and they may use audiovisuals to emphasize facts and add reality to a discussion. They also like to use course outlines and contracts with students. Their classroom discussion time with students is usually spent in teacher-led question-and-answer periods, brief lectures, and explanations of procedures.

Strengths

ISTJs usually know their place in the school hierarchy and expect students to respond appropriately to their authority. They usually spell out classroom requirements in concrete detail and make students aware of how they will be measured.

ISTJs are skilled at devising routines. They like to sort information in their inner worlds and devise efficient, step-by-step routines. Their logical, sequential thinking also helps them to be very effective logistically. ISTJ teachers are often particularly gifted in helping students to sort and classify things. They are masters of facts and data and present information in a very sequential fashion.

ISTJs do not like disorder, either internally or externally. They like to have physically orderly classrooms that make clear to the students where supplies are kept and which areas are designated for special work.

The ISTJs' propensity for order and structure leads them to develop thorough and well-thought-out lesson plans and activities. One ISTJ elementary teacher, who realized that different students liked different learning activities, worked all summer to design a series of student packets for each teaching subject. Each packet included standard worksheets, as well as word finds, logic puzzles, crosswords, and puns and riddles to provide some activities that would appeal to each student. The students worked individually on the packet at their own pace, but the packet had to be turned in by a given deadline. Her packets were very popular with the students, who looked forward to the games and puzzles in them.

The knowledge and procedures of an ISTJ are typically organized in a very step-by-step, logical manner; therefore, they do not like to be interrupted. If a student interrupts to ask for an explanation, the ISTJ teacher will usually take extra time to explain, ensuring that the student understands exactly what is meant. Clarity in speech is a hallmark for the ISTJ.

When an emergency arises, ISTJs are likely to seem very calm. Since they usually pride themselves on acting sensibly and doing what is expected of them, they will often work industriously to fix a problem, even though they would prefer to avoid problems altogether. Their well-organized and logical procedures are designed to prevent problems from occurring.

Since ISTJs tend to take their obligations seriously, they will usually not accept new assignments impulsively. They like to take time to ensure that they will be able to fulfill an obligation. Once they accept an assignment, they will usually carry it out with diligence and they expect their students to do the same.

Since they learn best from past successes, ISTJs help their students see the relationship of the students' past successes to their future achievements. They often excel at detailing specific tasks or projects for students to accomplish. When students turn in assignments, ISTJs examine them carefully for discrepancies and inaccuracies. Students will find that ISTJ teachers will go out of their way to help them improve their ability to be more accurate.

ISTJs often enjoy helping students learn how to take care of themselves. They like to see students become more self-reliant and responsible. Students are likely to learn economic facts in their classrooms. When discussing an occupation, ISTJs are likely to emphasize the responsibilities and the steps needed to get to that position. ISTJs tend to be the embodiment of commitment and endurance.

Like ESTJs, ISTJs will ensure that the assigned curriculum for the year is covered in their classrooms. ISTJs may experience some dilemmas between ensuring that the complete curriculum is covered and that the students receive solid grounding in all of the curriculum. At times, they feel that there is not enough time to do everything thoroughly.

Potential Weaknesses

ISTJs are sometimes seen as too perfectionistic. Their attention to accuracy and detail can at times be taken too far. The student who works quickly and hastily can be judged as not being responsible by the ISTJ teacher. ISTJs need to recognize that accuracy and responsibility are not synonymous. Since ISTJs tend to be good at categorizing, they can help themselves by determining which assignments call for high accuracy and which ones call for speed with the potential for reduced accuracy. Both of these skills are necessary in the world of work, and ISTJs can assist their students in learning them.

ISTJs have difficulty changing priorities quickly. Their step-by-step routines are not easily changed on short notice. When sudden changes occur, they need time to adjust. It is often difficult for them to depart from their routines. Sometimes they may seem like a steamroller to other people, going along with their processes even when others protest. Others may see them as coldhearted and uncaring. Explaining their processes to others can sometimes mitigate hard feelings. Although it may be difficult for them to stop their processes and listen to other people, there are ways for them to develop this skill. For example, jotting down a note or two before listening to the other person may lessen their anxiety about losing their place in the routine.

ISTJs may have difficulty spending relaxed or social time with the students in their room. Because they are so focused on the tasks they must accomplish, they sometimes have difficulty allowing themselves and others to simply rest or play. Because ISTJs typically have more task-focused endurance than most of the other types, they may discourage their students by unrealistically expecting them to display the same ability. If they can consciously cultivate a sense of humor or play, they will become more effective in helping all of their students stay on task.

ISTJs tend to be primarily visual, and too much auditory stimulation may bother them. They are likely to prefer a very quiet classroom, which may be a problem for some of their Extraverted students. When ISTJ teachers take control of the discussion and set aside time for it to occur in the classroom, both ISTJ teachers and their Extraverted students will become more comfortable.

ISTJs may find it difficult to delegate classroom chores to students and may thus find themselves overworked, especially in their efforts to keep the classroom orderly. ISTJ teachers are sometimes bothered when students do not complete a job or do not perform a job in what the ISTJ teacher perceives as the correct step-by-step manner. Sometimes ISTJ teachers need to accept the work done by students, even if it is not as thorough as they would like. They also need to understand that the processes that are efficient for them may not be so for other people.

Since ISTJs are so reliable and dedicated, they sometimes overcommit themselves. To prevent this problem, they need to become proficient at risk assessment, which includes a cost-benefit analysis of doing a job and the level of accuracy that is required. Sometimes ISTJs must cut their losses and back out of a commitment. This is usually a painful process for them. They may find it helpful to renegotiate a deadline. ISTJs often do not let themselves rest until all their work is done, so they need to find ways to protect themselves from overwork.

Causes of Stress and Possible Solutions

Environmental and Systemic Stressors   While ESTJs tend to focus on school or school district policies, ISTJs tend to focus on material content. Changes in textbooks or curricula may be upsetting to them. They usually develop detailed processes—many of them written—on how to teach or explain material, such as a particular chapter in a textbook. While they are not afraid of hard work, they do not look forward to redeveloping their system to teach the new material. Giving new material to them suddenly may be upsetting. *Solution:* If ISTJs are involved in curricula reform, they are more likely to champion the necessity of reworking material. If they are not involved in the development, they fare better if they are given ample time to read and absorb the new material.

When ISTJs Bring Stress to Others   Sometimes ISTJs are so intent upon their own step-by-step processes that they do not pay attention to others. They may also act oblivious to others' needs or denigrate the requests or demands of others. If they proceed from process to process without keeping up with other people's needs, they may find themselves friendless. *Solution:* While ISTJs find it difficult to stop themselves in mid-process, they can take time to ask other people about their needs when the process is completed. Next, they need to take the time to evaluate their processes in light of the feedback they receive. Other people will respond better to their procedures if ISTJs demonstrate a willingness to consider their point of view.

When ISTJs Are Stressed by Others   If ISTJs do not receive feedback from others that their hard work is respected, eventually they will begin to experience stress. Since their focus is on being accurate, responsible, and reliable, signals that others do not see them in this light will lead them to question their hard work. Their habits will not allow them to stop working, but they will begin to feel exhausted and pessimistic. Others will likely begin to hear self-pitying messages, something along the lines of, "Poor me; I've worked so hard...." *Solution:* First, ISTJs must find ways to ensure that they get enough rest. Second, they need to determine in which areas they have been too perfectionistic. In their search for perfection, they often do not allow others to be responsible in their own way. Third, they need to experiment with play and humor; they can treat them as skills to be learned. These skills will then provide more balance to their lives.

Personal Stressors   Like all types, ISTJs can bring stress upon themselves by overusing their gifts. Too much hard work, too much routine, and too much perfectionism will begin to take their toll, and, under such circumstances, ISTJs can sometimes begin to lose control over facts and details. *Solution:* Since ISTJs are so hardworking, they need to treat play as a job that can be incorporated into their schedule. This play must encompass their students, family, and friends. Without play, ISTJs can become too one-sided. They sometimes need to say no to responsibility in order to allow themselves time for needed play. This can be done in a variety of ways, such as getting involved in sports and hobbies they enjoy. For example, one ISTJ high school teacher enjoys sports such as skiing and bowling; another performs with a madrigal group. Both say that finding enjoyable outside activities enables ISTJs to return to their work with more energy.

Summary

ISTJs are gifted organizers of data and materials. Their classrooms are usually organized and well run. They excel at helping students become responsible and self-reliant. They work to thoroughly understand and communicate the school curricula and help students learn effective thinking processes.

SFJ Providers

SFJ Providers would rather give information than orders, the preference of STJ Monitors. Since SJ Guardians have many "shoulds" and "oughts" about the right thing to do, SFJ Providers will also give orders, but they will typically soften the way they phrase the directive. For example, the SFJ might say something like, "Now's the time to put your books away and prepare for our next topic," whereas the STJ might say something more along the lines of, "Put away your books." SFJ Providers are concerned with getting things done, but they spend more time ensuring that people are comfortable achieving the objective. They give a cooperative tone to their communications with others.

ESFJ Caretakers

Basic Characteristics

Adjectives that describe the typical ESFJ are caring, sympathetic, and warmhearted. They tend to be very sociable and work with others cooperatively and harmoniously. When dealing with others, they are both responsive and tactful, and they often go out of their way to be helpful to others.

Where They Are Found in Education

ESFJ teachers are found at all grade levels. The primary grades particularly attract them because students at that level have dependency and nurturing needs. They also teach reading, special education, mathematics, English, health, art, drama, and music. As administrators, they are most often found in elementary and secondary schools, but they can sometimes be found as administrators in colleges and technical institutes. The sequence of teaching level that is typically preferred by ESFJs is adult education, elementary school, preschool, middle school, community college, and university. ESFJs are best at helping students use values and tradition in their relationships to create and maintain social harmony.

Preferred Teaching Techniques

ESFJs enjoy talking with their students and are often found explaining the importance of courtesy and procedures. They enjoy teacher-led discussions, question-and-answer time, oral drills, and memorization. Course outlines and contracts with students are also favored by ESFJs as a way to help students assume greater responsibility. For quiet time, they use workbook assignments and, occasionally, audiovisuals.

Strengths

ESFJs can have a tendency to classify things as either good or bad and can be fierce protectors of all of their charges. Safekeeping and concern for others' welfare are their hallmarks. Their skill at promoting socialization is especially needed in the early grades to help students establish acceptable patterns of social interactions. Students often learn a sense of membership and affiliation with group norms in ESFJ classrooms.

One first-grade ESFJ teacher who exemplifies these socialization patterns uses a calm and friendly voice. She ensures that no child is mistreated or left out. When a difficulty arises among students, she calmly reminds the disagreeing students of classroom rules that are posted on the chalkboard. She is careful not to make any individual child feel that she or he is being a scapegoat or unfairly disciplined.

Since they usually have high respect for traditions, ESFJ teachers like to ensure that students have a solid grounding in traditions. No student in the typical ESFJ classroom, for example, can have an excuse for not knowing how Thanksgiving was started. Students will learn such things as what the Pilgrims and Native Americans wore and what they ate. This theme of socialization is still evident at the high school level, where the ESFJ English teacher might talk about the customs, mores, and style of a period described in a novel.

ESFJ teachers are often good at calmly and consistently making decisions and giving specific instructions to meet each student's needs. They tend to dislike chaos and are usually able to manage multiple interactions in a classroom to remain in control. Most typical ESFJ teachers want the interactions in their classroom to be harmonious and well ordered, and will often insist on courtesy rules to ensure that this happens.

ESFJs are usually conscientious about teaching all of the school curricula, although they are less insistent that each item is taught than ESTJs or ISTJs, and will allow for extenuating circumstances that may necessitate some revision. In general, though, they will meet the overall objectives of the school year as closely as possible.

ESFJs will often extend themselves to ensure that a student understands the material and is comfortable with it. Their ability to nurture extends to an ability to listen to the student and determine where the student is having difficulty. They like to find the exact tool (book, artifact, etc.) that will help the student understand, or they will tell stories about other students to help illustrate how the specific difficulty can be overcome.

Touch is an important part of an ESFJ teacher's communication to students to show their caring. They may pat a student on the back or even hug them. One ESFJ elementary teacher is very aware of her sensitivity to those students who need affection. She sees touch as a way of reaching out to those children. Many of her elementary students will not begin their daily work until she has hugged them.

ESFJs have the ability to ensure comfort for themselves and everyone around them and because of this are often put on committees where concrete tasks address the comfort of others. It is not unusual for ESFJs to bring special treats to share with their co-workers. Good conversation, physical comfort, and nourishing food provide real pleasure for them.

Potential Weaknesses

ESFJs may sometimes be accused of having teacher's pets. Since they are often kind and caring, they will usually recognize that ability in their students, and these students may get more attention than others.

ESFJs often have a need to like their students and be comfortable in their surroundings. They strongly support rules and regulations that help enforce discipline, although they do not aspire to be known as "tough." They do best in a friendly atmosphere, and having a system in the school where they are supported when sternness is needed is helpful for ESFJs.

ESFJs often have well-developed "shoulds" and "should nots." Students with values that sharply contrast with those of the ESFJ may have difficulty. In a multicultural classroom, it is imperative that ESFJs take the time to learn the customs and values familiar to all of their students. If they do, they are likely to find a way to harmonize other specific patterns and customs with their own. If they do not, they may find themselves in conflict with some of their students.

ESFJs often decide quickly on issues concerning social interactions and customs. They are usually dedicated to traditional values. Sometimes they become involved in arguments about the "right" and "proper" way to do things with students or peers. Adding an extra phrase such as, "In these circumstances, it has traditionally been best to. . . " can sometimes mitigate the sense that they are insisting that things be done their way and only their way. Of course, that may be exactly what they mean, but since ESFJs are hurt by conflict, they can usually find an effective solution that meets all perspectives if given enough time.

ESFJs usually express their emotions and opinions easily. They can be seen as wearing their hearts on their sleeves. Typically, if you want to know where they stand on an issue, you can learn by just asking them. They spend a lot of time discussing how things seem and focus on their own and others' opinions of social standards. At times, they put off students and colleagues by being too judgmental of perceived violations of these standards.

When there is a lot of conflict in a classroom or school, ESFJs will go to great lengths to solve the problem. If the problem is too great for them to handle, they will enlist the help of others. When these efforts go unrewarded, ESFJs may begin to blame themselves and others for the problem. They can sometimes get caught up in a litany of complaints. If this occurs, they can become quite uncomfortable with themselves and others.

Causes of Stress and Possible Solutions

Environmental and Systemic Stressors   When personnel changes or curriculum changes occur, ESFJs may experience stress. They may strongly resist changing standards. Their dilemma is that they need these standards to help them recognize the "right" thing to do to ensure that things remain harmonious between people. Since they like to be in control and ensure that relationships are harmonious, they may sometimes spend too much time worrying about potential problems. *Solution:* When ESFJs are given enough notice and have adequate time to discuss the social implications of change, they begin to feel more comfortable. They are particularly good at recognizing contrasts and similarities and may be given the task of identifying these elements. Once contrasts and similarities are identified, integrating new elements is easier for the ESFJs. The more hard facts they are given and the more they interact with new personnel, the higher their comfort level will be.

When ESFJs Bring Stress to Others   In their need to achieve harmony and order, ESFJs can become overly critical of others. They can assume that everyone either shares or should share the same view of traditional values and behavior as they do. This critical behavior can cause others to withdraw their support from ESFJs. *Solution:* ESFJs can learn to identify when they are experiencing a values conflict with another person. Instead of lecturing the other person on what are correct values, they can learn to ask questions about the other's values. If they can learn the reasoning behind how and why these values were established—that is, what life experiences led to this behavior—they usually can become more accepting and tolerant of the other's values.

When ESFJs Are Stressed by Others   ESFJs can get locked into their own standards of behavior and experience difficulty with others who have different values. If a high level of conflict in the relationship develops, ESFJs may first blame the other person, then move on to blame themselves. Important relationships gone astray may begin a downward spiral for ESFJs, with them first blaming the other person for their own sadness and then blaming themselves for the sadness of the other. If the pattern is not broken, ESFJs can become caught in a chronic melancholy. *Solution:* In this case, ESFJs are caught in looking only at the dark side of life. Instead of being so highly engaged with the conflict, they need time for personal renewal. They need to stop working so hard to solve the problem and start focusing on personal activities that they find pleasurable. Only by doing so can they recharge themselves so they can continue to help others. They may need help from others in doing this.

Personal Stressors   ESFJs often have difficulty when they do not feel appreciated. Since they go to great lengths to ensure the comfort of others, they become troubled when these abilities are not acknowledged. They do not expect praise for all of their work, since they see themselves as only "doing their duty." They do need feedback affirming that their overall contribution is valued. A simple statement like, "You did an excellent job on the progress report," is a great energizer for them. If they do not get this recognition, they may redouble their efforts to do their work. If still no recognition is forthcoming, they may begin to be critical of others' efforts to "do their duty." This is a loud signal that they need personal recognition. If the problem continues, ESFJs may begin to underuse their gifts of harmonizing and increase their critical behavior. In extreme instances, they might use convoluted logic and compulsively search for truth. *Solution:* Since they are so good at helping other people to be comfortable, ESFJs can apply the same principle to themselves. When they find themselves becoming overly critical, they need to purposely increase the time they spend with people who gave them an emotional lift through praise or appreciation. By recognizing that they, too, need some of the comfort they so freely give to others and ensuring that this support is available, ESFJs can do a great deal to prevent themselves from moving into the critical and melancholy spiral.

Summary

ESFJs like to create harmony in their environment and effective socialization in their students. They like to integrate human courtesy and rules of interaction into the curriculum. They will go to great lengths to ensure that students have academic and personal skills that lead to stable and successful lives.

ISFJ Protectors

Basic Characteristics

Adjectives that describe the typical ISFJ are considerate, dedicated, and service minded. In their quiet and conscientious manner, they will often go to great lengths to protect the well-being of those around them. They usually are loyal and devoted and have great patience in helping students learn to perform detailed tasks.

Where They Are Found in Education

ISFJ teachers are found at all grade levels. Like ESFJs, they are often found in the primary grades, where children have dependency and nurturing needs. Subjects such as reading, mathematics, English, special education, health, art, music, and drama attract them. The sequence of teaching level that is typically preferred by ISFJs is preschool, elementary school, middle school, adult education, high school, community college, and university. ISFJs can be very effective at modeling quiet perseverance on tasks regardless of the obstacles.

Preferred Teaching Techniques

ISFJs prefer more quiet work than ESFJs. They use pencil-and-paper drills, workbook assignments, and quiet desk work to teach their lessons. They often use course outlines and contracts with students. Their students are encouraged to memorize facts and will be exposed to audiovisuals as a way of teaching them about reality. ISFJ teachers also like short periods of teacher-led questions and answers, and brief lectures. Their explanations of courtesy and procedures often are provided on a one-to-one basis as needed.

Strengths

ISFJs usually like to provide high predictability and comfort in their classrooms. They have a need to bring things under control so that surprises and changes are kept to a minimum, and sometimes go to great lengths to prevent feared problems from occurring. It is important to them to help others avoid becoming upset by unforeseen circumstances. Preservation, prevention, and protection is a natural way of life for them, and they are sometimes surprised when other people do not have the same needs. Their concern for safekeeping is very valuable in the lower grades, where students generally have a greater need for personal protection.

An ISFJ high school algebra teacher was a favorite of one student. The teacher's daily procedures were very predictable. Each day, she would do a short lesson, giving examples of each kind of problem in the homework. The problems were done in a very step-by-step fashion, with no explanation of the theory behind them. Students would spend the rest of the class period doing the homework quietly, while the teacher roamed the classroom to find any students who were having problems. She ensured that no student was left behind and that all students thoroughly understood the processes she was teaching.

ISFJs are very attuned to what other people say. They might even seem to have a hidden tape recorder in their heads because they can often accurately recount a conversation days, weeks, and years later. One ISFJ teacher used this ability to notice even the slightest bit of progress by a student. She would make the student aware of his or her improvement by comparing present work to previous work. Through an elaborate recognition system using rubber stamps and stickers, she would reinforce the student's success.

ISFJs provide a model for their students with their quiet sense of affiliation with group needs and their ability to work cooperatively. For ISFJs, no job is too small to be ignored or left undone. They often accept jobs that others look on as too menial or unglamorous. To the ISFJ, work that needs to be done must be done. To them, *all* elements of a job *must* be done, and they will usually persevere, continuing to quietly serve and do whatever is needed long after most of the other types have relinquished the task.

ISFJs are usually good at breaking down complex tasks into small manageable ones. When a student is having a problem with learning a concrete skill, an ISFJ teacher will usually have the patience to observe the student and let them know how other students in a similar situation became successful. ISFJs are particularly good observers of human nature and behaviors. When they have diagnosed the problem, they will quietly assist the student in gaining the specific skill needed to overcome the problem. They require no praise for their dedication—the student's success is the teacher's own reward.

Potential Weaknesses

ISFJs may be uncomfortable with public praise. They usually wish to be seen as being dedicated to doing their duty, not as seeking public recognition. Sometimes they need to have it pointed out that others may need to be praised even though they themselves do not. However, ISFJs do need appreciation. Appreciation is best shown by quietly remarking on the effects of the ISFJ's dedication.

If an ISFJ pays more attention to one particular student, it is usually because that student is experiencing some difficulty. They are not likely to have "teacher's pets," but they can be taken advantage of by a student in need of help. By confirming the student's needs with too much attention, they may only compound the problem.

ISFJs tend to have a quiet manner. A student who behaves inappropriately, in the eyes of the ISFJ, may provoke discomfort in his or her teacher. If ISFJs begin to experience this discomfort, they need to guard against forming a negative image of the student. When ISFJs become disappointed with a student's behavior, such as bullying or talking back, they may choose to withhold attention from that student. Within the mind of the teacher, the student may become labeled as "bad." ISFJs need to be especially sensitive to putting pejorative labels on students. One ISFJ junior high teacher found himself thinking about one student as *always* being disruptive. When another teacher questioned him about the student, he realized that the behavior occurred only under certain conditions. By identifying the conditions, he was able to minimize their occurrence and then identify and reinforce the student's positive behaviors.

ISFJs sometimes experience conflicting loyalties. They may fail to meet a student's need out of fear of being disloyal to the principal or the department head. They do not shortchange a student willingly, however, and they experience much inner conflict over such issues. But their sensitivity to positional power, authority, and responsibility means they will not take their own status and burden lightly, nor will they fail others they report to. On the other hand, some ISFJs are so willing to take a backseat that they may become too willing to serve others and let other people, including their students, take advantage of them. They can sometimes swing from being either too superior or too servile, so they need to take care not to find themselves exercising such extremes.

ISFJs can become too caught up in their need to prevent conflicts between people. In their desire to have things go smoothly and prevent anyone from becoming angry or upset, they can end up overworking and exhausting themselves. They can also push themselves to the point of martyrdom. If these efforts are not seen in a positive light but are viewed as either too controlling or overprotective, ISFJs may begin to receive negative feedback or criticism.

Causes of Stress and Possible Solutions

Environmental and Systemic Stressors   ISFJs do not like things to be too unpredictable. They are especially sensitive to the degree of control they have over their own space. Redesigners of classroom space may receive a lot of resistance to changes from ISFJs, for their classroom, like their home, is their castle. They adapt more easily to changes in curriculum than changes in environment, as they expect to have less control over curriculum than their classroom. However, any sudden change may trigger excessive worrying. *Solution:* The more lead time and the more concrete information they have about a change, the less ISFJs will worry. It is also helpful for them to spend time in a small group reviewing the changes. In regard to classroom space changes, they adjust better if some area of the classroom remains untouched. ISFJs have a strong need to control some degree of personal space or they experience stress.

When ISFJs Bring Stress to Others   ISFJs often stress others by being overprotective or overworried. Both worrying and overprotectiveness are connected to their need to prevent problems for themselves and others. When they begin to worry about a situation, they respond by increasing their helpfulness. If the help is seen as intrusive, people will begin to avoid them or make disparaging remarks. This may lead to increased worry and intrusion as the ISFJ makes a greater effort to solve the problem. *Solution:* ISFJs need to recognize that they can sometimes be too helpful. If they see others withdrawing or making negative remarks, they need to experiment with being less involved. ISFJs need to ask others if they need more help or if they prefer to take care of the situation alone. The simple act of asking may keep ISFJs from helping in ways that others do not appreciate. As ISFJs gain experience, they learn to give differing degrees of helpfulness, depending on the people involved and the situation.

When ISFJs Are Stressed by Others   In most cases, ISFJs are well respected for their generous giving to others. In their desire to contribute to the group, ISFJs may exhaust themselves from overwork in trying to serve everyone. Occasionally, they can be taken for granted and be underappreciated. While ISFJs do not want frequent exhibits of appreciation, they also do not like being ignored. Even worse for them is when others give them feedback that their efforts are unwanted. Then the ISFJ may worry about being rejected as a member of the group. They may globalize the problem and begin to worry about everything. ISFJs can worry themselves to the point of physical illness. *Solution:* ISFJs must make a point of having some personal quiet time when they are not serving anyone else. They need renewal time, time to do something just for themselves, time away from their worries and responsibilities. Such action can consist of very simple things, such as getting a new hairstyle, taking a walk in the park, or reading a book for pleasure. ISFJs can also learn to seek feedback from individuals they trust in order to get other perspectives on their situation—for example, they can brainstorm ideas on how to improve relationships.

Personal Stressors When too many negative things occur within a short period of time, ISFJs begin to see the world as being out of control. When they have labeled something as "bad," they are not likely to see it differently. They can generalize this feeling of negativity to other things that are similar. In such instances, their imagination can seem to run wild and these seemingly practical people can lose touch with reality and invent all sorts of catastrophes that they foresee occurring. *Solution:* Instead of trying to deal with this problem after it occurs, ISFJs are better off preventing the problem. The basic issue is a lack of balance in their lives. They need to ensure quiet time for personal pleasures and renewal. Without this quiet time, they will not experience the renewal and balance that they need.

Summary

Along with ESFJs, ISFJs are the most service oriented of all types. They serve with humility and endurance and often take on chores that other types see as too menial. They have a practical sense of life and assist their students in dealing with practical daily problems. Their ability to care for others, protect them, and endure provides a model for others and is communicated through all of their actions to others.

Chapter 5

Sensing–Perceiving
Artisan Teachers

Sensing–Perceiving (SP) Artisan teachers often need excitement and variety in their classrooms. There are fewer SP Artisan teachers in formal elementary and secondary schools than SJ Guardians. The traditional SP style of teaching is not unlike what one might find in the world of construction, where the master teaches the apprentice. The apprentice (the student) works right along with the master (the teacher) in the actual process of work. The teacher instructs the student only when a mistake is made or when a new technique is introduced.

In traditional classrooms led by an SP, instruction is likely to change pace—with fast-paced action in place at times, and a slower, more relaxed style in place at other times. SPs like variety, but as they gain greater mastery, the variety is likely to be within some loose-knit standard that they have found to be effective.

Self-actualization for SPs comes from the freedom to act on impulse, that is, the ability to move into action. They admire courage and risk taking. SP teachers like to make an impact on their environment, on materials, and on people. They like to experience the joy of being alive. A love of life in the moment defines teachers in this group. They are aware of the past and the future, but they are most intimately connected with the here-and-now. Students in a typical SP classroom are encouraged to be autonomous and bold and to exhibit personal virtuosity.

Typical SPs need their lives to be filled with a variety of sensory experiences. This is the group that most enjoys the sensual experience of food, clothes, music, and art. SPs cannot shut out the signals from their environment that they take in through their senses. Environments that give high stimulation to the senses, such as a loud and exciting sports event, often attract them. The classrooms of SP teachers often have multiple areas of stimuli. They may contain many objects or bright colors that stimulate the eyes or use variations in sound to stimulate the ears. Or they may encourage student movement and mobility in their classroom to heighten the level of sensory stimulation.

Colloquial phrases are often a common part of the language of SPs. SP teachers are likely to use some of the current language of their students when talking to them to increase fraternal bonding and camaraderie. They also use story-telling techniques to add fun and excitement to the classroom.

The work speed of SPs can vary greatly. They can easily shift from idle to overdrive if the need arises. In fact, they seem to enjoy being in idle, overdrive, and reverse more than they enjoy being in the customary drive mode. The pace in an SP classroom reflects this need for variety and improvisation. SP teachers will quickly adapt their lesson plans to seize an unexpected opportunity. A pragmatic immediacy infuses the SP teacher's classroom.

Gifted troubleshooters and tacticians, SPs can manage a crisis as if it created a fine adventure. Students learn from them that crisis and trouble do not equal a paralyzing fear of failure. The brave "can do" spirit of the SP teacher transmits the same kind of energy to their students.

SPs can quickly move from a state of high energy and excitement into a state of relaxation, and vice versa. This need for a variety in pacing is evident in the classroom as students move between fast-paced activity and periods of calm study.

SP Artisan teachers are good at making learning fun. They have lively classrooms that may be chaotic but where lots of hands-on learning occurs. They can usually tolerate a lot of noise and apparent confusion in the name of learning. SPs may enjoy shocking students slightly to get their attention. They can be unconventional and keep students on their toes. Extraverted SP teachers often enjoy being the star of the classroom and having students as their audience. Introverted SPs enjoy getting involved in student-generated excitement. SP teachers dislike giving busy work. They are often willing to take risks in teaching that others are unwilling to take. They are also good at allowing their students the freedom to fail and, thus, the freedom to succeed. SP teachers may find themselves stifled by administrators who like orthodoxy and lesson plans that must be followed. Students often like SP teachers because they can be exciting and entertaining.

There are two major categories of SP Artisan teachers: STP Operators and SFP Performers, which are illustrated in table 9.

Table 9 SP Artisan Teachers	
STP Operators	**SFP Performers**
ESTP Promoters	ESFP Entertainers
ISTP Troubleshooters	ISFP Composers

STP Operators

STP Operators tend to give more directives than SFPs. A need for quick timing or efficiency usually drives their directives to others. However, they generally give orders only when necessary, as they enjoy a personal sense of freedom and prefer to extend as much freedom to others as possible. STPs are extraordinarily observant of details and movements that contribute to a student's success or failure. This skill is demonstrated by the woodshop teacher who points out that the student is not angling the drill in an effective manner and by the basketball coach who tells her players exactly how to move to make a play work.

ESTP Promoters

Basic Characteristics

Adjectives that describe the typical ESTP are active, energetic, and versatile. With their pragmatic view of situations, they are the adaptable realists of a school faculty. They are alert to clues from both the environment and people. This ability to be highly observant allows them to make quick assessments and take quick action.

Where They Are Found in Education

It is uncommon to find ESTPs within the ranks of teachers. When they do teach, they are often coaches or in trade, industrial, or technical fields. Some become administrators at the elementary- and secondary-school levels. The sequence of teaching level that is typically preferred by ESTPs is adult and trade/vocational education, middle school, community college, university, high school, and elementary school. ESTPs are best at teaching students to "read" situations so they can get desired results. This "reading" includes seeing the motivations of participants and other factors influencing the situation.

Preferred Teaching Techniques

ESTPs enjoy a gaming relationship with their students. They seldom give dry lectures; rather, they will demonstrate techniques, give entertaining illustrations, and encourage student experimentation. They enjoy oral playfulness with materials and competitive games. For quiet times, they use hands-on manipulatives and handicrafts.

Strengths

ESTPs are experts at observing and quickly reacting to signals from the external world. Often the motivations of others become apparent to them as they carefully observe body language. This skill allows them to be excellent negotiators. Being keen observers of things and people, they can determine what is needed to get the results they want.

ESTPs tend to love challenge and excitement. Crises often bring out the best in them as they boldly put out the fires. Their ability to "read" people makes them good motivators of groups. They are not usually long-winded, but their talks are filled with picturesque stories or images that get people excited and ready to respond.

When a program is in trouble or has become bogged down, ESTPs can get it moving again. No established procedure is sacred if it is getting in the way of making things happen. ESTP administrators can often cut through red tape to get things moving again. They strive for the most pragmatic solution. ESTPs will make the changes, but they often need the SJs to establish effective standard operating procedures after the ineffective roadblocks have been torn down.

In the trade or vocational schools, ESTPs teach in those areas where their ability to influence others and their desire for excitement can be an asset. In the classroom, they may set up team contests. They often like to encourage the attitude of "beat your buddy" just to keep the excitement going. They also like a friendly, relaxed atmosphere for a change of pace. Students in their classrooms report that it is "challenging but fun."

Since they are good observers, they can remember and apply many facts. Having little patience for theory, they prefer facts to be based on experience. ESTPs have a tactical awareness and focus their teaching on things that can be applied right now, not at some remote future date. For example, if an ESTP is teaching auto shop, students will repair a real car that will have practical benefit to someone in the class.

ESTPs can be firm when they have to. They prefer to be friendly and relaxed but do not hesitate to give an order when an immediate situation calls for it. In such cases, they can give out an order without hesitation or compunction. To them, it is something that is needed right now to get on with the action. An ESTP baseball coach reports,

> my team does better when we have a change of pace between being "laid back" and going for broke. Keeping the tension up and ordering players around works for some coaches, but not for me. The guys let off steam by joking around, and I encourage that. But things change when it's time to compete. There's no more monkeying around and they need to listen up. When I talk, it's time to jump. We know how to play, *and* we know how to win.

ESTPs like to teach their students how to enjoy living. They often surround themselves with things that are stimulating to the senses, such as good food, clothes, music, and art. Their avid curiosity about objects, places, and people propels them to seek new experiences. Life is rarely dull around an ESTP.

Potential Weaknesses

The ability to sustain long-term concerted effort is not as natural to ESTPs as it is to SJs. Therefore, ESTPs need work that is full of action and variety. ESTPs like to work on large projects, as long as the day-to-day operations of the project carry some excitement and variety. If ESTPs envision schemes that are too grandiose or have too long-term a focus, they may get bored with the process and opt for the quick fix.

ESTPs may need to find someone to take care of critical details after they have achieved the grand flourish. One ESTP teacher managed to convince the principal, school board, parents, and students that they could raise enough money to visit Washington, D.C. He was quite persuasive, and the students rose to the challenge. In record time, they raised the money. Then a parent discovered that the budget was based on another school's trip that had been underwritten by a benefactor. The ESTP, of course, was up to the crisis. The ISTJ mother who had discovered the problem reworked the budget to reduce costs, while the teacher personally visited some local merchants who helped him cover the budget shortfall.

ESTPs sometimes sidestep authority and find ways to bend rules and regulations that they find too confining. They need to be careful that their students do not see them modeling behavior that would get the students in trouble. Since they delight in their own ability to "get away with things," they usually laugh off student antics and are amused by the student's courage. However, when they think the student has pushed the limits too far, they may respond harshly. Without some guidelines, their students may not understand what risk-taking behaviors will result in punishment or a laugh. Sometimes ESTPs do not fully adhere to their principal's priorities. They like to respond to the moment and this sometimes takes them far afield. ESTPs may not complete all of the elements of the prescribed curriculum. The side adventures they take seem much more important to them, and they believe that students learn more from these spontaneous undertakings.

The ESTPs' need for novelty may make them stretch the boundaries of what is approved or acceptable. They may occasionally find themselves in trouble over something that is, to them, a very trivial matter. With their verbal fluency and ability to accurately guess what others are thinking, they are usually able to talk themselves out of trouble.

Since ESTPs enjoy games so much, they may overuse this technique in their classroom. The more cooperative types, such as SJs and NFs, may become stressed if too much of the curriculum has a competitive theme.

ESTPs love a good time and they usually can spot the most efficient route to get there. They may be criticized for having too much fun or laughter in their classes. If they sacrifice student learning and achieving of objectives for this fun, the criticism will be deserved. Successful ESTPs learn how to blend learning objectives and fun in a very pragmatic way that makes their classroom a fun and exciting place to be.

Causes of Stress and Possible Solutions

Environmental and Systemic Stressors   ESTPs become stressed by too many restrictions, so if a school system becomes too rigid with too many rules, ESTPs will often rebel or leave. Changes in curriculum will be resisted if they do not fit any of the ESTPs' life experiences. If after offering verbal resistance there is no likelihood of changing the circumstances, ESTPs will adapt and at least for appearances seem as if they are carrying out the change. *Solution:* When ESTPs are involved in a change, they must ensure that the change is practical, makes sense, and is not too complicated. Like most people, ESTPs adapt more easily and contribute more positively when they are included in the communication loop.

When ESTPs Bring Stress to Others   ESTPs are so good at getting what they want that they sometimes overpower other people. ESTPs do not steam roll over others the way that ESTJs and ENTJs have a tendency to do; they simply convince the affected individual to see the world in a different way and take action based on that perception. *Solution:* ESTPs can actively seek opinions and ideas from others whose views are different from their own. Strengthening the art of listening without trying to convince the other person to see things differently is an added skill for the ESTP.

When ESTPs Are Stressed by Others   ESTPs do not typically require much recognition from others and tend to be very pragmatic by nature. They are sensitive to others' lecturing them about their faults. If the lecturing continues over a period of time, it can sometimes produce thoughts of revenge within ESTPs, possibly in the form of petty actions against the lecturer. *Solution:* Although ESTPs can be good at persuading others to do what they want them to, they need to learn that they cannot truly control another's behavior. ESTPs need to empathize more with others and avoid thoughts of revenge. They also need to put their sharp minds to work on a win-win solution for both sides and present the solution in a way that includes a stop-nagging element. For example, an ESFJ teacher and an ESTP teacher shared the same classroom. The ESFJ wanted it kept tidy, but the ESTP had so much excitement going on that the students did not have time to put things away before they left. When the ESTP promised to have a big surprise for the ESFJ if she would not remind him about the classroom mess for one week, she grumbled a bit but agreed. Then he told his students that they would play a joke on the other teacher. On the first day, the room was a little cleaner. The second day, even better. The third day was a pleasant surprise. By the fourth day, it was neat as a pin. Finally, on the fifth day, she found the room smelling of disinfectant and furniture polish with a chalkboard drawing of the ESTP teacher as "Mr. Clean." His students had spent the last fifteen minutes of class cleaning the room. Everyone had a good laugh. They also liked how clean the room was so it never went back to its previous sloppy state.

Personal Stressors   ESTPs in general have an aversion to being hemmed in. They want life to be filled with excitement, challenge, relaxation, and fun, which they cannot experience if they are feeling confined. When other people try to constrain them too much, they will first try to talk themselves out of the trap. When that does not work, they will do less talking and take more action. *Solution:* One way they can rid themselves of anger and frustration is through physical exercise. Engaging in an activity that allows them action, change of pace, or change of scenery is helpful. One teacher goes camping with her family when she becomes stressed.

Summary

ESTPs usually have classrooms that are fun and full of activity. They are gifted in finding the "teachable" moment and are effective at responding to crises with immediate solutions. Their negotiating skills make them persuasive teachers and coaches. They like to show students how to look at all angles of a situation and to devise solutions that help them get what they want.

ISTP Troubleshooters

Basic Characteristics

Adjectives that describe the typical ISTP are independent, adventurous, and expedient. They are cool observers of life. Their concrete analytical skills enable them to effectively teach the how and why of things. ISTPs often have abundant physical energy and find effective and efficient ways to apply their skills.

Where They Are Found in Education

Like ESTPs, ISTPs are infrequently found in the teaching field. When they do teach, they are often coaches or in trade, industrial, or technical fields. With their strong preference for the more hands-on or action-oriented areas of learning, they are most commonly found in adult and trade/vocational education. Occasionally, they teach at middle school, elementary school, university, high school, or community college. ISTPs are best at modeling any skill that requires a high degree of hand-eye coordination.

Preferred Teaching Techniques

Often economical with words, ISTP teachers prefer to engage their students with handicrafts and hands-on manipulatives. Like ESTPs, they enjoy competitive games and are likely to give small group or one-on-one demonstrations of techniques, followed by student experimentation. They encourage physical playfulness with material.

Strengths

ISTPs, like ESTPs, like to gather lots of concrete data, especially of a visual nature. They have the ability to see the essential information that zeros in on a problem. Most ISTPs are gifted with their hands and are often found teaching in areas that deal with manipulatives, such as shop classes. They usually prefer to demonstrate or model a skill rather than describe a skill with words. This can often be done one-on-one on an as-needed basis. They can also be virtuosos of improvisation, using their keen senses to troubleshoot immediate problems.

While many ISTPs find the technical or mechanical fields attractive, some prefer to logically manipulate facts or data and often have an uncanny ability to see interactions in motion. ISTPs often have a highly developed sense of action relationships, that is, they have an awareness of how all things impact each other. This differs from the ISTJ's step-by-step organization of data. The ISTP's steps are multiple and in action.

ISTPs believe in economy of effort. Getting a lot of work done with the least amount of effort is an ISTP gift. They use their well-developed logical abilities to see how multiple actions can be done simultaneously. Their students learn how to break down projects into components and how those components relate to each other. If multiple components can be worked on simultaneously, they show their students how to do so. Their instructions are given more by actions than words.

ISTPs can be as hardworking as ISTJs, but tend to work with more changes of pace. The work being produced is not motivated primarily by the desire to meet objectives, but from a need for action. Although ISTPs enjoy relaxing for a while, they often get restless and put their bodies into motion. The classroom for the ISTP needs to have plenty of areas for action.

An ISTP's classroom is likely to be full of motion but unlikely to be noisy. ISTP teachers tend to be on the quiet side. For them, action truly speaks louder than words. Too much talk seems to interfere with their motions. They do, however, like to have some relaxed time, and quick banter and jokes are often encouraged.

ISTPs often have a wry sense of humor and use it to add excitement to the classroom. Sometimes they will purposefully keep a student guessing. For example, one ISTP physics teacher deliberately models techniques incorrectly, expecting his students to catch his error. If the students fail to identify the mistake, he repeats the error, exaggerating it and acting out consequences for the error. Many ISTPs have taught themselves by trial and error, and they often like to set up situations that force their students to experiment to find solutions. ISTP teachers often like to use their dexterity and wit to solve problems.

ISTPs are often good at fixing things. They like to see how things work and are often adept at creating adaptations to make things work. ISTPs often do not look at directions when assembling items. If they must read directions, they will—but usually only after their efforts weren't successful.

ISTPs who are athletic coaches are often found in individual events such as track and field, swimming, or tennis. When they coach team sports, they like to spot how each individual works best and set up team actions to maximize each player's abilities. Their focus will be on how to enable each individual to work toward a personal best rather than on elements such as team spirit.

ISTPs typically love a challenge. They often use challenge as a way to motivate students. If it is an area they are interested in, they will go to great lengths to demonstrate that they can succeed. An ISTP teacher had a parent donate a computer to her classroom, but the parent forgot to bring the manuals for the software. The students wanted to use the computer right away. One student said, "I'll bet you can't figure it out so that we can use it tomorrow." Naturally, the ISTP teacher stayed after school, hooked up the computer, played with the software, and created a lesson for the students to use the next day.

Potential Weaknesses

ISTPs value their freedom and do not like others telling them what to do. They usually remain cool and detached observers of what is going on around them until they feel compelled to take action. Their reluctance to become too directive and their bias toward detachment may cause problems for those students who crave more direction. With experience, the ISTP teacher can learn how to identify students who need more assistance and give them more guidance.

ISTP teachers usually give praise infrequently. Praise is less likely to come through words than through such signals as a thumbs up, a raised eyebrow, or a quick toss of the head. Students need to learn that ISTPs often praise them by giving them opportunities for more action.

ISTPs are bored by routine. Doing the exact same lesson plans every year to meet curriculum goals can seem constraining to them. They need stimulation and variety, and if it is not in the curriculum, they will often create it. The variety they provide can sometimes be surprising. In an urban high school that had an agricultural program, students had traditionally competed for prizes at the county fair with their animals. To add some excitement to the program, the ISTP teacher had the students compete among themselves to see who could teach their animals tricks.

ISTPs sometimes wait until the last minute before beginning a task. As they get older, their ability to determine the amount of time it takes to get things done usually improves. If they do not achieve this improved sense of timing, they are not likely to achieve their objectives. This is especially important in a school setting where there are specific objectives to be met.

ISTPs are very independent and can be infrequent talkers. Sometimes they can be so cool and collected that they appear to have no feelings. Because some students perform better if they perceive that their teacher feels some warmth toward them, ISTPs can compensate with their sense of humor so students receive some attention. ISTPs sometimes do not give enough consideration to other people's values. Values are strong motivators for many students and ISTPs need to learn how to be sensitive to others' values in the teaching process.

Causes of Stress and Possible Solutions

Environmental and Systemic Stressors   ISTPs, like ESTPs, become stressed by too many rules and regulations. They accept only those rules and regulations that they see as necessary and practical. They will often either ignore or work around excessive regulation. ISTPs do not necessarily communicate their resistance to such rules; they simply act in ways that make sense to them. If the rules are so detailed that they tell the teacher exactly what to do, it is likely that the ISTP will leave. In their minds, there is always another place to play the game when the game's rules become boring or too restrictive. They also tend to pay little heed to social conventions and can alienate those who find meaning in social requirements, such as the ESFJs and ISFJs. *Solution:* Viewing social customs and rules through a playful and gamelike outlook can help ISTPs become more aware of conventions that are important to others. Recognizing the negative consequences of not playing by the rules can help the ISTP see which rules are vital and which are not. When ISTPs experience real-life consequences that result from their tendency to ignore significant rules or social conventions, they learn very quickly what behavior they want to change.

When ISTPs Bring Stress to Others   Since ISTPs are more action oriented than communication oriented, others can sometimes be left in the dark about what ISTPs are thinking. Partners and co-workers can sometimes be left feeling ignored or abandoned. *Solution:* Since their natural mode is action, some ISTPs can learn to use action as their main mode of communication. One ISTP teacher shows that he appreciates others by buying "junk" from garage sales, restoring the items, and giving them to fellow teachers.

When ISTPs Are Stressed by Others   Emotional issues are often stressful for ISTPs. When a student, partner, or friend has an emotional difficulty, ISTPs are likely to either avoid them or try to tease them out of the problem. ISTPs will go to great lengths to avoid an emotional scene. They have been known to walk out of meetings and even disappear for a while. First, ISTPs are likely to try to defuse the situation with humor, which works as a distractor. If this does not work and the other person feels belittled by this behavior, ISTPs may respond with a quick unemotional statement of facts. They hope this will suffice to end the problem. If the other person continues to respond to the ISTP with negative emotion, the ISTP may become angry. Sometimes it is much better for the ISTP to leave a situation and cool down rather than strike out with anger. *Solution:* If the traditional defenses of the ISTP do not work, it is usually best to step away from the problem and come back to face it another time. ISTPs, who can sometimes be calm and cool loners, can become hypersensitive to relationship issues if they become involved in stressful interactions. Sometimes using another person, whom both parties respect, as a mediator can help restore effective communication.

Personal Stressors   If ISTPs do not have enough personal freedom, space, and alone time, they can become tense. They usually work off personal tension through action, which they often turn to good use. If they receive too much criticism or if their actions turn out in some way to be ineffective, they may turn outward with anger. They may also feel stressed if they feel their lives have become too bland and lack excitement. *Solution:* ISTPs need to have plenty of options for positive action. The more options they have for positive action, the less likely they are to turn that action into negative use when they are stressed. They often choose hobbies that can be done alone or with an adventurous friend. Some ISTPs enjoy action sports, such as skiing, tennis, and soccer, while others enjoy quieter activities, such as reading and model building.

Summary

ISTPs, like ESTPs, have classrooms focused on action and are able to teach their students to solve problems with an economy of motion and words. They show their students how to solve problems logically and quickly by manipulating data or materials. They challenge students to solve their own problems.

SFP Performers

Like STPs, SFPs need to feel a sense of personal freedom. SFPs are among the types least likely to give orders. They much prefer to give information and let the listener decide what to do with it. When SFPs must give orders, they sometimes give them harshly, which demonstrates their personal discomfort with the process. SFPs, particularly ISFPs, can get so caught up in what they are doing that they lose track of time. But they often use their grace and flair to make up for lost time.

ESFP Entertainers

Basic Characteristics

Adjectives that describe the typical ESFP are playful, vivacious, and out-going. They tend to demonstrate acceptance and tolerance for others. With their talkative, exciting style, they can be very entertaining. ESFPs can also help others to relax and take time to enjoy life.

Where They Are Found in Education

ESFP teachers are found in areas where they can be expressive and create an atmosphere of excitement and variety. Though not found in teaching as frequently as ESFJs, they are often found in preschool and kinder-garten, where their motto is often "learning is fun." They may coach or teach reading, special education, health, art, drama, music, mathematics, or English. They may be administrators for special programs in elementary school, secondary school, colleges, and technical institutes. The sequence of teaching level that is typically preferred by ESFJs is pre-school, elementary school, adult education, middle school, community college, high school, trade/vocational school, and university. ESFPs are best at helping students to use values and tradition in their relationships to create and maintain social harmony.

Preferred Teaching Techniques

ESFPs tend to be fluent talkers. Through the use of dramatization, demonstration, and student experimentation, ESFPs keep their classes lively. They are likely to engage students in playful games. Their students often are encouraged to enjoy sensory experiences and use speed and action.

Strengths

ESFPs are the most fun loving of all the types, and their students experience much play and laughter in their classrooms. They are very observant and have a natural ability to see exactly what is needed to make something work. If a student is working on an art project, ESFP teachers are most likely to appear at the student's side at exactly the right moment with a new tube of color saying, "Here, try this." The color will usually be the exact thing that will help increase the painting's impact.

ESFPs are exceptionally good at observing body language, making them good coaches and vocational arts teachers. An ESFP typing teacher achieved a high success rate with beginning typists. She constantly scanned the classroom as she casually strolled around the room. She could tell if students were holding their fingers incorrectly over the keyboard just by the tilt of their heads and the movement of their shoulders. In a very low-key manner, she would show the students just how to hold their fingers. Students did not feel they were being criticized for poor performance because she made an entertaining exercise of how they should stroke the keyboard.

ESFPs are usually very alert to sounds. One ESFP English teacher, who was working in a multicultural classroom, realized that many of her students were concerned about obtaining good-paying jobs. Some were concerned that their accents might affect their ability to obtain such jobs. When her class decided to experiment with accents, the teacher actively encouraged them to playact and experiment. She also used oral reading as a vehicle for giving her students tips on how to sound out words to produce different accents.

The ESFPs' playful style is a natural stress reliever and an energizer for most groups. They can tolerate more differing activity in their classrooms and a greater level of noise than most other types. Their classrooms are also likely to be full of stimulating color. Zest for life is their motto, and they energize other people around them.

ESFPs are usually very tolerant of individual differences and accepting of people for what they are. Their relationships with their peers and students send messages of fraternal goodwill. They project an easy camaraderie with others, and their actions and speech express an excitement for life.

ESFP teachers use humor to defuse the negative aspects of life. If they have a problem, they are likely to belittle it by laughing at themselves. With their gift of exaggeration, they can make something very serious suddenly become ridiculous. They teach their students to see problems as things to be disposed of as quickly as possible so they can return to the joy of living. Because they are so in tune with the moment, they can often see new ways of using materials and utilizing people to solve problems.

One ESFP first-grade teacher put on a class play. Fifteen minutes before show time, a student came to him in tears because her mother had forgotten the black cape she needed to wear for her role. "Don't worry," consoled the teacher. "We'll figure something out." With the children helping to tape and staple, a cape was soon created with construction paper and crepe paper. The problem was solved and the play was a great success.

Potential Weaknesses

ESFPs occasionally find themselves in trouble because of their spontaneous actions, which, while they may solve one problem, can create another. Usually ESFPs can find some quick solution to solve that problem as well. In their efforts to allay such problems, ESFPs may find themselves forgetting or ignoring rules and regulations. They want to get along with others, and their easygoing enthusiasm and excitement often persuade others to go along with their schemes.

ESFPs need many opportunities for socialization. They express their joy of life with other people through communication. Normally gifted as very persuasive talkers, they can sometimes talk other people into exciting, risk-taking adventures. If the other people are very conservative, the results may not work out as well as the ESFP had expected. However, since they are such good talkers, they may not give the quieter people any time to express their opinions.

ESFPs are often very generous, and they expect others to be the same. They tend to give freely without the expectation of receiving anything in return. If another teacher needs to borrow some supplies, generous ESFPs are often their first target. When ESFPs need some assistance, they expect the same treatment from others. If it is not forthcoming, they may become resentful and seriously curtail their former generosity, which is a loss for everyone invovled.

ESFPs tend to love good food, good life, and good times. Occasionally, they may go overboard on spending to achieve these things. One ESFP teacher had a chronic problem of running out of materials before the end of the school term. She would then find ways to barter time or finished materials with other teachers in order to make it through the year. She also persuaded local merchants to give her castoff materials.

ESFPs are among the most positive and upbeat of teachers. They prefer life to be an exciting adventure, full of surprises and stimulating sensations. They are likely to focus much more on the positive than on the negative. At times, this may lead them to ignore unpleasant situations. If this situation is a one-time occurrence, ignoring the problem may have no negative consequences. If the situation is recurring, ESFPs may need some support. ESFPs often find it useful to discuss the particular situation with other teachers to see what others have done in a similar situation. As they gain more experience, ESFPs usually identify problems early and prevent them from escalating.

Causes of Stress and Possible Solutions

Environmental and Systemic Stressors   ESFPs usually do not like learning theoretical material. They are very practically oriented and learn best by doing. Although they are highly adaptable, they are likely to have trouble with curriculum changes that are highly theoretical. *Solution:* ESFPs do best when theoretical areas are translated into practical applications. In-service training might help them with this. For example, ESFPs might teach the new math approach to addition and subtraction by the very useful method of making change. If ESFPs are given the opportunity to actively practice new learning and talk about it with others, they are likely to adapt quickly.

When ESFPs Bring Stress to Others　While the ESFPs' approach to life as an adventure of fun and pleasure is enjoyed by those around them most of the time, there are times when it creates problems. ESFPs are often reluctant to face problems, which may result in a compounding of the problems. Other people in their lives may be hurt by this tendency, and they may be left to pick up the pieces. Others may feel compelled to bail ESFPs out of the difficulty they have created for themselves. *Solution:* ESFPs need to talk to others about occasions when they successfully addressed problems and balanced their obligations with their need to have fun. They can also recruit the help of a friend who will let them know when they are avoiding difficulties. They can enlist the friend to help them talk through their solutions.

When ESFPs Are Stressed by Others　ESFPs do not like to have other people tell them exactly how to do things. If the person also monitors the ESFP's behavior to ensure that she or he is doing something right, the ESFP is likely to rebel by acting out in some way—possibly ridiculing the person. They may perform a charicature of the monitor, getting a laugh form their colleagues. *Solution:* When rules and regulations seem restrictive, ESFPs first need to ensure that they understand the rules and regulations and the reasons for them. Often when ESFPs understand the reasoning behind the rules, they are more motivated to comply with them. They can also discuss with the administrator different ways they might satisfy the rules' objectives. Sometimes a mediator can help solve the problem.

Personal Stressors　When ESFPs do not experience enough joy of life and excitement, they may complain about being bored. They may compensate for this boredom by engaging in pleasure binges. These binges may take the form of indulging in food, spending money on clothes, or taking risks. *Solution:* ESFPs need to ensure that they have variety in their lives. Activities that allow them to be in the limelight can be energizing. They are often sociable, communicative, and humorous, which makes them natural performers. Many ESFPs benefit from honing these skills. Their natural talent in performance may be used in teaching, selling, acting, dancing, persuasion, and negotiation. Exploration of things that are new—new events, new restaurants, and new sites—enlivens ESFPs. Experiencing freedom and variety usually reenergizes ESFPs and helps them to deal with stress.

Summary

ESFPs have active, colorful, and fun-filled classrooms. They are often natural performers and keep their classrooms lively. Their students are likely to feel accepted for who they are and have experiences that play to their own strengths. ESFP teachers express their love of life to their students and provide them with spontaneous excitement and fun.

ISFP Composers

Basic Characteristics

Adjectives that describe the typical ISFP are modest, gentle, and trusting. They are observant and understanding of others. They are very adaptable and become loyal followers, unless the leader's values are contrary to their own. In their quiet, warm way, they retain the quality of free spirit.

Where They Are Found in Education

ISFPs are not found as frequently in teaching as ISFJs. Like ESFPs, they are usually found in the more expressive and action-oriented areas of teaching. The subjects they may teach include speech, art, music, drama, reading, mathematics, special education, health, and industrial crafts. The sequence of teaching level that is typically preferred by ISFPs is adult education, elementary school, preschool, middle school, high school, community college, and university. ISFPs are best at modeling for students an appreciation of the beauty of life and artistic form.

Preferred Teaching Techniques

ISFPs often provide their students with exciting sensory experiences. They encourage physical playfulness with material, artistic expression, and humorous subtleties. They engage students in playful, cooperative games and use small group or one-on-one demonstrations, which are then followed by student experimentation.

Strengths

ISFPs like to learn by doing and to teach by having their students do. ISFPs do not teach primarily by words but by actions. Their methods frequently involve the whole person in the sensing aspects of the moment. They are often found in the arts or other fields that involve body movement and creative expression.

In the arts, ISFP teachers often enjoy experimenting with patterns of movement and store the experience as knowledge. Their awareness to their bodies can be applied to various fields—from dancing to nursing care to word processing. For the ISFP, practice occurs not to master a set of movements, but to experience the action itself. ISFP teachers encourage their students to enjoy what they are doing while they are doing it.

ISFPs often express a quiet joy of living to others. They usually have a lighthearted sense of humor that helps them through troubled times. Since they prefer life to be more spontaneous than planned, their students often experience surprises in their classrooms—a new technique in art, a new piece of music, a schedule adjustment to make time for an audiovisual. They also often love the outdoors and are good at helping students explore nature, learn to garden, or raise small animals.

ISFPs have strong values and want to be free to live by their own values, although they have no desire to force them on others. ISFP teachers help students discover their own value sets in a very nonthreatening and supportive environment. They have a great deal of tolerance for human differences, as long as the differences are not in conflict with their own values.

ISFP classrooms are usually fun, experiential, and exciting. Since they enjoy student-generated enthusiasm, ISFPs may encourage their students to show off. There is likely to be an artistic flair to their classrooms that expresses the personalities of both the teacher and the students. Students are not overly constrained by rules in an ISFP classroom. They prefer students to have as much personal freedom as possible. If a student crosses too far over the line, the ISFP teacher will take action but is not likely to scold.

Their students are encouraged to be cooperative and help each other. This attitude is modeled rather than discussed. ISFPs quickly attend to the real needs of others. However, they are good at identifying when students are merely playing to get their attention and seldom fall prey to them.

ISFPs are similar to ISFJs in that they are both very loyal and prefer that the people around them have harmonious relationships. A key difference is that ISFJs work hard to prevent potential problems, while ISFPs cope with problems as they occur. If a tempest comes, they will scramble to address the problem. Through their highly developed sensitivity toward others, they have the ability to diagnose and solve problems quickly.

ISFPs are compassionate toward students or friends who are having difficulties. For example, an ISFP will impulsively give up his or her free time to help another teacher who has just received emotionally upsetting news. ISFPs translate caring into immediate action and do not concern themselves about the time they are giving up in the process of helping.

Potential Weaknesses

ISFPs are so easygoing most of the time that it can sometimes be hard for their students to recognize that they mean business until they become angry. One ISFP teacher found that she was not getting her students to respond to her warnings to stop inappropriate behaviors until she became visibly angry. She felt they were taking advantage of her. She realized that she needed to issue consequences immediately for at least some behaviors if she wanted her students to listen to her. She focused on two unacceptable behaviors and moved into action to stop them as soon as they occurred. For behaviors that were not as serious or occurred less frequently, she used a signal that alerted her students that she was becoming frustrated and that they should pay attention.

ISFPs are likely to allow papers that need grading to accumulate until the workload becomes overwhelming. They will then spend time doing nothing but grading papers. They almost seem to enjoy helping to set up a crisis situation and launching into an adrenaline high to solve the problem.

ISFPs often fail to plan ahead for issues that occur on a daily basis. They are capable of dealing with just about any emergency, but are not as skilled with things that require planning, such as lesson plans. It is more natural for them to adapt to the moment.

ISFPs are so adaptable that they sometimes do not make others aware of their needs. One ISFP teacher allowed his students lots of freedom. The classroom was fun and a great deal of learning took place. There was a lot of experiential learning and a lot of experimentation. But when the teacher needed more order in the classroom, he found it very difficult to tell his students directly what his needs were. He would make remarks, such as, "It looks like a herd of elephants has been tramping through here," instead of telling the students what he wanted them to do to clean the classroom. Finally, when one student asked, "What do you want us to do?" he realized he had not given instructions. Now he tells his students, "It's five-minute pick up time," and they clean up the room.

ISFPs can take action very quickly. Sometimes they startle their students by moving into action precipitously. If the students recognize a need for immediate action, no problems are created. However, if the need for quick action isn't clear to the students, it would be helpful for the teacher to explain the need for immediate action. One teacher learned that she needed to talk to her students when there was a fire drill. She tended to move immediately and begin herding the children out of the room. Since she responded so quickly, some of her students began to panic. Now she uses a calming voice but encourages her students to move quickly to get out of the building safely.

Causes of Stress and Possible Solutions

Environmental and Systemic Stressors   ISFPs, like other SPs, do not like to be fenced in by limits. They are more likely to ignore such restrictions rather than fight them. As long as curriculum changes and rules are made concrete by true examples and hands-on experimentation, ISFPs can adjust to them. Until they experience the new rules through their own actions, they do not truly "know" them. If they are denied the opportunity to experiment with and test the new rules, they may ignore them. Should administrators become more forceful in setting rules and limits, this can become an escalating problem for the ISFP. *Solution:* When ISFPs get involved with specific concrete elements of curriculum changes, they will test the new material to see if it is presented in a way that works for students. For areas that are totally new to ISFPs, in-service training is essential to help the ISFP gain experience and confidence. They want to experiment with the new ideas rather than learn them from routine use.

When ISFPs Bring Stress to Others   ISFPs are often very adaptive to circumstances. Others may see them as hard to pin down. Their need to experiment and adapt to present circumstances may make their specific behavior hard to predict. They sometimes find it difficult to follow through on commitments. For example, an ISFP may express a desire to meet with a friend but fail to specify a time or cancel plans when something else comes up. *Solution:* ISFPs need to train themselves to plan for multiple options. Some ISFPs ask their friends who have a higher need for specific plans to take charge of the planning and keep them informed of the plans. Communicating more frequently and relying on the skills of those who are better planners will be beneficial to ISFPs and those around them.

When ISFPs Are Stressed by Others   ISFPs become stressed by people who do not follow through with their promises, especially if it prevents them from taking action. ISFPs are often so easygoing that others may not be aware when they are upset or disappointed. *Solution:* ISFPs need to learn that sometimes it is necessary to give directives. Normally, they prefer to give and receive information. They do not like to give orders. For some, a course in assertiveness training can be helpful so that they can become more comfortable asking or telling others to do things.

Personal Stressors   A conflict over values is likely to be the most personally stressing to an ISFP. Since they are such adaptable people and prefer to let others "dance to their own tune," they find it difficult to state their own preferences and needs. They may find themselves avoiding the person with whom they are in conflict and may make unflattering remarks about that person to mutual acquaintances. ISFPs may also lash out with highly emotional statements. *Solution:* Again, assertiveness training can be an important solution for ISFPs. When they learn to express what they want in simple, unemotional terms that do not attack the other person, they will find they do not need to carry resentment against them.

Summary

ISFPs model a special grace and quiet zest for living and teach their students to appreciate the wonder and beauty of life. They allow their students to experiment with actions and concrete materials. Results are seldom labeled as "wrong," but are accepted "as they are." This quiet acceptance allows students to seek their own definitions rather than having them imposed from outside themselves.

Chapter 6

Intuitive–Feeling Idealist Teachers

Intuitive–Feeling (NF) Idealist teachers tend to prize their own unique identity and to try to encourage their students to authentically express themselves as individuals. They often rely on creative and individualized teaching methods to reach their students. It is not uncommon for students to see NF teachers as inspiring catalysts for their own personal development.

NF teachers commonly use praise to encourage their students' individuality and creativity. Sometimes the praise can be verbal; at other times, it may consist of informal notes. Other teaching techniques favored by NFs include group discussion, creative writing, and peer tutoring. NF teachers like to give assignments that encourage divergent thinking, that is, assignments that encourage students to think of multiple ways of approaching a subject. Such assignments stimulate their students to become more creative and individualized.

Self-actualization for NFs comes from pursuing the development of their own and their students' highest potential. They help their students see the need for improvement, cooperation, and being the best that they can be.

NFs are usually connected to the idealized world—the world of the future. Their idealistic view of the world can sometimes cause them to have an almost romantic drive for unity and rapport with others. They fantasize about realizing their dreams and goals and imagine the best future possible. They find meaning in making their own contributions to make the world a better place.

The language characteristic of NFs is global and metaphoric. Of the four temperaments, NFs are the most likely to customize instructional techniques to enhance an individual student's learning. NFs are often seen as excellent and enthusiastic communicators. People listening to an NF will often hear about people issues. NFs are concerned that people have lives that are filled with meaning and worth. Their use of similes and symbolic metaphors allows students to supply personal meaning based on their own experience.

From a values standpoint, they tend to prize sentiment and affiliation. They are usually sensitive and empathic teachers, and they benevolently focus on individual needs and aspirations. They may often notice when one of their students is feeling depressed or appears to be stressed and can sometimes become emotionally involved in helping that student solve his or her problem. They like to believe the best in people and sometimes gain a reputation for being too credulous, but their positive attitude helps facilitate their diplomatic approach to others.

NF Idealists often have excellent listening as well as verbal skills. They can often detect the frame of mind of others based on the tone of their voice. This skill helps them to be attuned to their students.

NF Idealist teachers are skilled at individualization. They are the best of all the types at determining accurately what each student needs emotionally to achieve success. They like to ensure that each student gets their individual needs met. NFs are good at identifying and drawing out the potential in each student. They like to encourage students to express themselves and their opinions. NFs are likely to conduct a democratic classroom. They also look for and encourage creativity. NF teachers prefer to create their own curricula rather than use preplanned curricula consisting of such things as workbooks. NFs work hard to create a harmonious classroom in which each student feels valued and accepted. NFs must be careful not to burn out in their quest to help all students reach their potential. Students often like NF teachers because they tend to be inspiring and value each student as an individual.

There are two major categories of NF Idealist teachers: NFJ Mentors and NFP Advocates, which are illustrated in table 10.

Table 10 NF Idealist Teachers	
NFJ Mentors	NFP Advocates
ENFJ Mobilizers	ENFP Enthusiasts
INFJ Developers	INFP Questors

NFJ Mentors

NFJ Mentors tend to be better than other NF types at giving orders. Since they want to get along with everyone, they give orders mostly when circumstances demand them and state the directives so that others are not entirely aware that they are being told to do things. The good of the organization frequently serves as the basis for their orders and they prize cooperative behavior. NFJ Mentors like to create meaning in their lives by helping others, often in organizational settings. They often like to use their gifts to help other people develop.

ENFJ Moblilizers

Basic Characteristics

Adjectives that describe the typical ENFJ are charismatic, congenial, and personable. The needs and welfare of their students often bring out their supportive and caring nature. Their sensitivity, along with their highly developed verbal skills, enables them to be both tactful and persuasive. With kindness and compassion, they are often able to foster feelings of worth in their students. ENFJ teachers strive to make education a meaningful and inspiring experience.

Where They Are Found in Education

ENFJ teachers are found at all grade levels. They may teach art, music, drama, English, or reading. Some become school administrators, usually at the elementary- and secondary-school levels. Some choose specialties such as speech therapy, counseling, and special education. The sequence of teaching level that is typically preferred by ENFJs is high school, university, preschool, community college, middle school, elementary school, and adult education. ENFJs tend to be the best at guiding students in developing their capabilities as fully as possible. They inspire and challenge their students to work toward their dreams.

Preferred Teaching Techniques

ENFJ teachers often use mini lectures followed by classroom discussion. All of their students receive encouragement to participate in classroom discussions, and they try to ensure that no one's ideas are belittled. Much of the ENFJ's time is spent ensuring that all students are progressing to the best of their ability. They roam the classroom to answer questions and ensure that children don't become stuck while doing desk work. Small group cooperative learning and peer tutoring are encouraged by ENFJ teachers to promote both learning and affiliation in their classrooms.

Strengths

ENFJs have been named by Keirsey and others as natural-born teachers. They are driven to guide others through growth experiences and help them unfold future possibilities. With natural ease, they learn about others and their interests. Information about human events and issues fascinates them, and they transmit this knowledge enthusiastically. Many ENFJs can recall childhood experiences in which they enjoyed actively helping another person to learn.

ENFJs are often chosen for leadership roles, such as department or committee heads. They enjoy leading others toward a future ideal for the good of all. Their persuasive abilities help them enlist others in cooperative efforts aimed at achieving long-term goals. They tend to be very diplomatic, skilled at problem solving, and able to value the opinions of others. They can often find ways of harmonizing differing opinions so that everyone gets something desirable. People usually find themselves attracted to ENFJ teachers because of their natural enthusiasm and the genuine warmth they demonstrate toward others.

One of the most sociable types, ENFJs are excellent communicators and particularly enjoy face-to-face interaction. They like to observe facial clues to read the mood of their listeners. This sensitivity allows them to adapt their presentation to the needs of their audience. They are also able to create effective two-way communication by providing other people with adequate speaking time.

ENFJs are often skilled classroom lecturers. They illustrate their talks with similes and metaphors and allow students to fill in the blanks from their own experiences. At times, they may almost seem to have an easy inattention to logic; nevertheless, they are effective in getting their main points across. Public speaking and lecturing are talents most ENFJs can develop with little effort. Their advantage comes from their ease with words, their ability to understand students, and their gift for speaking directly to student concerns. They often have a gift for inspiring creativity in their students.

ENFJs are usually very sensitive to the welfare and feelings of others. Being very nurturing, they will often go to great lengths to ensure that each student gets whatever she or he needs. They will also go out of their way to fulfill their responsibilities, particularly when others are relying on them. They are very generous with their time to ensure that the relationships around them are healthy and harmonious.

In their desire to meet individual learning needs, ENFJs often have many activities occurring at once in their classrooms. An ENFJ first-grade teacher's custom was to have many projects underway. At one point, the class made butter, built and painted a farm, took a field trip to a farm, and raised ducklings. The class also performed several plays and held contests in learning skills.

ENFJs are sensitive to individual needs in personal development. They almost seem to have an innate ability to identify what each individual needs to help them grow more effectively. To help students develop, they will often customize lessons so that students with different needs will have the optimum chance of understanding new concepts. Both in and out of the classroom, they work very hard to ensure maximum growth for others. They tend to be organized and dependable. With their dedication and devotion, they may have trouble finding time for themselves.

Giving tokens of appreciation comes naturally to ENFJs. They are masters at spreading the good news of each new success of their students.

With their skill at recognizing student growth, they create a climate of warmth and appreciation. As one ENFJ English teacher explains, "I like encouraging my students through notes that show that I see their successes and breakthroughs. I can't imagine not telling students where they are doing well. It would be as if I were leaving them blind."

In an ENFJ classroom, emotions can be shared without embarrassment. They often find it almost impossible to hide their own emotions and are excellent at helping students deal with their emotions. It should be noted that many ENFJs are found at the high school level, where students are often dealing with new emotions and addressing value issues. ENFJs are particularly adept at helping students through these kinds of transitions.

Potential Weaknesses

Since ENFJs are often so good at appreciating others, they find themselves more energized if they receive positive feedback, too. If ENFJ teachers receive little or no recognition for their efforts, or, worse, they receive criticism unaccompanied by any positive feedback, they will begin to respond negatively. For example, they may begin to actively criticize the administration, and they can inspire others to do the same. Fortunately, this problem seldom occurs, since ENFJs prefer harmonious relationships. Recognition of their efforts does wonders for restoring their positive outlook.

ENFJs usually get along well with their students. They are organized and give clear directions. They look for the best in each student. Occasionally, a relationship will temporarily deteriorate. When this occurs, ENFJs may engage in a compulsive search for the truth, asking themselves what went wrong with the relationship and how they might prevent this from happening in the future. They will usually initially take personal responsibility for the failing relationship, but if they cannot solve the problem, they may begin to blame the other person and be more critical toward them. Taking time away from the problem usually restores their perspective and allows the relationship to begin healing.

ENFJ teachers are bothered if one of their students seems to dislike them. They will usually try to get the student to change his or her opinion, and will continue searching until they can find the root of the problem. Sometimes they need to learn to live with the animosity, but accepting it may not be easy for them. By listening to a student's concerns and responding to them, ENFJs usually can change a student's attitude.

Occasionally, ENFJs can begin a new project without finding out enough about the requirements beforehand. They may sometimes begin a project without having all the necessary materials in place. Sometimes ENFJs can make their explanations of new material too complex and convoluted. In their haste to move toward the ideal future, they can sometimes omit the details. Usually, their students understand this oversight. Given time, ENFJs will find ways to make things run smoothly again.

Causes of Stress and Possible Solutions

Environmental and Systemic Stressors   Even though ENFJs encourage personal growth and change in others, they still may experience stress when personnel changes occur. They invest a lot in their relationships with others and like to work with each other as an effective team. While they can accept changes on a team and even decide to move on after the changes occur, the severing of personal attachments can be painful for them. *Solution:* When ENFJs have adequate time to consider the social implications of a personnel change, they can begin to see how the change can be made positive for everyone involved. They may be inspired to create events that help integrate new team members or say goodbye to departing ones. The ceremonies they create can help them and others to see the change as a desirable outcome that need not sacrifice a caring atmosphere.

When ENFJs Bring Stress to Others   Sometimes ENFJs can overdo their need for harmony and order. Being the most directive of all the NFs, they may stand in the way when others try to air their differing views. ENFJs can sometimes become excessively helpful in their efforts to solve conflicts. They can also at times become too intrusive into other people's private space. They sometimes tend to insist that their set of values are the only "right" ones. They can sometimes make value judgments that are harsh and overly constraining of other people's options. *Solution:* ENFJs can learn to identify signs that they are being too intrusive. ENFJs can also learn to identify when they are in a values conflict with another person.

If they make an effort to learn what life experiences contributed to the development of the other person's values, they can become more accepting of them.

When ENFJs Are Stressed by Others   ENFJs are stressed when personal conflicts occur with people who are important to them, even if the conflict does not directly involve them. Regardless of the circumstance, ENFJs often feel compelled to help solve the relationship conflict and have a desire for everyone to get along. *Solution:* While the preservation of harmonious relationships is a worthy goal, ENFJs must recognize that, at times, the price associated with this goal may be too high. ENFJs need to first become aware of their tendency to want to bring calm to most conflicts. They also need to recognize that sometimes the best solution can be to engage in active disagreement. Classes in debating can help ENFJs recognize the fun aspects of conflict. In addition, ENFJs need to recognize at what point they've done all they can—accepting that some problems will solve themselves over time, while others may be insolvable. They may need to step back and gain some distance from the conflict or to do something pleasurable for themselves, such as taking a walk in the park or seeing a play. ENFJs may find themselves in conflict with others simply because they are too tense and have not given themselves enough personal renewal time.

Personal Stressors   ENFJs tend to work above and beyond the call of duty. They may exhaust themselves with their need to develop each individual student fully. Some ENFJs decide they need to leave the teaching profession because they have worn themselves out from giving so much and fear that their efforts have not made a significant enough difference. *Solution:* ENFJs need to balance their ability to customize with the SJ ability to standardize. They need to recognize that personalizing learning for each of their students is not possible. Finding a reasonable balance between customization and standardization may be difficult for them, but will be easier to achieve if they observe a few guidelines. Customization can be done when it is (1) fun and rewarding and/or (2) likely to have a real payoff. Standardization can be done (1) when there is not enough time to customize, (2) when everyone needs to be exposed to the exact same experience, and (3) when the ENFJ is feeling signs of burnout from overwork. Finding the balance between meeting the needs of others and their own needs is also crucial if ENFJs are to remain effective. Others can best be helped when ENFJs have enough energy to give help. By planning personal renewal time, ENFJs can maintain the energy level they need to customize learning in the way they want. If they fail to meet their own needs, however, the stress of continually giving to others will eventually lead to burnout.

Summary

ENFJs are inspiring teachers who specialize in helping their students develop effective communication skills. They actively praise students in an effort to spur personal and emotional development. Their caring attitude and personal attention help students to learn.

INFJ Developers

Basic Characteristics

Adjectives that describe the typical INFJ are compassionate, empathetic, and intense. They tend to commit to achieving their goals and pursue them with great determination. In their drive to serve the common good, they exert quiet forcefulness and are good at empowering others. Since they tend to be both complex and deep, they like to examine and interpret the emotional states of themselves and others. With their strong intuitive abilities, they can quickly identify ways to develop rapport with their students and empathize with their needs.

Where They Are Found in Education

Like ENFJs, INFJ teachers are found at all grade levels. They may be found teaching English, art, drama, music, science, or the trades. Some choose special education, counseling, or speech therapy. Those who choose administrative positions are more likely to be found in colleges or technical institutes. The sequence of teaching level that is typically preferred by INFJs is high school, university, preschool, elementary school, community college, middle school, and adult education. INFJs are very good at helping students become aware of their personal gifts and preferences.

Preferred Teaching Techniques

INFJs often involve students in creative writing projects. They invite students to help each other in a quiet manner. Small group discussions in their classes provide springboards for new ideas and cooperative learning. Many INFJs use notes to students as a way of giving personal attention and encouragement. Their lectures are usually followed by classroom discussions. They often emphasize desk work that helps students with skills they will need in future careers.

Strengths

INFJs like to contribute to the welfare of others and are often seen by others as one of the most empathic of the teacher styles. Whereas ISFJs want to serve others, INFJs tend to want to create something new that will help improve the human condition. INFJs tend to be quietly forceful and enjoy conceptualizing and creating work that others can benefit from.

If a task is complex and involves many people, INFJs can be excellent at orchestrating harmonious interaction. Their kind of leadership contrasts with that of ENFJs, who can become the center of attention. INFJs prefer the role of the behind-the-scenes director. They ensure that everyone knows what to do and that all the needed materials are at hand.

INFJs usually are gifted listeners who seek rapport with others. They are able to hear fine distinctions and nuances in others' conversations. Some INFJs become school counselors. In this role, they focus on the issues of concern to a person, the person's identity, and their personal preferences. They often interpret and share insights about human behavior. INFJs who counsel like to educate their students about common life patterns.

INFJs often enjoy developing their student's imagination through creative writing. When students are new to creative writing, INFJs generally praise improvement and are cautious in their criticism. As students improve their creativity and communication skills, INFJ teachers begin to shift their focus from global praise to more specific suggestions for improvement.

Like the other NFs, INFJs like giving and receiving praise. They seem particularly attracted to students who respond well to positive feedback. Helping individuals grow and become self-actualized is important to the INFJ. Both INFJs and ENFJs are good at guiding and nurturing others. While ENFJ teachers like to inspire group members toward a common goal, INFJ teachers like to nurture individuals more on a one-on-one basis. They use their listening skills to diagnose issues, then give pointed and brief individualized feedback.

Many INFJs have visionary insights. They seem to collect patterns of human growth and development and are able to predict future developments for individuals or systems. INFJs and INFPs are often in touch with universal behavior of human beings. It is not uncommon for an INFJ to foresee a difficulty that is likely to occur for a student. Experienced INFJs search for the reasons they have this insight before they talk to the student.

Because of their ability to see patterns or associations connecting seemingly unrelated material, INFJs are often able to recognize the key elements in complex systems that make them more understandable to others. With this ability, they can help students comprehend difficult ideas. INFJs can also often make connections between concepts that may not be obvious to others, which enables them to be very creative. They nurture creative insight in their classrooms and become excited when one of their students has an intellectual breakthrough and can suddenly see something they were unable to perceive before. They nurture both the individual and creative thought processes in a very personal, caring way.

INFJs are attracted to thematic presentation of materials, such as using the Westward movement theme across math, English, and social studies classes. While this thematic presentation is often part of curriculum design, INFJs seem to enjoy its use more than most other types of teachers. As one INFJ sixth-grade teacher explained:

> I use themes to show my students how all learning is interrelated. For instance, we've explored the development of logical thinking in the fields of math and English. Currently, I'm using a Gilbert and Sullivan play to help students see changes in customs and language. Not only do they practice mastering writing, spelling, arithmetic, and so on, they are learning about changes in human culture.

Potential Weaknesses

INFJs can sometimes become so concentrated on a project that they become irritable if they are interrupted. Explains one fifth-grade teacher:

> Sometimes I find it hard to get back into the classroom mode. Then I may ask my students to give me a few minutes of quiet time to complete my work. Most of the time they do. We've talked about my need for some quiet concentration during the day and they usually respect my need.

INFJs are generally sensitive to disorder. They may experience tremendous tension if disorder becomes too great. It can even affect their mental functioning. "I run in cycles," says an INFJ sixth-grade teacher.

> I work very hard to get the classroom looking orderly, and I work hard and have my students pitch in to keep it that way—for about two weeks. By then I have other more important interests and I am using my energy elsewhere. I don't have time to worry about keeping the classroom so perfect. Eventually, the place becomes messy enough that I sense myself becoming confused. It is as if I can't stand too much visual stimulation. When it gets like that, I seem to go on overload. Eventually, the students and I will put the place in order again.

INFJs are usually sensitive to conflict and criticism. As new teachers, they may need assistance in dealing with discipline problems. Ideas and support from co-workers can help them find strategies to deal with challenging students. Their cooperative attitude usually prompts cooperation from students, but sometimes they need to be more assertive. The more strategies they can learn for dealing with discipline, the more comfortable and effective they will become.

INFJs often understand human behavior and speech patterns so well that they can sometimes complete sentences for the person who is speaking. They should try to understand, though, that others may become annoyed when they do this.

INFJs are often such complex people that few others have a complete understanding of them. This can include other teachers, students, and even members of their own families. To bring out another aspect of their complexity, INFJ teachers may renovate their teaching techniques to incorporate new talents or interests. They enjoy the challenge of developing new skills, but once the skill has been mastered to a reasonable degree, they may move on to a new challenge and drop the old one. This change of teaching style may cause some students discomfort. Experienced INFJ teachers hold on to enough of the old technique to make students feel comfortable, while they are in the process of incorporating the new technique.

Causes of Stress and Possible Solutions

Environmental and Systemic Stressors   INFJs do not like to work in a crisis mode. They have a strong vision of where they are going and do not like surprises from administrators that upset their plans. They are usually able to respond to crises, but they can become tense and irritable when incidents occur frequently or become lengthy. *Solution:* INFJs should ask their administrators if they can preview proposed changes. They also should make an effort to get plenty of rest, eat well, and exercise to help reduce stress.

When INFJs Bring Stress to Others   Sometimes INFJs can be so driven by moral imperatives that they may feel compelled to take stands. At such times, they can use their talent with words to personally attack anyone who does not agree with them. They may then become increasingly tense or begin to obsess about problems. *Solution:* INFJs are usually very tolerant of differences, so it can shock co-workers when they demonstrate intolerance for differing ideas. INFJs need to remind themselves of their desire to understand others. If their tension starts turning into anger, they need to take time away from the issue to let themselves cool off. Physical activity, such as taking a walk or going on a bike ride, is very helpful. Working on some creative project that has nothing to do with the original problem is also helpful. With their perspective back in order, they are likely to discover that the issue was not such a great problem or that they have come up with an ingenious solution.

When INFJs Are Stressed by Others   INFJs often have difficulty with confrontations. Some types can be energized by them, but INFJs work hard to prevent problems. When one occurs, they are as upset about their inability to prevent the problem as they are about the problem itself. *Solution:* First, INFJs need to recognize that confrontation or severe criticism can be very painful to them. They need to allow themselves time to recover. Some may find comfort in music. INFJs should also try to seek solutions to the issues brought up during the confrontation before too much time passes. The longer they wait, the more difficult it will be for them to address it.

Personal Stressors   INFJs often have unusual insights into the human condition and a tendency to make predictions. It can be painful for INFJs if they have no one with whom they can talk when their ideas come to fruition. They tend to be such good listeners themselves that others often expect them to always fulfill that role. When they need to be the primary talkers themselves, they may have a difficult time being heard by others. *Solution:* It is important for the friends of INFJs to become accustomed to listening to them and for them to learn effective ways to talk about their insights. INFJs can practice talking to a few close friends and then gradually progress to talking to small groups. They might also find it helpful to express their predictions as merely hypothetical results of cause-and-effect relationships.

Summary

INFJs like to concentrate on serving the common good. They tend to be insightful and are able to discern subtle patterns in human behavior and ideas that allow them to accurately interpret complex ideas to their students. Their quiet concern for their students is plainly evident, and they are particularly good at listening to their students on a one-on-one basis. They often encourage their students to express themselves through writing.

NFP Advocates

The NFP Advocates are among the types least likely to give orders. They tend to be naturally curious and are collectors of information. When they give out information, they may use a persuasive tone, but are not apt to order their listener to respond in prescribed ways. They focus on the good of the group. NFP Advocates actively encourage new ways of relating to information and people. They seek out the new and unusual to enrich the learning process for their students.

ENFP Enthusiasts
Basic Characteristics

Adjectives that describe the typical ENFP are charming, communicative, and enthusiastic. ENFPs are very people oriented, and their restless, curious nature leads them to become highly informed about many issues. Their imaginative perception allows them to recognize concerns that may go unnoticed by others. While maintaining a diplomatic approach, they are often able to help others expand their insights so they can grow and change.

Where They Are Found in Education

ENFP teachers are found at all grade levels. They may teach art, drama, music, English, reading, or physical education. Some become educational consultants or choose specialties in counseling, speech pathology, or special education. The sequence of teaching level that is typically preferred by ENFPs is community college, preschool, high school, middle school, elementary school, university, and adult education. ENFPs are particularly good at helping students become effective team members. They also encourage creativity.

Preferred Teaching Techniques

ENFPs encourage student participation in their classrooms. Their lectures may be very dramatic and they may allow students to interrupt them. Their attitude seems to be that the whole classroom is a team. Discussions are encouraged, with particular emphasis on divergent thinking. Peer tutoring is likely to occur spontaneously. ENFPs often have their students participate in group projects, some of which may be major undertakings, such as large murals or plays.

Strengths

ENFPs are often warm and enthusiastic teachers who can be inspirational for their students. They are able to cast new light on the unnoticed aspects of everyday life. They are excellent at building new sets of cultural expectations with students who have diverse backgrounds. Their avid curiosity adds a spark of life to the classroom.

ENFPs often have an uncanny ability to perceive the harmony or disharmony of others. This ability attracts ENFPs into such positions in education as school counselors, which enable them to effectively use their diplomatic and empathic talents. They are often able to get people to talk about issues of personal importance. Students may find themselves pouring out their souls to an ENFP when they did not intend to say very much. ENFPs can often pick up the slightest nuances in another person's conversation and make intuitive leaps about what concerns the other person. Students often feel personally understood by ENFPs.

ENFP teachers consider themselves to be more like peers of their students than rigid, authoritarian figures. When they talk to students, they get down to their level and meet them eye-to-eye. Students are likely to find their ENFP teachers working right alongside them, especially in art and drama classes. By working with their students in this way, ENFPs show their enthusiasm for what their students are doing. The classrooms of ENFPs are usually filled with fun and laughter.

ENFPs have faith in an ideal world. As eternal optimists, they can sometimes be seen by others as too credulous, but their positive attitude encourages others to support them. They are good at innovatively solving problems. In fact, challenges stimulate them. They are one of the ebullient, high-energy types, and they have the ability to handle many projects simultaneously.

In the classroom and in any organization, they are the ultimate team builders, functioning as "cheerleaders." As teams can be built faster when the members know what abilities each member can contribute to the team, ENFPs are true team-building catalysts. Says one ENFP fifth-grade teacher, "One way I encourage team behavior is by noticing what each student likes to do and then promoting their talent to the rest of the team."

There is generally a great deal of creative activity in an ENFP classroom. ENFPs stimulate imaginative and creative forces in their students. They are particularly drawn to the expressive arts such as art, music, drama, and writing. It is not uncommon to find ENFPs serving as advisers to their school newspapers.

ENFPs are usually flexible and adaptable. Many seem to enjoy a sense of adventure. They have the unusual ability to be trusting of the world and to take risks, which others might find uncomfortable. Their trust of others sometimes prevents them from recognizing the degree of risk they are taking. Since others usually work hard to live up to the ENFP's high expectations, they are likely to be successful in their risk taking.

In a high school setting, ENFP teachers are often given a variety of courses to teach over the years. They are quick to study new material, and like rising to the challenge. Said one ENFP teacher,

> Since the administrators found I like having new challenges, I have been given opportunities to teach English, math, drama, and journalism. Now I've gained a reputation for being able to handle the "problem kids." The next thing I want to do is to become a counselor.

ENFPs are usually more effective with ongoing processes than they are with step-by-step goal-oriented achievements. This is not to suggest that they do not have achievements. While they may harness themselves to a distant goal, they have felt their greatest joy in experiencing the process that occurs along the way. While ENFPs live primarily in the here-and-now, they seem to swing back and forth between their future dreams and their joy of living in the moment. For them, life is a journey with movement and action, with delightful new surprises occurring along the way. They are often finding and developing some new aspect of themselves.

ENFPs are very accepting of a wide range of individual differences and foster understanding of others in their classrooms. They need to be cautious about overreacting when they encounter intolerant behavior in students. One ENFP music teacher says,

> I have students from diverse backgrounds in my class. I encourage disadvantaged students to experience the joy of music. What I can't stand is the student who deliberately tries to hurt someone else or damage someone else's property. They shape up real fast or else they're out of my class. Students know I'm tough about treating others with respect.

Potential Weaknesses

Sometimes ENFPs can be so attuned to helping their students have a positive life experience that they overdo things. They may become almost completely preoccupied with helping one or two students. But even those students who are being singled out by the ENFP teacher may begin to see themselves as dependent upon the teacher. Since ENFPs need challenge and variety in their lives, they usually begin to focus their attention else-where. The students who were once the focus of their attention may then feel abandoned.

Since ENFPs enjoy new challenges, they may begin too many projects at once. They may overload or overcommit themselves to the point of exhaustion. So many different things attract their attention that they find it difficult to narrow their focus. Also, other people naturally gravitate toward them because of their cheerfulness and sympathy and may over-burden them with their requests.

ENFPs may also become distracted from the main objective of a par-ticular project and go off on tangents because something inspired them. If they have not adequately developed the general outline of a project, they may find themselves leaving out details that are necessary for the project's success. They may have problems with managing the time and resources—including their own energy—necessary to bring projects to successful completion. Since ENFPs are excellent at beginning projects but less skilled at reaching closure on them, they will benefit from getting others—students or co-workers—to help them focus on closure. ENFPs tend to be most effective when they are part of a team, so gaining the cooperation of others is usually very easy for them.

ENFPs often dislike being alone. Some ENFP teachers encourage stu-dents to stay in their rooms after school and talk to them while they grade papers. Because of their ability to perform multiple tasks, ENFPs can manage this kind of arrangement successfully.

Causes of Stress and Possible Solutions

Environmental and Systemic Stressors ENFPs are adaptable to changes in curriculum, as they enjoy having the opportunity to be cre-ative with new material. They are, however, more sensitive to personnel changes. They can become concerned that their own efforts are not being appreciated. ENFPs have a high need for personal independence as well as involvement with others. *Solution:* Administrators should be clear to ENFPs about where they stand. ENFPs do best when they are given feed-back about their contributions. If they are given critiques, they need to receive both positive and negative feedback. Administrators should encourage ENFPs to brainstorm ways to make improvements rather than give detailed instructions on proper procedures. ENFPs need to ensure that they find a way to comply with standard procedures that have high priority.

When ENFPs Bring Stress to Others ENFPs enjoy their ability to be creative and adventurous. Sometimes they apply their gift so much that they almost seem to leap from adventure to adventure. Since about one-third of most classrooms are made up of SJ Guardians who prefer stability, too much adventure can be stressful for these students. *Solution:* ENFPs need to strive toward achieving a balance between adventure and stability in their classroom. Holding classroom discussions about the advantages and disadvantages of change and stability might be helpful. Such discussions will allow students to make their needs known. Individual conversations with students to determine their needs might also be helpful. They can use the results of their discussions to design a better balance for their classroom.

When ENFPs Are Stressed by Others ENFPs put a lot of energy and enthusiasm into their activities. These activities are intended to benefit everyone. If their efforts are ignored or criticized, ENFPs often interpret this feedback as personal rejection. *Solution:* ENFPs need to recognize their tendency to heighten both negative and positive thoughts. When they begin experiencing negative thoughts, they should try to counteract them by taking positive action. Some examples of positive actions include brainstorming solutions to a problem or talking about the problem with a trusted friend to get a clearer perception of it. Positive visualization—that is, envisioning that the problem doesn't exist—is a very powerful tool for ENFPs. It is also helpful for ENFPs to treat themselves to a positive experience that is outside the realm of the problem at hand. A weekend activity that is pleasurable and fun can help take their minds off a problem that exists at school.

Personal Stressors ENFPs can overstimulate themselves sometimes to the point of exhaustion or physical illness. In the extreme, they can become hypersensitive to body signals and may even suffer from panic attacks. ENFPs can sometimes deny that a problem exists. *Solution:* ENFPs need to be sensitive to their bodies' needs. They need to learn about balancing activity with proper rest and nutrition. ENFPs can often benefit from relaxation techniques and positive visualization. These activities will enable them to slow down. Making their bodies effective partners in their joyous journeys through life can extend and enhance their adventures.

Summary

ENFPs are energetic and enthusiastic teachers. They often stimulate students to seek out what is unknown and to make it known. They promote imagination and creativity in their classrooms through many different kinds of activities. Their students usually feel that their ENFP teachers understand them and help them to deal with their personal problems.

INFP Questors

Basic Characteristics

Adjectives that describe the typical INFP are devoted, deeply caring, and virtuous. The most idealistic of all the types, they are also the most individually unique. In their drive for unity, they often function as peace-keepers who actively work to keep harmony among their students and peers. In the classroom, they are adaptable and actively bring new information and new ideas to their students.

Where They Are Found in Education

INFP teachers are found at all grade levels, but they generally cluster at the higher levels. They may teach art, drama, music, English, and reading. Some choose specialties such as counseling, speech therapy, special education, or administration. The sequence of teaching level typically preferred by INFPs is university, community college, preschool, high school, adult education, middle school, and elementary school. INFPs are best at helping students become aware of their personal values. They can help students express their personal passions.

Preferred Teaching Techniques

INFPs nurture the creative gifts of their students. Creative writing, poetry, and/or journal writing often receive a prominent place in their teaching. They also may encourage science projects. The teaching technique they use will depend on the student population and their unique gifts. Like ENFPs, INFPs are in tune with the group and may use small-group projects or discussions. No matter what the technique, it will often be delivered with a unique twist.

Strengths

INFPs value uniqueness and encourage individuality in all of their students. Showing a genuine concern for their students' welfare, they seek to set up a cooperative environment where students can take the time they need to grow. INFPs are usually inspiring teachers, and they are careful not to press students too deeply into an area of discomfort. They prefer to let their students explore at their own pace. INFPs view each student as an individual who knows what will best meet his or her own needs. INFPs do not like a rigid curriculum. They prefer to find a holistic way of achieving the objectives and requirements while allowing their students adequate time for growth.

INFP classrooms are usually interactive. Students are given plenty of opportunity for experimentation and individually paced growth. Outsiders sometimes wonder how INFPs manage to maintain discipline. INFPs often change classroom pace and adjust their voice pitch to keep students alert. They insert bits of humor, use clever words, and give students plenty of personalized attention to keep them working effectively.

While ENFPs often think of life as a journey of change and adventure, INFPs tend to view life as a journey of internal discovery. They absorb the outer world into their inner being. Their personal values evolve over their lifetime based on their external experiences. INFPs are often driven by their values. They help their students examine values and create a personal set of ethics.

INFPs experience words as being value laden and are sensitive to emotional overtures. They are as sensitive to words as INTPs and will carefully choose words based on their exact meanings and nuances. INFPs are very aware of the emotional overtones of words. Because of this sensitivity to the feeling of words, they are often poetic. They use their gift with words to help students increase their ability to richly express themselves in a personal manner.

INFP teachers seek a sense of inner harmony and do their best to help others achieve a similar state. They like to devote some part of each day to a period of calmness in which students have an opportunity to regroup their energies. Their classrooms are also the scenes of lighthearted fun, sprinkled with enthusiasm. INFPs are gifted at helping students deal with complex issues. The range of experience in their classrooms is usually wide and diverse.

INFPs are complex, and it is often difficult to get to know them well. They may appear to others as calm, complex, and somewhat reticent. INFPs often carry within them strong passions connected with values, and they can become spirited advocates for causes that interest them. INFPs also encourage their students to express their personal values. It is not unusual in an INFP classroom to find students focused on issues. As one INFP sixth-grade teacher explains,

> each year my class chooses some project that is important to the group. We have been active in recycling, cleaning up graffiti, and writing to politicians about issues we are interested in. As a result of increased student awareness of how each person can make a difference, some students have visited nursing homes, given help to elderly neighbors, and tutored other children. When a student goes beyond the school-sponsored activities, the student has made a personal choice. Their personal action gives them a sense of being important in the scheme of life and increases their self-esteem.

Potential Weaknesses

INFPs like to reflect and dream. In fact, if they do not have enough time to dream or fantasize, they may find it difficult to keep their sense of balance. Their dreams and fantasies help to renew them. By setting aside some classroom quiet time, INFP teachers may achieve some personal renewal. They also need to have some time to pursue interests outside of the classroom.

Sometimes INFPs can take on too many activities and overburden themselves. If they become overloaded, they may appear to others as very unfocused. They may also feel as if they are losing their sense of focus. INFPs normally feel uncomfortable delegating responsibility to others, but doing so is a necessary part of their personal maturity and a key to addressing the issue of being overburdened.

Since INFPs enjoy their personal freedom so much and dislike commanding anyone, they may fail to make their expectations clear to their students and co-workers. This can be a source of frustration for everyone involved. INFP teachers normally ask their students if they need some help; experienced INFP teachers also ask their students if they know what to do.

They often fail to use the help of others. Their discomfort with asking others to do things is a factor in this behavior. If others can make it clear that their assistance is being offered willingly, INFPs will be more open to involving them. One INFP history teacher says he feels more comfortable when other teachers or students spontaneously offer to help him. He usually gives a few generalized instructions, then lets the other people act independently.

INFPs are normally very caring. They are, like all NFs, very good at giving positive feedback to others. Their praise tends to be very personally focused. They may have creative and fun ways for giving positive feedback. If they become overly stressed for some reason, however, they can run the risk of becoming aggressively critical. This is most likely to occur if a student openly challenges one of their personal values.

INFPs are curious about new ideas. They can take their students on many interesting explorations. Sometimes they do not adequately explore a new area well enough to realize that it may be too complex for the students at their current state of development. It is for this very reason that INFPs are most attracted to the higher levels of education.

Causes of Stress and Possible Solutions

Environmental and Systemic Stressors   INFPs need room for personal expression. If the curriculum or rules and regulations do not support student needs, they may rebel. They use actions and words to focus attention on their cause and can often persuade others to rally behind them. *Solution:* If an INFP rebels against the system, the worst tactic would be to dismiss the teacher's concerns. To prevent such a problem, administrators need to listen to the INFP concerns, then search for a win-win solution that will help bring about a resolution. INFPs can prevent such a problem from occurring when they communicate with administrators regularly, and not just at times when they have a specific concern.

When INFPs Bring Stress to Others   While INFPs are usually positive people, they can sometimes focus more on the negative. This usually occurs when they feel overwhelmed from having taken on too many obligations and are unable to have enough personal time. When they experience this feeling, they may communicate a negative attitude to their students and become overly critical of their students' work. *Solution:* To solve this problem, INFP teachers need to first recognize that unscheduled personal time is essential for helping them to restore their positive attitude. This may mean that some of their obligations have to be turned over to others so that they can meet their own needs as well as their students' needs. Once INFP teachers have resolved these problems, they then can identify the students who have been most affected by their negative attitudes and consciously give more positive attention to these particular students.

When INFPs Are Stressed by Others   Conflicts over values often create stress for INFPs. Since they find meaning in life from their personal values, a threat to their values can often put them in conflict with others. INFPs may report being out of touch with themselves and others when such conflicts occur. They may also experience a loss of energy, and may even withdraw from others. *Solution:* INFPs can avoid many such problems by simply recognizing when they are becoming involved in a values conflict. When such conflicts occur, they can identify their negative responses and share with others the experience that contributed to such feelings. Sometimes the disagreement stems from differing definitional and emotional connotations to specific words. Often substituting a different word or phrase that is more acceptable to both parties can help solve the problem.

Personal Stressors   INFPs can sometimes set unrealistic expectations for themselves, stemming in part from their desire to do exceptionally well in the things that they value. If they continue to experience difficulties with meeting their high standards, they may become depressed or overly tense. *Solution:* INFPs need to ask themselves whether the standards they've set for themselves are attainable given their current circumstances, whether they can set new standards that are obtainable if circumstances change and they are able to focus on them, and what that new standard might look like. When INFPs allow themselves a reasonable way to escape from self-imposed difficulties, they can avoid excessive tension or depression.

Summary

INFPs approach their work and their students in a very personal manner. Pursuing their values with passionate conviction, they demonstrate for their students the importance of a cause or meaning in life. They encourage all students to strive toward achieving their own uniqueness.

Chapter 7

Intuitive–Thinking Rational Teachers

Intuitive–Thinking (NT) Rational teachers encourage individualism, autonomy, and achievement in their students. They are driven by a desire for competence, and they expect their students to want to learn and to have at least some self-motivation. NTs want their students to be rational, critical, and independent thinkers. When students ask insightful questions, NT teachers feel that real learning has begun. NTs pursue excellence in themselves and their students, and they encourage intellectual curiosity.

NT teachers are found more often in the higher grades and college than other areas of education. They prefer to teach one or two subjects in which they feel completely competent. Most NTs seek to achieve expertise in the subjects they teach.

One of the favored techniques of NT teachers is individual study. Since NT teachers tend to take a skeptical view of knowledge that they have not personally verified, the assignments they give will often challenge their students to question assumed knowledge. Students in NT classrooms are often expected to do research and will be recognized for exhibiting curiosity about the world and how it operates. NT teachers appreciate students who are ingenious.

Self-actualization for NTs comes from a sense that they and others believe they are knowledgeable and competent. NTs live in a world of concepts and ideas, and their ideas often provide them with their primary sense of self. They continually challenge themselves to know more, and they search for theories that illustrate truths about the world. Since they highly value intelligence, they often seek relationships with others who are experts in their field. They look for consistency in thought, logic, and the ability to state general principles. Their somewhat abstract vision of reality helps them to perceive long-range consequences and to apply inventive new approaches to solving problems.

The language of NT teachers tends to be precise. They often have excellent grammar and an extensive vocabulary. In lectures or conversations, they tend to carefully choose specific words that get the correct nuance of a meaning across. NTs usually stress to their students exact definitions of words.

NT teachers will often talk about visions or designs. They like to compare and differentiate their thoughts to communicate the correct conditions that will help explain their vision. They carefully describe relationships and systems and can often spend hours discussing strategies and precise categories. To succeed in an NT classroom, students must demonstrate an ability to use logic and reason.

NT teachers are often experts in their fields. NTs tend to structure their lessons logically, tying each statement they make into the theme of the lesson. NT teachers typically love their subject and are able to communicate this enthusiasm to their students. They like to challenge their students intellectually with such things as puzzles. NT teachers delight in seeing recognition or understanding occur for their students. They are pleased when students ask questions that demonstrate a high level of reasoning. NTs are the most likely of all the types to create tasks for their students that fit the growth and development of each student. NT teachers may become dissatisfied if they see themselves expending a fair amount of energy performing tasks they feel are insufficient uses of their time, such as doing a great deal of paperwork or attending unproductive meetings. Students often like NT teachers for their intellectual style and thorough knowledge of a subject.

There are two major categories of NT Rational teachers: NTJ Organizers and NTP Inventors, which are illustrated in table 11.

Table 11 NT Rational Teachers	
NTJ Organizers	**NTP Inventors**
ENTJ Directors	ENTP Innovators
INTJ Planners	INTP Definers

NTJ Organizers

NTJ Organizers are among the most directive all the types. They are usually comfortable with delegating tasks. Like the STJs, they find it easy to assume authority, particularly the ENTJs. Most NTJs have an inner drive to achieve objectives. These objectives are often visionary in nature. NTJs like to continually refine and improve the knowledge they teach in their classes. They focus their energies on creating the best strategy for accomplishing a task and on challenging their students intellectually. It is more important to them that their students know *how* to think than they know *what* to think. More NTJs are attracted to teaching than NTPs.

ENTJ Directors
Basic Characteristics
Adjectives that describe the typical ENTJ are dynamic, controlled, challenging, frank, and decisive. ENTJs are natural leaders who think strategically and futuristically. They work directly toward their goals. Each of their goals and objectives is underpinned by logical principles.

Where They Are Found in Education
ENTJ teachers are found at all grade levels, but many favor the higher levels of education. They often become administrators at all levels of education, particularly in colleges and technical institutions. Some become educational consultants or educational specialists. ENTJs may teach

reading, English, special education, or trade and industrial education. The sequence of teaching level that is typically preferred by ENTJs is university, community college, adult education, elementary school, preschool, middle school, and high school. ENTJs are best at helping students to plan the course of actions that will enable them to achieve their goals and objectives.

Preferred Teaching Techniques

Since ENTJs tend to be orally adept, they often use Socratic questioning to challenge their students to think for themselves. They also encourage debates among their students. Their students are challenged to state their positions as clearly as possible and to show all the possibilities and ramifications associated with each idea. NT teachers also often give lectures and then engage students in question-and-answer sessions. However, they do not want want their students to give them rote answers; they want insightful thinking.

Strengths

ENTJs, like ESTJs, are often found in administration. However, whereas ESTJs focus on having well-run operations, ENTJs tend to focus on policy and goals. Underlying these objectives is a well-tested set of conceptual principles. These principles are the rules governing the logical operation of the system or bigger framework. This ability to comprehend and operate in large systems makes them effective big-picture strategists. They often use the assistance of others, particularly other Sensors, to deal with follow-up details.

ENTJ teachers are usually aware of administration priorities and school board decisions. They see themselves as connected with the structure or larger framework of their educational system and regularly keep up with priorities. If the institution is moving in a direction that seems detrimental to ENTJs, they will make themselves heard. Inefficiency and illogical actions are particularly unsettling to ENTJ teachers and rarely go unchallenged.

Natural-born leaders with a "commanding tone" to their voices, ENTJs are clearly in charge of their classrooms. Their students may try to challenge their control, but they are very unlikely to succeed. ENTJs take immediate obedience for granted and are usually low key but firm in their reprimands. They do, however, value leadership in others and expect to be challenged. They encourage their students to refine their logical arguments, especially in the area of strategy. ENTJs also encourage students to develop their abilities in classification, summarization, generalization, and citing of evidence. They challenge students to develop cogent arguments for their beliefs and actions.

They often exude confidence in their ability to solve problems and chart the right course. They tend to be dynamic and are often energized through personal willpower. They control as much of their environment as possible and constantly organize and plan ahead. Having little tolerance for inefficiency, they will usually single-mindedly meet their stated goals. Their students are exposed to methods for strategizing action to achieve their objectives. ENTJ classrooms often do not seem as routine as those of ESTJs, and they generally have a purpose or focus for each event that takes place in their classroom. An ENTJ sixth-grade teacher commented on his style of teaching by explaining, "Some teachers think I allow too much freedom for my students. They see this activity as chaotic. It may seem that way, but it is actually *organized* chaos."

ENTJ teachers like to use innovative approaches to their subject matter. One ENTJ high school history teacher explains her approach to history:

> Students need to learn more than dates. They need to see how the geography, food and shelter sources, weaponry, the arts, and major assumptions of the time influenced what actions people took. All these factors interrelate. I like to ask questions like, "What influence did the development of the Erie Canal have on American trade and economics? Did it do anything to change the life of the commoner?" Questions such as these help students to see relationships and the development of new possibilities.

ENTJs are usually very well informed about the curriculum and subjects that they teach. They tend to seek truth and accuracy, both in the theoretical and the real world. If they are challenged on a point they do not know about, they will either gather the information themselves or delegate that task to another person. If they consider the information important, they will research it. Like all NTs, they do not like to appear incompetent.

Students usually know where they stand with an ENTJ teacher. ENTJs use their logical abilities to critique students' thinking or performance.

They will often search for strategies to help students improve and prescribe actions that they believe will help students make improvements. When they analyze a situation, they usually take multiple factors into consideration, such as the specific description of the problem, the student's past academic record and areas of difficulty, the location of the student's desk, the noise level of the classroom, and the student's family situation. If the first effort does not bring about a resolution, ENTJs will typically reexamine their initial hypothesis and rework it based on the new evidence.

Potential Weaknesses

ENTJs may get into leadership conflicts with their peers. This is more likely to occur if one of the peers is also an ENTJ who has a conflicting philosophy. In such instances, the two can solve the problem by agreeing to each choose a different sphere of influence. ENTJs may need to take care to be less critical in their remarks and show more respect for other people's opinions. Their difficulty with peers can often result from a tendency to not listen carefully to others' positions.

Occasionally, ENTJs have power struggles with their students. This is not a common problem, but can occur if a student consistently challenges them for control. Usually, the ENTJ will outlast the student and gain the student's respect. If parents become involved in an issue, it may be useful to have a diplomatic administrator available to offset the ENTJ's tendency toward bluntness.

Sometimes ENTJs can overpower a group or an individual. This may be a particular problem for their more introverted students. ENTJs who are aware that they overwhelm some students make a point of spending some individual quiet time with those students to build rapport.

Some ENTJs are not generous with praise. They are insightful with their critiques and exceptionally capable of finding solutions to problems. If they seldom include praise in their communications, students may come to believe that the main form of personalized communication from the ENTJ teacher will be in the form of criticism. One ENTJ high school English teacher explained how this played out in his classroom:

> I didn't realize how personally some students received criticism until one yelled at me, "Can't I ever do anything right?" Now I make sure that they know what they do right as well as what they do wrong.

Since ENTJs operate from logical principles that describe how the world functions, they do not change their ways easily. These judgments about reality can underlie their behavior. To change behaviors, they need logical reasons for the change and need to rethink their assumptions to form a new logical system.

Causes of Stress and Possible Solutions

Environmental and Systemic Stressors   When the institution such as the school district or the school itself moves in a direction that the ENTJ finds illogical, the ENTJ teacher usually will object. ENTJs will express indignation toward district policies that they perceive as poorly thought-out changes. *Solution:* When ENTJs are actively involved in evaluating or creating the changes, they will help ensure that the strategy is well designed. ENTJs do not want to be bothered with small matters, but major changes are important to them. Their involvement in the process is likely to prevent future difficulties.

When ENTJs Bring Stress to Others   Sometimes ENTJs can become overly controlling or demanding. They may become impatient, particularly when others do not come to understand their ideas quickly. Making their own point can sometimes be so important to them that they may fail to listen to the viewpoints of others. Students and co-workers may sometimes become so overwhelmed by their verbosity that they may leave without ever stating their thoughts. *Solution:* ENTJs need to take time to seek the input of others. They can also paraphrase what others tell them to ensure that the other person knows they are understood. Increasing their listening skills also increases their leadership skills.

When ENTJs Are Stressed by Others   ENTJs believe their strategies are the logical course of action. If they cannot convince others to follow their strategies, they may become stressed. If their ideas are ignored, they may begin to spend more time focusing on their past successes. They may emphasize how brilliant their strategies were and point out that no one else had come up with the same idea. If this tactic does not succeed in getting others to follow their ideas, they may begin to focus on some subject outside of the school arena, such as their golf game or their stock portfolio, and talk about it endlessly. They may also engage in emotional outbursts. *Solution:* Taking a long weekend or doing some kind of activity that enables them to get away from things may help the ENTJ put things in perspective and relieve the tension. They should take care to get adequate rest, nutrition, and exercise. ENTJs can also experiment with talking less and listening more. Sometimes they can become so wrapped up in advocating their viewpoint that they miss some vital information. By examining conflicting basic assumptions and making them apparent to all parties, ENTJs can often reach new agreements or simply agree to disagree.

Personal Stressors   ENTJs can get themselves so tightly wound up in their strategies that they can alienate others and lose their own perspective. They can become ineffective by overusing their gifts as big-picture strategists. They can also experience stress if they become too involved in mundane daily tasks and have no time to look at the overall picture. At either extreme, they do not appear as their normal competent selves. They may begin to obsess about small matters. *Solution:* ENTJs need time to themselves to reexamine their perspective. Often they are so involved with influencing others that they have little time to themselves. Getting themselves out of the action/crisis mode and allowing themselves the time and space to contemplate often does wonders to relieve their stress. It also helps them to engage in activities that are outside of their ordinary experience and which are relaxing.

Summary

ENTJs lead their students toward long-term goals. They hone their students' perceptions of interrelations between events and help to develop their critical thinking skills. They challenge their students to develop effective arguments for their actions and beliefs.

INTJ Planners

Basic Characteristics

Adjectives that describe the typical INTJ are autonomous, high achieving, and deep thinking. Often visionaries, they use their single-minded concentration to develop complex systems. In their pursuit of the truth, they can become demanding, critical, firm, and tenacious.

Where They Are Found in Education

Like ENTJs, INTJ teachers usually prefer the higher levels of education. Some become administrators of their schools or colleges; others become educational consultants or specialists. They may choose to teach mathematics, special education, English, art, drama, music, or trade and industrial courses. Some become coaches. The sequence of teaching level that is typically preferred by INTJs is university, community college, high school, middle school, preschool, adult education, and elementary school. INTJs are best at helping students to create long-term visions and strategize a system that will help them achieve their objectives.

Preferred Teaching Techniques

INTJs love complex mind puzzles. They may challenge their students with written activities that encourage strategic thinking. They are also apt to favor the use of independent study. They encourage their students to engage in complex thinking. They usually follow their lectures with challenging questions, either verbally or in writing. They often ask students to make inferences from facts to an ensuing possibility.

Strengths

INTJs are innovators of thought. Most often found in the higher levels of education, as well as in administration, they are the long-term visionaries of the future. They have an interest in conceiving new structures as well as seeing them built. They share the ENTJ drive to achieve objectives. However, unlike ENTJs, who adapt their vision to changing circumstances, INTJs want the new reality to conform to their perfect vision or theory. Like ISTJs, they can be gifted at identifying discrepancies. Whereas ISTJs see reality discrepancies—such as the wrong number in a spreadsheet column—INTJs see visionary discrepancies—for example, identifying that two policies work together now but will probably conflict when a new law is enforced.

INTJs tend to have original minds and are often creative thinkers in such diverse fields as philosophy, religion, science, engineering, mathematics, business management, and politics. Their lectures will typically contain well-reasoned information seasoned with visionary insight. Students usually find their lectures clear and informative, with facts positioned in a way that illustrates underlying structures or concepts. To them, understanding the overall picture is the objective and facts are simply the logically organized data that are necessary but of lesser significance.

INTJs have a gift for envisioning the future. They help students see future trends and possible consequences of their currents actions, and they become highly energized when they talk to their students about new ideas. They encourage their students to engage in speculative thinking and challenge them to solve complicated problems and debate the merits of various actions. Their students are encouraged to discover alternative viewpoints, to work from hypotheses, and to uncover facts that prove or disprove each hypothesis. INTJ teachers search for the "right" vision or overarching truth and help students to do the same.

INTJs are the most self-driven of all the types and they achieve their objectives through willpower. Others may sometimes see them as arrogant or insensitive when they are simply busy creating their vision. Unlike the NFs, who like to empower individuals to be their own unique selves, INTJs like to build better thinkers. It is not unusual for INTJs to view their classroom as a laboratory in which actions or teaching techniques are tested to determine which has the best results. One INTJ English teacher explained how she wanted to encourage students to think in her classroom:

> I want them to be able to see how an author achieved the tone and outcome of a work. They need to be able to state the differing points of view of the characters and describe how the interaction of these viewpoints helps lead to the story's climax. I want them to be aware of the social forces that impact the decisions the characters make and to identify crucial decision and action points in the story. By opening their minds to the complexity of life choices, they may learn to engage in more effective critical thinking.

INTJs tend to work tirelessly on behalf of their visions. They will often work long and hard to ensure that students have a clear concept of a given subject matter. In administrative positions, they may spend countless hours thinking and planning to ensure that objectives are being met. It is particularly important to them to avoid duplication of effort and inefficiency. They rarely allow events or individuals to stand in their way when they pursue an objective that they believe is essential. They can be quietly forceful and decisive.

INTJs are usually good at solving complex puzzles. They may be found in curriculum development, where they enjoy designing effective new strategies for learning, and are often at the forefront of applying new concepts in the classroom.

Many INTJs use computers as a tool for education and are often at the forefront of introducing computer technology into the classroom. Most are at home with technology and will willingly spend whatever amount of time is necessary to learn a new software program. As a result, they often function as their school's computer expert.

Potential Weaknesses

Sometimes INTJs overintellectualize concepts, providing little or no factual information. Without concrete facts, Sensing students, in particular, may have problems making connections to the concepts. Feeling types may also experience difficulty if the INTJ teacher makes concepts so impersonal that they seem to have no connection to real people. INTJs who illustrate their points with factual examples and show connections to real people are very effective in reaching all types.

Like ISTJs, INTJs may have difficulty changing activities in midstream. But while ISTJs do not want to lose track of their sequence, INTJs do not want to experience delay in reaching their goal. To keep on track of their goals and to prevent unnecessary interruptions from occurring, INTJs may develop rules about classroom behavior. Otherwise, they generally see rules as arbitrary. They only want rules that are personally useful to themselves or to their students.

INTJs enforce their selected rules with consistency and determination. Explains one INTJ chemistry teacher,

> I prefer to have few rules, but those rules I do have, I fully enforce. Horseplay around chemicals, for instance, is not tolerated. When this occurs, students are sent to the dean's office. No explanations are allowed and no pleas for mercy are tolerated. I made a convincing case to the administration about possible safety hazards and now they back me fully.

INTJ teachers usually insist on a high standard of intellectual performance. Sometimes these standards can be too high for most students to meet. The higher levels of education can tolerate increasing levels of standards. Some INTJs find their style more compatible with the higher grade levels and therefore may change their teaching level. The higher levels of teaching also tolerate less social interaction with others, which may suit some INTJs who are not fully skilled in everyday conversation. They may be adept at critiquing ideas and yet have little ability to offer praise. They need to be aware that students in the lower grades need more encouragement in the form of praise. INTJs need to learn to give effective feedback in both positive and negative terms.

INTJs may resist being told what to do and how to do it. They may be overly insistent on having their own way and mount cogent arguments on why their way is best. INTJs often reserve their respect for administrators who will at least listen to their arguments and restate them. If a decision goes against them, they usually return to the event in their minds to determine how they might have argued their case more effectively. They then think of a new strategy that will help them achieve their long-term objective.

Causes of Stress and Possible Solutions

Environmental and Systemic Stressors   While ENTJs like to focus on policies, INTJs like to focus on the intellectual content of textbooks and curricula. INTJs do not like changes that are not well thought out. They usually develop effective systems for teaching or explaining particular concepts. As a result, too much of their time may be spent envisioning all the possible ways of effectively integrating a new textbook or curricula with their current system. *Solution:* INTJs can try to be involved in curricula reform or textbook selection so they can help others determine if the new material can easily be integrated with existing material. INTJ teachers can be relied on to carefully examine the new material to determine if it is logically presented. If they are not part of the development or selection committee, their stress level can be reduced if they are given more time to prepare the new material.

When INTJs Bring Stress to Others   When INTJs become too wrapped up in their own visions or thoughts, they may stop being aware of events occurring in the classroom. They can ignore a student who tries to interrupt their concentration with a question. Students may believe that the INTJ teacher is intentionally ignoring them. *Solution:* They need to stop what they are doing to perform regular reality checks. They may find it useful to set up a feedback loop with a few trusted people as a way of allowing others to give them input. They can also determine which activities can stand interruption and which cannot. For example, one INTJ teacher allows students to interrupt her when she is grading homework but not when she is grading tests.

When INTJs Are Stressed by Others   INTJs may become stressed if others ignore them or give them messages that they are incompetent or stupid. When stressed by others, INTJs tend to withdraw, and they can become obsessed with their own intellectual processes. Since they tend to be very independent, their infrequent opportunities to talk about their visions and ideas with others can make it difficult for them to recognize their stress. *Solution:* INTJs need to seek more healthy social interactions and try to develop a more playful side to offset their serious thinking nature. They should also try to find activities to shut down or redirect the mind, such as relaxation techniques or recreational activities. They should also make an effort to find a few people whom they can be playful with and who will help them to avoid obsessing about things. They can also establish relationships with people to whom they can express their ideas and visions.

Personal Stressors   INTJs like to have control over themselves and their part of the world. If they feel that someone else is encroaching on their freedom in this area, they may begin to engage in negative thinking about their own and others' abilities and try to work even harder to regain control. *Solution:* INTJs need to talk about the issue of control with those who seem to be encroaching on their freedom. When both parties clearly know their area of authority, everyone involved can relax. They also need to give themselves regular mental breaks and make an effort to engage in play. Cultivating a sense of humor can help relieve tension in their relationships, as can engaging in recreational activities or learning relaxation techniques. Regardless of the activity, it needs to be one that enables INTJs to relieve their minds of problems or visions of the future.

Summary

INTJs are visionaries who drive themselves and others to attain institutional goals. They challenge their students to engage in critical thinking and defend their hypotheses. They also expose them to complex systems thinking and encourage them to develop an awareness of the most efficient and effective choices available to them.

NTP Inventors

Unlike NTJ Organizers, NTP Inventors would rather provide information to others than give them orders. Like the STPs, they prefer a sense of personal freedom and do not like to be controlled. They are among the most pragmatic and curious of all the types, particularly ENTPs. They readily absorb information. ENTPs communicate information, whether or not they are asked to, while INTPs prefer to be asked for information. NTPs tend to be keenly observant of patterns and processes that define systems. The systems analyst who unerringly uncovers the broken or missing element in a software system, or the theoretician who lays out the underlying patterns of a system and defines the logical connections of its elements are common roles of NTPs.

ENTP Innovators
Basic Characteristics
Adjectives that describe the typical ENTP are clever, ingenious, and resourceful. Their natural curiosity and questioning style often lead them into enterprising pursuits. They can be stimulating company as they argue both sides of an issue. They are often creative thinkers who unwind systems problems and can be outspoken.

Where They Are Found in Education
ENTP teachers are found less often in the field of teaching than ENTJs. This may be due, in part, to their inventive nature, which may cause them to feel constrained by the many rules and regulations that can be so common in the field of education. Like ENTJs, they tend to prefer to teach at the higher levels of education. Some choose to become coaches, while others choose to be school administrators. Others teach mathematics, reading, special education, art, music, or drama. The sequence of teaching that is typically preferred by ENTPs is university, community college, middle school, high school, adult education, and, much less commonly, elementary school or preschool. ENTPs are particularly gifted at helping their students to expand their creative thinking. They are also skilled at encouraging their students to brainstorm and think in new and unusual ways.

Preferred Teaching Techniques

ENTPs, like ENTJs, tend to be orally adept. They, too, use Socratic questioning, but typically with a lighter touch. They expect their students to be as creative as possible with their ideas. They encourage divergent thinking. When using debates, they often encourage students to develop the ability to argue both sides of an issue. When they give lectures, they like to follow with a question-and-answer time that is dedicated to bringing out all the possibilities.

Strengths

ENTPs are one of the most curious of the personality types. Always seeking the next new idea and facet of knowledge, they are propelled through life with high energy and optimism. They continually seek information that they unconsciously sort into patterns. They are natural systems thinkers who quickly perceive relationships within complex structures, and they usually are able to hone in on the missing or broken elements in any system. This gift makes them effective problem solvers of complex structures.

ENTPs are typically excellent sources on a school staff for finding new ways of solving old problems. Involving them in new projects that give them opportunities to find unique solutions provides an effective way to use their high level of energy for starting up a project. When long-term implementation of their ideas is needed, however, it is usually best to partner them with others who are skilled at detailed maintenance work and who are able to put the final touches on a project. The more complex and daunting the project, the more inviting it often is to an ENTP.

ENTPs tend to be creative thinkers and gifted talkers who can easily argue both sides of an issue. They often encourage their students to engage in debates and to think innovatively. Their highest praise frequently goes to innovative thinkers, and they more highly prize an ingenious solution than a tried-and-true solution. Innovation and creativity are typically their hallmarks. Student debates in an ENTP's classroom can be very stimulating for all parties, as both participants and listeners typically learn a great deal.

ENTPs encourage their students to believe that they can solve any problem if they just apply a little ingenuity. They can help the more hesitant students learn to take at least some degree of risk, and they can help the risk takers learn to examine the level of risk they may be taking on. Since ENTPs are so attuned to systems, they are usually good at estimating the probable downside and benefits of changes to a system. As a result of this gift, many ENTPs engage in entrepreneurial activities.

ENTPs usually have exciting classrooms. They are particularly adept at using multiple sensory inputs in their teaching. "I love multimedia presentations," explains one ENTP middle-school teacher. "And one of my favorite things about teaching is parents' night. The walls and desks are covered with information…groups of students are explaining their projects to parents…there is stimulating music in the background. At times like that, my classroom is really *alive!*"

ENTPs do not keep their classrooms static. They like to fill them with stimulating objects and pictures that they change regularly. Even when they are teaching the same curriculum, they find a new way to illustrate a point. If a student brings forward new information, the ENTP teacher may discard the planned lesson and simply improvise. In a sense, they like to seize the teachable moment.

ENTPs are resourceful at gathering materials that will help develop inventive skills in their classrooms. They usually have a wide network of friends and can be very persuasive in convincing others to donate materials for classroom use. ENTPs can also have an ability to make multiple uses of things.

ENTPs strive to understand their students. They like to know about their students—what makes each one tick, what fascinates them, and what their ideas are. ENTP teachers can appear to pay little attention to a given student, when suddenly they will come up with the perfect thing to spark that student's enthusiasm. Sometimes their unpredictability can add to the excitement of learning.

ENTPs seldom make judgments about their students. If a student is having difficulty in a given subject, the ENTP teacher usually believes that a solution to the student's problem will soon be at hand. Their next way of explaining a problem that has stumped a student will be just what is needed to get the student back on track. Students enjoy being around ENTPs because they seldom appear discouraged with their students' progress.

Potential Weaknesses

ENTPs sometimes let their natural curiosity override set curriculum. Administrators, who are responsible for maintaining school standards, often do not approve of this behavior. Provided the ENTP can show that the innovation is meeting the principle objective, administrators may be able to allow some room for their inventive talents.

SJ students who want predictable classrooms may find the constant innovation of ENTP teachers too overwhelming. ENTP teachers need to realize that some students do best with at least some degree of structure. Experienced ENTPs develop strategies to provide for both structure and innovation in their classrooms.

The attraction that ENTP teachers have for innovation may sometimes cause them to overextend themselves. They can attempt to take on too many projects and commit to too many new ways of presenting information. As a result, they may not be able to meet all of their commitments or, if they are able to, they can end up feeling exhausted. ENTPs need to make regular reality checks and estimate how much time they will need to spend completing the small details of a project. ENTPs sometimes allow their their enthusiasm to override their good judgment and significantly underestimate the time and resources needed to complete a project or lesson.

Sometimes ENTPs can get behind on maintenance tasks such as cleaning the room, grading papers, or filling out paperwork. They can become so caught up with their systems thinking that they fail to pay attention to sensory details.

ENTP teachers may fail to provide their students with step-by-step methods for solving problems. This is due both to their tendency to pay limited attention to details and their reliance on intuition rather than linear thinking to solve problems. ENTP teachers who become aware that they are having difficulties in this area can usually address this problem by investing time in reading the teacher's manuals, which typically provide this kind of detail.

ENTPs are often so quick and clever that they may find themselves playing intellectual games. They find the game of one-upmanship very stimulating and enjoy being challenged by students. Such verbal bantering often fosters their creative instinct. They may try to steal the student's arguments to support their own position. As long as the game continues in a playful manner, it can add some spice to the classroom. Sometimes ENTPs play the game too seriously or for too long and students may become upset.

Causes of Stress and Possible Solutions

Environmental and Systemic Stressors   ENTPs can become stressed by too many rules and regulations and they often have a difficult time with consistency, since they are so inventive. If a school system becomes too bureaucratic, the ENTP may ignore the rules or merely pay lip service to them. If administrators wind up overmanaging rather than openly discussing what problem the rules are intended to solve, the ENTP may become stressed. This may lead to avoidance behavior, such as forgetting the rules or behaving in ways that are entirely outside of the rules. *Solution:* ENTPs need to identify this problem early, perhaps by becoming part of the rule-making group. They can encourage the development of a few, flexible rules. If a particular rule cannot be rewritten, ENTPs need to understand the reason behind the rule and any potential consequences for not enforcing it. They do best when they can discuss the issue. They often find inventive ways to prevent the problem from occurring.

When ENTPs Bring Stress to Others   ENTPs can become so involved with invention that they forget all about the need for maintenance. No classroom activities can survive without some degree of maintenance—such as recording grades or ensuring that the room is not a fire hazard. ENTPs may not communicate classroom standards for behaviors and grades, which can leave SJ students, in particular, feeling anxious. Administrators may sometimes wonder if institutional standards are being kept in their classrooms. *Solution:* ENTPs may choose to avoid maintenance as a daily chore, but they do need to recognize that it needs to be done fairly regularly. Most ENTPs tend to do maintenance chores during bursts of energy. They also need to set a few samples for behaviors and grades, which they are willing and able to enforce. This puts students and administrators more at ease.

When ENTPs Are Stressed by Others   ENTPs are often stressed when they are not allowed to be inventive. They require a certain amount of freedom to explore their curiosities. When others stop listening to their free-flowing ideas or they are actively discouraged from being inventive, they may lose energy and become less effective in the classroom. *Solution:* If possible, ENTPs should get away on a curiosity adventure. This will help to release some of their inventive energy. Finding other arenas in which to be inventive can also release stress. ENTPs can also recognize that in order to have their ideas heard, they may need to spend some time listening to others. ENTPs, like ENTJs, benefit from learning how to paraphrase the words of others so that others believe they have been heard. ENTPs can also put their understanding of a problem in writing. They are natural systems thinkers who usually like to come up with spontaneous solutions. By spending quiet time working through a problem, they may find a way to improve the situation.

Personal Stressors ENTPs may become so busy with their many projects and their insatiable curiosity that they can burn out. ENTPs who continually burn up energy and never allow themselves time for reenergizing can find themselves becoming anxious and fearful. *Solution:* ENTPs need to learn how to take care of themselves. Rest, exercise, and proper nutrition can be crucial to ENTPs who often take on too much at once. Some ENTPs allow themselves to go into a sort of hibernation phase before they become exhausted. As a specialist who teaches computer programming explains,

> I go through phases. Most of the time I am up and optimistic. Then, suddenly, I run out of gas. It is as if I have no energy, no curiosity about anything. I get so lethargic that, finally, I can't stand myself. Then, suddenly, I seem propelled to be up and at things again. Once I am active, I become my normal optimistic self.

Summary

ENTPs are natural innovators. They like to encourage their students to be verbally expressive and to take risks. They model an optimism for solving problems in their classrooms and they expect their students to be successful. Their classrooms are generally stimulating and challenging. Their students are challenged to understand systems concepts and to be creative.

INTP Definers
Basic Characteristics

Adjectives that describe the typical INTP are detached, precise, cognitive, reserved, and impersonal. INTPs live in a world of ideas constructed on logic. Their speculative abilities are used to construct new theories that they subject to critical thinking. They can be skeptical and are self-determined.

Where They Are Found in Education

INTP teachers, like the rest of the NTs, prefer the higher levels of education. Of all NTs, they are the least commonly found in teaching. They may teach mathematics, trade, industrial, or technical courses. Subjects such as art, music and drama, and coaching also may attract them to teaching. Some become administrators, usually at the higher levels of education. The sequence of teaching level that is typically preferred by INTPs is university, community college, high school, middle school, preschool, adult education, and elementary school. INTPs are skilled at helping students learn precise definitions of words and terms. They challenge students to express themselves accurately and clearly.

Preferred Teaching Techniques

INTPs often favor independent study and simulations of processes. They like to challenge students to come up with new ideas and show the workings of a complete system. Their lectures often focus on exact definitions of terms and the relationships of all the elements. The question-and-answer period that follows their lectures is often intended to ensure that students understand the ideas thoroughly and know how to use the terms. INTP teachers commonly use essays to determine how well students understand the concepts they have been taught.

Strengths

INTPs tend to be the most theoretical of all types. The subjects that attract them usually allow them to organize ideas into new ways of seeing things. Often their insights result from years of pondering over the ideas and information they have gained from others. Because of this tendency, INTPs in education are usually found at higher levels, such as in universities. Some are engaged in educational research. They may also consult in staff and organizational development for school districts.

INTPs are very aware of processes. They differ from INTJs, who tend to concentrate on future strategies, and ISTPs, who tend to notice the interworking of actions. Unlike them, INTPs notice the interworkings and flow of ideas. One INTP explains her style with her students:

> I design situations in which my students must use multiple sources of information to solve problems. My students are forced to be inventive. When an exercise is completed, my students know how well they understood and applied the concepts during the process. Real learning has taken place. Sometimes I gain new insights from watching the process.

INTPs are the architects of ideas. They deal with knowledge in all of its complexity and are often excellent at logical analysis. They use their analytical ability to design new solutions to complex problems. INTP staff consultants, for example, are often energized by the perceptions of previously unknown nuances of knowledge that were triggered by the process they designed. They may adjust their original design so that these new insights are more likely to occur for the participants. It is the precision of design of their model that excites them. For them, the results of effective learning prove the competence of their model.

INTPs prize intelligence, both in themselves and others. For them, the world is a place to understand, in all of its complexity. In a search for accuracy and truth, they often form theories and hypotheses and then test them. Since the amount of knowledge in the world is too great for any one person to know, INTPs usually find some specific areas that are particularly attractive to them. INTPs are not as driven to learn everything about a subject in a short period of time in the way that INTJs often are. They continually absorb the knowledge as it appears in their personal world. Their search for knowledge is driven more by curiosity than by time bound targets.

Their students benefit from being able to learn from their knowledge. The students who benefit the most from them are those who ask well-formulated questions. The INTP knowledge bank is often so complex that they find it impossible to share everything they know about a subject.

Students often benefit from the impersonal criticism an INTP can provide. INTPs seldom attack a person, although they will attack what appears to be sloppy thinking. They do, however, phrase their words so objectively that students seldom take personal offense.

Potential Weaknesses

INTPs are the most particular about words of all the NT styles. They can even use their talent at precise definition of words to use words sarcastically, ironically, or bitingly. They can be quite pedantic over words. By gently insisting upon accuracy in word usage, INTP teachers can help their students expand their vocabularies. If they are too forceful about this, however, they can make students feel insecure or inferior.

INTPs are natural systems thinkers who are able to understand interworkings and relationships between multiple elements in a system. Because they tend to have such a depth of knowledge, they can sometimes make their explanations more complex than students can easily follow. Some INTPs can become so caught up in emphasizing the logic of a system that they ignore any human element within the system. If a particular student wants to spend more time on the human element, the INTP may avoid calling upon that student or ignore the student's questions. INTPs who focus on effectively answering the questions of all types of student will find their students more willing to devote their attention to the INTP's system of thought.

Sometimes INTPs can become so absorbed in academic or textbook knowledge that they have little or no ability to apply the knowledge. Unlike INTJs, who are driven to apply their conceptual structures, INTPs are satisfied with creating logically precise patterns and may never see any application from their creation. While colleges and universities provide forums for INTPs to communicate their insights to others, high schools and lower grade levels insist on a greater degree of application of knowledge. INTPs teaching at these levels need to make an effort to focus on the application of knowledge in the real world.

INTPs can sometimes become lost in their own mental processes. This can surface in various ways. Sometimes they can mentally drift off when involved in a conversation with another person, posssibly because some chance remark has led them onto their own mental trail. This tendency can be explained with a polite mention that something the other person said made the INTP think of something else. The other person often feels flattered that the INTP found their statement so important. By becoming lost in their process, INTPs can forget deadlines or important personal events such as anniversaries. Reminder notes left in obvious places may help, but since INTPs usually have such a collection of materials that they might want to access at any time, reminder notes may get lost. A better solution might be to keep a planning calendar or obtain agreed-upon reminders from a student or a co-worker.

Causes of Stress and Possible Solutions

Environmental and Systemic Stressors   INTPs are often stressed by too many fine rules and regulations, especially if they seem illogical. They generally do not like being told what to do or how to do it. Their ideas about the "truth" in the world of ideas can make them scornful of new textbooks that do not meet their standards. They may complain that new procedures or instructional aids are not intelligently designed or are in some way illogical. *Solution:* Because of their resistance to being controlled, INTPs do not generally do well at schools that have a multitude of rules. They observe the principle of the law, rather than pay attention to the fine details of them. Involving them in the process of writing the rules can ensure that any rule meets their standards. It is also a good idea to get their comments on new material whenever possible. If INTPs take time to organize the rules into a hierarchical system, they are more likely to use them effectively.

When INTPs Bring Stress to Others   INTPs can get lost in their own processes and fail to pay attention to details. They can stress others by failing to communicate clearly. Students can be left wondering what the next step in an assignment is. *Solution:* INTPs spend a lot of time organizing information in their minds. The most successful INTP teachers learn to do reality checks with their students from time to time. "I've learned to periodically ask my students how they are doing and what more they need," explains an INTP physics teacher. "I've learned that most students understand the concepts that I define, but they may have trouble seeing where we are going or what step to take next."

When INTPs Are Stressed by Others   INTPs dislike emotional scenes. If students become upset, INTPs are more likely to discuss the issue of fairness than the extenuating circumstances. If the level of emotionalism becomes too heated or appears chronically, the INTP may avoid dealing with that individual. A high degree of emotionalism may leave INTPs at a loss for words. *Solution:* INTPs should first try to constrain the length of time in which an emotional interaction will take place. By reducing the length of the interaction, the INTP's discomfort with the situation is less likely to be triggered. A second approach would be to paraphrase what the person who is upset is saying. INTPs may benefit from studying Carl Roger's (1942) technique of reflection, which places the emotionalism back with the sender and enables the INTP to remain calm. For consistent problems, the INTP can ask colleagues if they have found effective techniques for dealing with this type of behavior or situation. The INTP can then experiment with suggested techniques.

Personal Stressors   INTPs, like ISTPs, can become tense if they do not have enough personal freedom, space, and time alone. INTPs function best when they have ample time to organize their thoughts in a logical system. It is because of this tendency that they tend to be the supreme theorists of all the types. Not having this thinking space can affect INTP teachers' ability to explain their thoughts. *Solution:* INTPs need to have time they can call their own. They might enjoy reading, playing sports, traveling, or meditating, for example. How they spend their personal time is not as important as the fact that they have set aside time when no one else is scheduling their time. Sometimes the stimulation of seeing new things can provide them with a sense of renewal. At other times, relaxation techniques or simply relaxing the mind can give them time to recover.

Summary

INTPs tend to be the most theoretical of all the types. Their long-term accumulation of knowledge in areas that fascinate them often makes them expert teachers in their fields. They can be wonderful sources of knowledge for students who ask questions. They highly value students who use words precisely and organize supporting evidence logically.

PART THREE

Students and Learning Style

Different students need different things. For example, an SP student might not be happy in a classroom that an SJ would describe as ideal, and vice versa. An NF in an NT-style classroom might be starved for warmth; an NT in an NF-style classroom might be starved for intellectual challenge. A teacher's style will appeal naturally to some students and appeal less so to others.

Some teachers may read the sixteen personality type descriptions in chapters 8 through 11 and think that they must learn fifteen new ways of communicating, but this is simply not true. In fact, each type has something in common with fifteen out of the sixteen possible types. For example, if you are an ESFJ, you have at least one polarity in common with every type of student except INTPs. Your teaching strategies probably include useful techniques for the Extraverts, Sensors, Feelers, and Judgers in your classroom. Keep in mind that 98 percent of students will have at least one of those preferences. If you are already a successful teacher, you may only need to add a few strategies to better reach your Introverted, Intuitive, Thinking, and Perceiving students. The most valuable skills you can add are a tolerance of differences and an ability to recognize and value abilities that are different from your own. You cannot become all things to all people, but you can increase your ability to understand and appreciate all people.

Cautions About Typing Students

As you observe particular personality type characteristics in your students, remember to keep an open mind. Students often try on personalities much like hats, so their current behaviors may not be true indicators of their basic styles. On the other hand, some of the purest examples of type can be seen in young people because they have not yet learned adult ways of masking behavior.

Whenever possible, allow students opportunities to discover their own personality styles. One good resource is the *Murphy-Meisgeier Type Indicator for Children* (MMTIC; Murphy and Meisgeier, 1987), which requires only a second-grade reading level and is appropriately administered to students. This personality inventory requires a trained professional to administer it; often school counselors choose to receive the training. MMTIC results have consistently shown that children are more likely than adults to score as Feelers and Perceivers.

Keith Golay's (1982) *Learning Patterns and Temperament Styles* contains an assessment form on which teachers can record observations of student behavior to help them determine a student's natural style of learning. Golay's four categories correspond to the temperaments as follows: SJ Guardian = Actual-Routine Learner; SP Artisan = Actual-Spontaneous Learner; NF Idealist = Conceptual-Global Learner; and NT Rational = Conceptual-Specific Learner.

Above all, keep in mind that *all* children—like all adults—have Extraverted *and* Introverted, Sensing *and* Intuitive, Thinking *and* Feeling, and Judging *and* Perceiving abilities. Children are more likely than adults to have an unclear preference on one or more of the preferences. They are also more likely to experiment with the different preferences. If, on two different days, you allow students to choose between doing a Sensing task or an Intuitive task, some, perhaps many, students will choose the Sensing task one day and the Intuitive task on the other. Sometimes this is because they are still trying to determine their preference. In determining the type of children, the MMTIC uses a "U" if a child's preference seems undetermined.* For example, an IUTP would be a student who seems to be an Introverted Thinking Perceiver but whose preference on Sensing–Intuition is unclear. This student would probably have some of the strengths of both INTPs and ISTPs and would probably also have some of the weaknesses of both types. Allow your students the right not to have a preference.

Sometimes when you are observing type characteristics in a person, you may feel that you are sure of most of the preferences but that one is unclear. Here are some guidelines.

If you think you know most of a person's preferences but you are vacillating between:

- The realistic temperaments, SJ and SP, choose SP; it is easier for an SP to look like an SJ than for the reverse to be the case.

- The futuristic temperaments, NF and NT, consider the person's sex; since NFs are more likely to be female and NTs are more likely to be male, if you are unsure, it is probably because the person is contrary to the norm.

- E and I, consider the cultural or group norm; since American culture emphasizes Extraversion, a borderline case is more likely to be Introverted.

- S and N, consider your own preference. If you are an Intuitive, the person you're observing probably is, too, but they may be a weaker Intuitive or simply Intuitive in different areas. If you are a Sensor, the person you're observing is probably, too, but they may have some Intuitive abilities that you do not have.

- T and F, consider the person's sex; since Thinkers are more likely to be male and Feelers are more likely to be female, if you are unsure, it is probably because the person is contrary to the norm.

- J and P, consider the cultural or group norm; since most schools emphasize Judging behavior, a borderline case may occur because the person is a Perceiver attempting to be a Judger.

---

*Undetermined or unclear preferences are usually indicated as "U" on the *Murphy-Meisgeier Type Indicator for Children*. Adult preferences that are unclear are often marked as "X." See C. Meisgeier and E. Murphy, *Murphy-Meisgeier Type Indicator for Children Manual* (Palo Alto, Calif.: Consulting Psychologists Press, 1987).

As you use this book more, you will become more accurate in observing and understanding personality type preferences in people. You will gain a better sense of the fundamental differences between the sixteen types. Many times, simply recognizing one preference can be very useful. Both teachers and parents can benefit from reading Elizabeth Murphy's (1992) book *The Developing Child* to learn about preference differences. As an example, she tells about a teacher who asked a student to go to the school office. The student said, "Make me." Remembering that Extraverts often blurt things out before thinking, the teacher asked the student, "Is that what you really meant to say?" The student said, "No"; in fact, he had no idea why he said that. This exchange defused a potentially explosive situation.

A Teacher's Response to Student Preferences

A student's preferences or personality type is an explanation, not an excuse, for his or her behavior. A teacher should not excuse an Extravert's talking out of turn by saying that Extraverts need to talk. The teacher may need to work with the student on keeping ideas fresh. The teacher may also need to reevaluate his or her method of teaching and decide to allow more classroom time devoted to talking activities, but a student's preference should never be used to excuse inappropriate behavior.

In the same way, students of all preferences need to learn certain things, so students of all types can be expected to complete well-designed classwork. In an article on type and education Elizabeth Murphy (1991) writes, "I have heard statements such as, He's a P. What would you expect? (when a child's assignment was turned in late). I would expect that I needed to help the student develop a more realistic plan for meeting deadlines." Some necessary classroom behavior does not come as naturally to some types as it does to others, but all students need to learn appropriate behavior. Some students may need more help than others in a particular area.

Teachers can praise students based on the preference they are currently using. For example, after a class has discussed a poem, the teacher may praise the student who demonstrated Sensing abilities by saying, "You helped us to understand what the author was saying by finding many descriptive words in the poem." The teacher may also praise a student for using his or her Intuitive skills by saying, "You did a good job of identifying the theme of the poem." To praise Thinking skills, the teacher might say something along the lines of, "You helped us understand the poem better by showing how it is organized in sections and how the author used repetition to highlight her idea." To praise Feeling skills, the teacher might say, "Thank you for sharing how the poem made you feel and why. That helped us understand why the author wrote the poem." A teacher who praises students' uses of their preferences shows a respect for the strengths of each preference, even when they are not the teacher's own.

Looking at Students

The following four chapters will describe characteristics of each of the sixteen personality types as they appear in students. Chapters 8 and 9 will discuss the Sensing students, the SJ Guardians and the SP Artisans. Chapters 10 and 11 will review the Intuitive students, the NF Idealists and the NT Rationals. The sixteen type descriptions include a discussion of each type's basic characteristics, potential career paths, preferred classes, common behaviors, discipline issues, academic issues, interpersonal behavior issues, and a concluding summary.

When you read the descriptions of certain issues or challenges, remember that most of these issues are not unique to one type. If you have a student who is a probable INTJ, you may want to read through all of the issues and challenges associated with each of the four NTs. For example, the student may experience difficulty shifting from one activity to another. We placed this issue under ENTJ because they are the most likely to confront it, but any of the NTs may struggle with this same issue.

The descriptions of the students are based on normal, average students of each type. With severely emotionally disturbed students or students experiencing other such challenges, the strategies may have limited usefulness. You may also find it difficult to even detect what type preferences they likely have. Also, every person does some things that are atypical for their type or temperament. Do not assume, for example, that a student who has trouble accepting authority cannot be an SJ or an NF. Students from *each* of the sixteen types can and sometimes will exhibit inappropriate behaviors. Likewise, students of each type can be and are a joy to have in the classroom.

Table 12 provides an overview summary of the key elements that teachers often need to consider when working with students.

Table 12 Student Preferences by Style		
Topic	SJ Guardian	SP Artisan
Instructional Mode	Lectures—procedures and past facts; how tos (the "right" way)	Performance—personal manipulation of materials to learn subject matter
Learning Mode	Workbook completion; paper-and-pencil drills	Experimentation with tools
Learns Best Through	Teacher-led question and answer; rote drill and recitation	Demonstration with action; results of hands-on work
Favored Activities	Review; repetition; practice for learning requirements	Hands-on manipulatives; personal experimentation
Reading	Factual and real; information about the past	Limited, but with action theme or facts in short sound bites
Writing	Directed and structured to include facts, reality-based stories	Limited; telling about observed exciting actions and events
Art	Structured homecrafts with exact procedures that are practical and useful	Handiwork with room for trial and error
Games	Emphasizing fairness and rules	Emphasizing fun and competition
Sensitive to	Unfairness	Confinement
Respects	Status	Ability
Praise and Rewards	Recognition of a job well done; school monitor; line leader	Recognition of flair, timing; free time; recess; games
Discipline	Clear, fair rules with follow-through	Follow-through and allowance for "wiggle room"
Areas of Interest	Business, health services, education	Music, drama, arts, crafts, mechanics, construction

Table 12 Student Preferences by Style (continued)

Topic	NF Idealist	NT Rational
Instructional Mode	Lectures—about real people; fantasy; unmet people needs	Lectures—abstract and intellectual; future trends
Learning Mode	Creative writing with a people focus	Intensive study of subjects that fascinate
Learns Best Through	Small group discussions; one-on-one interaction	Self-determined study; debates
Favored Activities	Group discussions or projects; opportunities for self-expression	Individual projects with emphasis on research and reports
Reading	Fantasy, make-believe, people-oriented works	Self-challenging; satisfy curiosity
Writing	Seeking to personally capture the essence of the world of people	Seeking to impersonally express ultimate truths and theories
Art	Personal expression, not to be judged	Experimentation with techniques; gaining mastery
Games	Emphasizing cooperative effort	Emphasizing puzzles and brain teasers
Sensitive to	Criticism	Humiliation
Respects	Personal values	Competence
Praise and Rewards	Recognition of unique self; personalized attention	Recognition of high competence; new intellectual challenge
Discipline	One on one, caring with affirmation of personal worth	One on one; discussion of assumptions and expectations
Areas of Interest	Humanities, social science	Math, physical science, theoretical development

Chapter 8

Sensing–Judging Guardian Students

Most Sensing–Judging Guardian (SJ) students thrive in school because it offers them the routines, customs, and procedures that are meaningful for them (Wirths and Bowman-Kruhm, 1992). Consequently, SJs are less likely than other temperaments to create discipline problems in school. Their need to belong to a stable and orderly social group that values their contribution generally prevents them from engaging in disruptive behavior.

SJs make up approximately 38 percent of the general population (Keirsey and Bates, 1984). They generally develop habits that enable them to keep on top of their schoolwork, often including an organizational system that helps them track homework and tests. It is often very difficult for them to function if they are not allowed to carry out their routine habits.

Teachers who give clear, precise, and concrete directions are highly regarded by SJs. Every detail of how to do an assignment is important to them. With a paper, for example, they want to know exactly what the title should be like, how long the paper should be, how many sources to use, how the paper should be presented visually, and so on. In their minds, meeting these measurable standards is the surest way to a receive a good grade.

Since most elementary school teachers are SJs, their classrooms naturally incorporate the routines that work best for SJ students. Some of the best techniques for working with SJ students include maintaining an organized schedule, giving lectures, and using workbooks. Repetition and drill exercises of facts will also appeal to SJ students. This will help them solidify their knowledge by building new skills upon old ones. They enjoy teacher-led question-and-answer sessions and benefit from paper-and-pencil drill exercises. Lectures that are most effective for SJs focus on facts from the past and present to help them understand material. Clearly outlined assignments that are broken down into concrete steps help SJs process and retain new knowledge.

SJs benefit from activities that develop foundational skills in arithmetic and spelling. In reading, they prefer factual material about people, inventions, or events. Writing activities, such as sentences, paragraphs, and essays, that emphasize organizational structure and factual details will help improve their ability to communicate. They prefer arts and crafts that are practical and useful. They enjoy games, provided the rules are fair and are upheld. SJs are particularly sensitive to unfairness.

SJs prefer lessons in which each point clearly follows the one preceding it. They are not particularly interested in the overall picture or in unifying themes. SJs are more likely to focus on the details of a story rather than its symbolism or underlying messages.

SJs generally like true/false or multiple-choice tests. They usually have a good memory for precise details and can often remember the exact wording from a book or lecture. They may have difficulty with timed tests because of their need to completely understand questions before answering them. Consequently, it is difficult for them to skip difficult questions and come back to them later, and they may fail to finish a test in the allotted time. SJ students who can be convinced to read questions only once before choosing an answer will usually perform better in such situations.

SJs are usually good team members. They often do more than their fair share of the work because of their responsible attitude and desire to receive good grades. They dislike group activities, however, when the team includes irresponsible or lazy members.

Reliability and dependability are common trademarks of SJs. If they have agreed to meet a friend at a certain time, they can be relied upon to punctual. They work hard to meet deadlines and expectations and are not likely to ask teachers for deadline extensions. They will usually either complete the work or turn in the portion they have completed.

SJ students are more likely than other styles to save money. They are usually very aware of the cost of things and they like to make price comparisons. Due to their strong sense of ownership, they respect other people's property and expect others to respect theirs.

SJs are grounded in the reality of the past and in how current events are like or unlike events of the past. They like to ensure that life will be at least as good today as it was yesterday. As a result, they often take on the responsibility for making life safe and secure. If things begin to go wrong and continue to do so, their optimism may turn into pessimism or fatalism. If a teacher notices that an SJ student frequently talks about things going wrong, the teacher can help the student by getting him or her to recall some positive events that have occurred in the recent past.

SJ students prefer to see people treated fairly and justly. For them, when rules and regulations are understood, everyone knows how to do things properly. Students who do not do things in ways SJs view as proper often receive criticism from their SJ peers. SJ students may have difficulty understanding peers who do not strive to be "normal." For them, being "normal" means being more understandable and predictable, which for them leads to less stress in human relations and an increased sense of community.

SJs do not expect or want praise for simply meeting standards. Although they have a difficult time accepting compliments and will seldom ask for praise, they do need messages of appreciation. If they must ask for recognition, they generally will not believe the answer. SJs want to earn praise for what is done above and beyond the call of duty. SJs like to be praised for accuracy, carefulness, responsibility, loyalty, and industriousness. They like praise to be very specific and to contain comparisons when possible. Using comparisons makes the recognition stronger and more believable to them. SJs constantly compare themselves to the norm and to their previous accomplishments. If the teacher does not provide comparisons for them, the SJ will. SJs like teachers to give them tangible recognition for their achievements, and appreciate such forms of appreciation as gold stars, smiley faces, stickers, and wall charts.

More than any other temperament, SJs desire routines. They do not experience the world as safe and secure if they are subjected to constant change. They like to know what is expected and to have a degree of predictibility to their daily events. It is not that they must always have a routine; in fact, they enjoy life more when it includes occasional variety. However, they are generally more comfortable with planned variety. Surprises are often unsettling for SJs. Small hints about possible upcoming surprises can help SJs prepare for and enjoy the surprise. SJs often like to be on committees that plan surprises for others.

SJ students enjoy traditions and ceremonies. They work hard to maintain the organizations to which they belong and preserve the orthodox and conventional ways of doing things. One SJ student, for example, became very upset when she learned that there would be no sixth-grade class play due to a staff change. The sixth-grade class was known for its productions at her school, and this was a tradition she expected to participate in.

SJ Guardian students are good at fitting in, working hard, and following the rules. They generally take responsibility for completing their work. SJs are usually attentive and respectful of authority. They are good team players and work hard to help the group function. SJs often have rituals they practice before starting their work, such as sharpening pencils, putting them out, and creating an answer column. They like to know exactly what is expected of them and work hard to meet those expectations. SJs work at a slow but steady pace and will usually perform well when given ample time. An unexpected change in routine, such as a pop quiz, will generally be uncomfortable for them. SJ students can be enjoyable because they are generally hardworking, obedient, organized, and conscientious.

There are two major categories of SJ Guardian students: STJ Monitors and SFJ Providers, which are illustrated in table 13.

Table 13 SJ Guardian Students	
STJ Monitors	SFJ Providers
ESTJ Stabilizers	ESFJ Harmonizers
ISTJ Perfectionists	ISFJ Conservers

STJ Monitors

The STJ Monitors, along with NTJs, are often blunt and to the point. It is important to them that they are clear about authority figures, and they are comfortable giving and receiving orders. STJ students expect their teachers to provide them with routines and clear-cut directions. If directions are unclear to them, they will continue to ask questions until they know exactly what the teacher expects. They tend to be very conscious of the amount of time it takes to complete an activity and will pressure teachers to ensure that they have enough time to complete the tasks and assignments. If they have well-defined requirements, they can use their logistical skills to produce the appropriate work in a timely manner.

ESTJ Stabilizers

Basic Characteristics

Adjectives that describe the typical ESTJ student are decisive, direct, and matter-of-fact. ESTJs tend to be industrious and responsible. Structure or routines are the primary means that ESTJs use to get things done efficiently. They often act as if there were no time to waste when they take charge of events or tasks.

Potential Career Paths

ESTJ students are natural organizers and skilled decision makers. These talents often lead them to become managers or administrators. They prefer work that shows real-time results in well-developed career fields. Service occupations, such as police officer, insurance agent, real estate agent, and industrial arts teacher require interaction with people that leads to tangible results. Applied technical jobs such as engineer or computer analyst appeal to some ESTJs, while others seek out more physically demanding jobs such as construction worker or farmer. Professional occupations such as dentist or judge also appeal to some ESTJs.

Preferred Classes

ESTJ students often like math, physical education, history, government, speech, and debate classes. In a five-field comparison of study areas, their preferred sequence of interest was found to be business, liberal arts, engineering, medicine, and science.[1] They often have an inner drive toward goals and their extracurricular activities often are connected to helping them meet their goals. Classes that have specific goals and practical applications are usually considered the most worthwhile by ESTJs.

Common Behaviors

ESTJ students are usually good managers. Excellent organizers of people and materials, ESTJs will often take charge of any group they belong to and run it successfully. In whatever situation they find themselves, ESTJs usually enjoy being in control. Often they assume a leadership role in a group to ensure that the work is done properly and efficiently.

ESTJs like classrooms that are strictly fair. Too many exceptions to set rules can make them feel uncomfortable. They usually feel that rules should be consistently enforced. If other students do not follow rules, ESTJs may lose their patience with both the students and the teacher who allows the infraction. They prefer that a teacher errs on the side of justice rather than on the side of mercy. Classrooms with a certain noise level are acceptable to them, provided they are not chaotic. They prefer predictability with a minimum amount of unusual events. ESTJs also like classes that have clear grading standards, preferring objective measurements of grades to subjective ones.

ESTJs usually have a strong sense of ownership. They respect the property rights of others and expect others to respect theirs. People who ask to borrow things but fail to return them tend to cause them stress. ESTJs almost always meet their obligations. It is important to them to ensure

---

[1] Data for the five-field comparisons used in chapters 8 through 11 of this book are derived from Myers and McCaulley (1985), p. 124.

that they do not get too far in debt, so they keep careful track of who owes whom what.

Teachers need to be aware that ESTJs like to assume control in their desire to help things run efficiently. However, ESTJs will usually step down and relinquish control when they are firmly told to do so by an authority figure. Respecting the hierarchy of authority and their place in it, ESTJs are traditionalists. They often work hard to maintain traditional roles and cultural standards.

ESTJ students are usually very direct about things. What you see is essentially what you get with them. They do not usually have hidden or secret sides to them. If they have an opinion on an issue, which they often do, they do not hesitate to share it with others. Their frame of reference is generally standard operating procedures. When people deviate from these standards, ESTJs are likely to bring it to their attention. Both ESTJs and ISTJs are sometimes resistant to change, for they are more comfortable with routines that are tried and true. If the change is supported by solid facts and logic, they may reverse a particular stance and become avid supporters.

ESTJs often want to know the extent that their teachers will adhere to their rules. They expect their teachers to enforce the rules consistently and may argue over perceived unfairness. When ESTJs reach middle school and have many teachers, it becomes even more important for them to understand their teachers' expectations. As one eighth grader explained,

> I have seven different teachers, and they don't all enforce the rules. If I don't know the limits, I might step over the line by accident. I need to know what is important to each teacher.

ESTJs generally make efficient use of their time and turn in consistently good quality work. While not as perfectionistic as ISTJs, they often turn in work sooner, while still managing to be fairly neat and thorough. Compared to other SJs, they also tend to do well on timed tests.

ESTJs are likely to become officers or committee heads of the clubs they join. They are not always comfortable as rank-and-file members, but will feel more comfortable in such roles if they have responsibility for carrying out specific tasks. They are likely to join debate clubs, future business leader clubs, or service clubs.

Ken, an ESTJ sixth grader, was often chosen by other students to be the leader of talent show groups. The other students naturally gravitated toward him because he was a good regulator and commanded the attention of others. He ensured that something was accomplished at each practice session. Ken was not the imaginative one who designed the act for the talent show; instead, he took care of the logistics by organizing practice sessions and making sure that everyone had whatever they needed for the talent show performance.

ESTJs who see a purpose in school are generally obedient and hardworking and often perform well academically. They use their considerable leadership skills to encourage other students to keep the class running smoothly. They make good teacher deputies and are likely to be harder on their peers than are teachers.

Discipline Issues

ESTJs usually express themselves publicly and with great confidence. In fact, their directness in stating their desires and opinions can be very forceful. This behavior is sometimes trying for teachers if it occurs too frequently or at inappropriate times. Some ESTJs may take their ability to extremes, in which case they become argumentative. *Solution:* Teachers need to be very clear with ESTJ students about which behaviors are acceptable and which are not. ESTJs are not likely to pick up on subtle hints. Teachers should feel comfortable insisting on acceptable behavior. ESTJ students respect teachers who enforce rules fairly and consistently.

If the ability of ESTJs to persuade and manage are not used positively, they may channel them into inappropriate causes. For instance, they may become leaders of counterproductive groups and lead the members in disruptive behavior. *Solution:* Teachers should talk to ESTJ students privately and remind them of their responsibilities to those who look up to them. They should help make them aware of how they can influence the behavior of others, sometimes in negative ways. They should help ESTJs to appreciate the challenge and importance of influencing others in positive ways. Providing them with positive leadership roles and role models will often help. They will benefit if teachers help them to take charge of their abilities and apply them positively.

Academic Orientation Issues

ESTJs are generally take-charge people. If they have no opportunities to exercise leadership, they may do poorly in school. In extreme instances, they may drop out of school. *Solution:* When possible, teachers can give ESTJs leadership roles in the classroom. For example, they can ask ESTJ students to teach part of a lesson. ESTJs will do best if they are given plenty of time to prepare and are filled in on any necessary details. Teachers can also encourage them to run for class or club offices and select them as group leaders for projects. Group discussions about behaviors that make leaders and followers effective contributors to a project are helpful to ESTJs.

ESTJs may have difficulty with classes and lectures that deal with abstract subjects. The less the class or lecture has to do with practical matters, the more ESTJs are likely to be dissatisfied. Courses that do not follow their stated outlines will also often irritate them. *Solution:* When teaching subjects that are fairly theoretical, teachers should remember that most Sensing types, and ESTJs in particular, do better when they can follow an outline. Outlines should be broad enough to allow teachers flexibility but narrow enough to include plenty of specifics. It will also help if teachers point out at the beginning of a lesson how the theory applies to the real world.

Interpersonal Behavior Issues

ESTJ students can sometimes be abrasive and abrupt. They express judgments readily, sometimes without thought for the feelings of others. *Solution:* Keep in mind that it can be difficult to change the opinions of ESTJ students. Teachers will find that pointing out unacceptable behavior soon after it occurs will work best. At times, ESTJs may not respond unless the teacher provides a clear directive for them to stop a behavior.

ESTJs are very goal oriented and may not allow anyone or anything to come between them and their goals, including new information. They quickly reach decisions, often before they know all the pertinent information. Sometimes ESTJs are excessively driven to seek closure. *Solution:* Teachers can encourage ESTJ students to assess whether they have enough information to make good decisions. They can try to get the students to take some time to think before making a decision.

Summary

ESTJs are motivated by teachers who encourage them to assume some kind of leadership role. They enjoy opportunities to express their opinions and often have some influence with their peers. Teachers can help ESTJ students to do their best in school by outlining clear directions and expectations. ESTJs appreciate teachers who are consistently fair. They benefit from teachers who instruct in a step-by-step manner and avoid shifting rapidly from one topic to the next.

ISTJ Perfectionists

Basic Characteristics

Adjectives that describe the typical ISTJ student are dependable, reliable, and steadfast. They like to work in a systematic, step-by-step manner. Their work tends to be painstaking and thorough. They are usually true to their word and will complete their agreed-upon tasks, often in a serious and quiet way.

Potential Career Paths

ISTJs may use their gift for precision in financial occupations, such as estate planner or tax examiner. Their ability to keep things running smoothly is an asset in the business world, where they may become managers. Some ISTJs have a strong drive to serve and preserve their community. Civil service positions such as government employee, police officer, and military officer can help meet this interest. Educational positions such as school principal or mathematics teacher also attract ISTJs. Given their penchant for technical skills and exactitude of knowledge, ISTJs may be found in legal, technical, or medical fields.

Preferred Classes

ISTJs usually like math, accounting, reading, history, government, industrial arts, and physical education classes. In a five-field comparison of study areas, their preferred sequence of interest was found to be engineering, business, liberal arts, science, and medicine. Organized and logical classes that lead to practical applications strongly appeal to them.

Common Behaviors

ISTJs, like other SJs, generally enjoy school, especially at the elementary level. However, some teachers may see their ISTJ students as unenthusiastic. This can be frustrating to ISTJs, who may feel very enthusiastic about school but may not be able to express their enthusiasm outwardly. They are one of the most private styles. Their enthusiasm is usually expressed by the diligence with which they do their work.

ISTJs and ISFJs are the most likely to take care of their surroundings. Their desks are usually neat and organized, and they take care of their own and other's possessions. One ISTJ seventh grader stayed after school to receive some help in math. While talking to his teacher, he straightened up all the stacks of paperwork until every stack was neat and all the stacks were evenly spaced. ISTJs generally prize regularity. They are gifted at logistics, and are able to ensure that things are in the right place at the right time and in the right condition.

Most ISTJs are strongly committed to their agreements. If they say they will do something, they usually will do it, no matter the cost. They not only honor their commitments, they are also likely to do far more than the minimum that is required. An ISTJ eighth grader promised to help his classmate study for a math test. He not only wrote a sample of each type of problem that was likely to be on the test, he also made sure that his classmate could do at least three of each type of problem.

ISTJs respond best to a school environment that is predictable, traditional, neat, fair, and relatively quiet. They are usually uncomfortable being the first to try out new ideas. If the teachers of ISTJs try out new ideas in the classroom, they should not expect positive reactions from them until the idea has become well established. ISTJs like to know what to expect in the classroom. If they know that Friday afternoon is a time to try new methods, they will be able to adapt. Noisy, untidy, and unpredictable classrooms can be stressful for ISTJs.

ISTJs expect their teachers to fairly and consistently apply rules. They can be resentful when rules are broken by others, especially if no consequences or punishments result from the action. About the only thing that will bring ISTJs to break the rules themselves is when their sense of fairness or honor has been deeply insulted.

ISTJs, like ESTJs, expect everyone in a given hierarchy to follow his or her appointed role. However, they can learn to enjoy teachers who act like "one of the kids" at times but are able to revert to authority figures when necessary.

ISTJs work at everything they do. They usually work on some level, even when they play. For example, while they play sports, they might make a conscious effort to improve their skills. ISTJ students are usually focused on their tasks and seldom daydream. More than any other type, ISTJs must finish their work before they are able to relax. Even if ISTJs do not like a class, they will typically work hard to do well in it if they believe it is necessary for their future goals.

ISTJs are likely to believe that there are unalterable rules and regulations governing how to be a good group member and that everyone should follow them in order to establish their status in a group. ISTJs are apt to work hard at gaining status. ISTJs sometimes work hard to demonstrate Extraverted behavior because they feel that they should be Extraverted, believing that it is the norm.[2] This idea is likely to be reinforced by their parents, friends, and teachers. However, acting Extraverted can be very draining for any Introvert, so they often need extra time alone after demonstrating this kind of behavior.

Most ISTJs are quiet and hardworking. Their academic performance is often good or excellent, and they give their best efforts when they believe their grades are based upon objective and fair standards. As adults, they are likely to have positions that emphasize accuracy and responsibility, such as supervisors or managers. They are likely to turn in neat, painstaking work with few or no errors. They seldom turn in work late.

Discipline Issues

ISTJs like to have a place for everything and to keep everything in its place. If their environment or schedule gets out of order, they are likely to complain or become disruptive. *Solution:* Teachers can make an effort to warn ISTJ students of daily schedule changes before making them.

---

[2]Extraversion is the norm in the United States, but in a nation such as Japan, where Introversion is the norm, this behavior might not occur.

Teachers can also be sensitive to the ISTJ need for physical order in the classroom and might try to schedule regular cleanup times. Teachers should also try to keep in mind that ISTJs are unlikely to express their discomfort with an unsettling physical environment.

ISTJs often have certain rituals they perform when doing their work such as *always* sharpening their pencil before beginning an assignment. They are likely to become upset if these rituals are interrupted. *Solution:* Whenever possible, teachers should try to allow their ISTJ students to carry out their rituals. This may be frustrating, since some of their habits can be very time consuming. Although these behaviors seem inefficient, they often help the ISTJ to feel confident that their work is of high quality. Teachers trying to help ISTJ students relinquish one habit will probably need to substitute another. ISTJs need logical reasons and specific details for changing a behavior. When helping them change a behavior, teachers should focus on streamlining the behavior to make it more efficient while remaining effective.

Academic Orientation Issues

ISTJs tend to be perfectionists and may spend so much time on certain parts of their work that they fail to finish an entire project. They may work themselves to the point of exhaustion. *Solution:* Teachers can help ISTJ students to learn that there are various levels of thoroughness that can be used in completing tasks and to identify which levels different tasks demand: a perfect job, a reasonably thorough job, or a job that simply gets an item off a list. They can also help them to pace their work by doing it quickly initially and then returning later to clean it up. Giving them a sense of what grade their unperfected efforts would earn can help them assess how much work is really necessary.

ISTJs may have difficulty working in groups, particularly if the group seems disorganized and the ISTJ students do not have the opportunity to organize it. *Solution:* Teachers should try to explain to their ISTJ students that group members are not necessarily rejecting them or their ideas if they disagree with them, but simply want to consider multiple perspectives. They can emphasize that the other group members will appreciate their skills when it comes time to reach a conclusion.

Interpersonal Behavior Issues

ISTJs tend to find negative emotions particularly unacceptable and may resist acknowledging them when they have them. They can dismiss or suppress their feelings instead of resolving them, which can bring about negative consequences, such as stress or even illness. *Solution:* Teachers can try to help ISTJ students recognize their negative emotions by simply affirming that they exist. They might say, for example, "I see that you feel very angry right now," while refraining from making judgments about the validity of the anger. Modeling the acceptance of these emotions will help ISTJs. It might also help to remind them that suppressing emotions will not make them go away.

Young ISTJs may have difficulty understanding behaviors other than those with which they are comfortable. This can make them seem intolerant of other personality styles. *Solution:* Teachers can help the ISTJs by pointing out their own and other students' strengths and discussing their value. They can also give personal examples of how accepting diversity has helped them become more effective teachers. When ISTJs become more understanding and comfortable with differences, they will no longer seem intolerant.

Summary

ISTJs are motivated by teachers who provide them with clear rules and allow them adequate time to complete high-quality work. Teachers who discuss step-by-step procedures enable their ISTJ students to use their strengths to learn new material. ISTJs respect teachers who comment on their accuracy and the precision of their work. They prefer teachers who keep classroom noise and disorder to a manageable level.

SFJ Providers

Like STJ Monitors, SFJ Providers want teachers to tell them the "right" things to do, but they allow for a little more personal preference and expression. Because they often help their fellow students, many SFJs gain a reputation for being kind and cooperative. Having the right thing in the right place at the right time is important to them, just as it is to the STJs, but they get distracted more easily from their own objectives by their concern for another student's needs. Their personal generosity and desire for harmony often make them well liked by their peers and teachers. They usually are very conscious about not breaking rules and may caution others not to break them.

ESFJ Harmonizers

Basic Characteristics

Adjectives that describe the typical ESFJ student are caring, sympathetic, and warmhearted. They are very sociable and work with others cooperatively and harmoniously. When dealing with others, they are usually both responsive and tactful. They will often go out of their way to be helpful to others.

Potential Career Paths

ESFJs, who are good at creating harmonious relationships with others, are often found in fields where this talent is needed, such as in medicine or health care. Occupations such as physician, nurse, and physical therapist may appeal to them. Many ESFJs are found in the field of education. Their people skills are also valuable in jobs such as social worker or counselor. Some may choose service careers, like cosmetologist, flight attendant, or customer service representative. With their practical bent, they may also be found in business in such occupations as bank loan officers, telemarketers, and sales representatives.

Preferred Classes

ESFJ students usually like music, math, home economics, child development, and arts and crafts classes. In a five-field comparison of study areas, their preferred sequence of interest was found to be business, medicine, liberal arts, engineering, and science. They may enjoy athletic and social events as extracurricular activities. They prefer well-structured classes that also allow them to have some social interaction with others.

Common Behaviors

ESFJ students are often the most popular with teachers. They report that teachers like them, even in instances when they are not particularly fond of the teacher. Liking tradition and being eager helpers are two traits that probably endear them to their teachers. ESFJs seldom demonstrate problematic behavior. Like other SJs, they respect authority for authority's sake. Once they learn a set of standards, they work hard to preserve them. Their disobediences, when they occur, tend to be of a fairly mild nature, such as whispering or passing notes in class. ESFJs expect teachers and schools to provide them with security. They expect themselves and their possessions to be protected.

Peer relationships are very important to ESFJs. They work hard to keep peace with everyone, especially their friends. They enjoy working in groups and are often highly contributing members. ESFJs are likely to do more than their share of the work in a group project.

ESFJs are typically steady workers. Their work is not usually done quickly, but it is generally done thoroughly. Writing down a question often helps ESFJs feel that they understand what is being asked. (In contrast, NTs, NFs, and SPs often consider writing a question down to be busy work.) Although they usually do not come up with their own system for studying, they do appreciate being taught a system and will use it consistently.

Since they like belonging to a group, ESFJ students are often club joiners. Service clubs, in particular, seem to appeal to them. They may assume leadership roles when they are asked to do so or when no one else will take on such roles. Preferring to be encouraging of others rather than highly commanding, they act somewhat modest about their leadership abilities. They are more likely than most other types to define themselves by the groups they belong to.

ESFJs are at the center of the information chain. They, along with ESFPs, are usually the best informed about social happenings. If someone wants to know what parties are being planned, who is going out with whom, and what is the latest rumor about a classmate, they should probably ask an ESFJ. Because of their sense of responsibility, they are able to keep secrets, but they may find it difficult to do so, especially if they are not asked to keep it to themselves.

For ESFJs, organizing and throwing parties are two of their favorite activities. They carefully plan every detail of such events. The food they serve is often a work of art as well as good tasting. They will generally work hard to ensure that each of their guests feels welcome and included.

Other students naturally gravitate toward ESFJs and ask them for help because they project an image of being helpful, dependable, and optimistic. As adults, ESFJs often find it difficult to get their own work done because they are often so busy helping others. As children, ESFJs may have difficulty completing their homework. One ESFJ high schooler talked about a time when her favorite sixth-grade teacher disciplined her. During quiet time, the student had quietly answered another student's question. The teacher made her stay in at recess for the offense. She appreciated his actions for two reasons. First, his enforcing the rule proved he was fair; and second, it gave her a compelling reason to refuse to help others, enabling her to get her own work done.

ESFJs enjoy learning about social standards. They often like finding out about cultures of the present and past. History told from the human perspective often fascinates them. By showing the connection of the present to the past, teachers can help their ESFJ students broaden their understanding.

ESFJ students usually like to do work that produces a practical result. They often enjoy corresponding with pen pals. Their favorite art projects are usually crafts. Making a decorative gift or a piece of jewelry for a friend tangibly expresses their caring for others. They prefer math to be presented as a tool with practical uses, such as balancing a checkbook or doing taxes. ESFJs are more grounded in reality and practicality than most of the other types.

Discipline Issues

ESFJ students may talk out of turn or commit other minor infractions. They might become more strongly disruptive if they become members of a group that encourages such behavior. Punishing the ESFJ in front of their group may result in feelings of martyrdom and perhaps encourage the student to continue committing the offending behavior. *Solution:* Talking to the ESFJ on a one-on-one basis and appealing to their SJ sense of what is proper or to their feeling side will likely get better results. Teachers might help the ESFJ to think about their behavior by asking questions such as, What is the function of school? Is it a good function? Does your behavior help or hinder this function? What is the effect of your behavior on your friends?

ESFJs can become very bothered if they feel that someone has been treated unfairly. They may challenge the teacher by championing the other student's cause. *Solution:* The teacher may need to help ESFJ students see that problems are more easily solved when fewer people are involved. Thanking them for their concern and reemphasizing that the teacher will discuss the problem with the affected student should help.

Academic Orientation Issues

ESFJ students need to have someone show interest in their academic performance. Some ESFJs who have dropped out of school lament that their parents did not even ask them if they had done their homework. *Solution:* ESFJs need someone who will monitor their performance, either a parent or teacher or both. The person acting as monitor simply needs to ask the ESFJ student about schoolwork status and to look over samples of their work for each class periodically. ESFJs usually do their best work for another person because of their strong desire to please other people.

ESFJs may begin to slip academically if they make too many commitments. They are likely to become overcommitted because they often feel that if they themselves do not do a task, it will not get done. *Solution:* Teachers can sympathize with overcomitted ESFJ students and discuss with them how their overcommitment is affecting their performance in school. It may be helpful to point out to ESFJs that by taking on too much responsibility, they are preventing others from learning how to take care of things themselves. They can help the students to prioritize obligations and make choices, and then help them learn how to refuse to make inappropriate commitments to others. To avoid becoming overcommitted, young ESFJs often do well if they can attribute their inability to do something to someone else. They might say, for example, "I wish I could help you study for the test, but my parents say that I need to spend time with my aunt, who is visiting this week."

Interpersonal Behavior Issues

Since giving directives is unappealing to ESFJs, they may expect others to know what they want without being told. When others do not meet their expectations, they can sometimes become sharply critical and judgmental. *Solution:* Teachers can help ESFJ students learn how to express their wishes clearly and nonjudgmentally. They can also try to help them understand the many ways that miscommunication can naturally arise when only nondirective messages are given. It is important for ESFJ students to personalize and practice a new behavior. Teachers can help them by encouraging them to describe ways that they could help others better understand the messages that are most important to them.

In their desire to retain good relationships and be responsible, ESFJs sometimes allow others to take advantage of them. *Solution:* Because relationships are so important to ESFJs and they are not swayed by pragmatic considerations, it is generally best for teachers to simply sympathize with ESFJs' desire to keep their relationships intact. Teachers can use themselves as an example by discussing the need to avoid being overly responsible for their students because it can prevent students from growing and learning. Teachers can then engage ESFJs in a discussion of responsibility to others. They can point out how ESFJs are being irresponsible when they prevent other students from learning new skills or assuming their own responsibility. This discussion usually curbs the ESFJ tendency to overhelp or assume inappropriate blame.

Summary

ESFJ students are motivated by teachers who exhibit a caring and harmonious style and who set clearly defined standards for behavior. They also appreciate teachers who will listen carefully to their questions and take the time to ensure that they understand the answers. Teachers who emphasize practical application over theory will usually hold the interest of ESFJs.

ISFJ Conservers

Basic Characteristics

Adjectives that describe the typical ISFJ are considerate, dedicated, and service minded. In their quiet and conscientious way, they will often go to great lengths to protect the well-being of those around them. Loyalty and devotion to the people and groups they identify with are trademark ISFJ qualities. They have the ability to demonstrate uncommon patience and perform detailed tasks.

Potential Career Paths

ISFJ students are often involved in occupations that provide personal service to others. In the field of medicine, for example, they may be nurses, dental hygienists, and dieticians. They frequently find satisfaction through pursuing such social service occupations as teacher, librarian, guidance counselor, or probation officer. They may be attracted to business positions, such as secretary, administrator, computer operator, or bookkeeper. Since they tend to have a practical orientation, they are often attracted to occupations that deal with the needs of people in their community, such as innkeeper, retail salesperson, or electrician.

Preferred Classes

ISFJ students often like classes that focus on practical skills such as reading, arts and crafts, child development, and on-the-job training. In a five-field comparison of study areas, their preferred sequence of interest was found to be medicine, liberal arts, engineering, business, and science. For extracurricular activities, they may enjoy personal hobbies and one-on-one social interactions. Practical classes with real-world applications that help other people appeal to them the most.

Common Behaviors

ISFJ students generally work quietly and tirelessly in the classroom to get their own work done and to help the teacher or other students. They often take note of what needs to be done and do it without fanfare. They believe in the value of hard work and believe that relaxation must be earned. They are among the least likely of the types to use inappropriate behavior in the classroom, and may be favored by the teacher.

ISFJ students generally work well by themselves or with one or two others. They are usually self-motivated and can work for long periods without teacher intervention. They prefer to do written work or a project rather than give an oral book report or other public presentation. Their work is generally thorough and neat.

ISFJs are usually obedient, and their misbehavior is typically of a fairly mild nature, usually along the lines of chewing gum or passing notes. Sometimes ISFJ students will follow their friends in misbehavior in order to remain an accepted member of a group. Intensely loyal, ISFJs will often support their close friends at almost any cost. However, they will with-draw from a group if the behavior is offensive to them. Staying in line with authority figures is one of their primary concerns. They not only obey the teacher; they also often feel personally responsible for the mis-behavior of others around them.

ISFJs are often likely to join library clubs or service clubs. Libraries meet two needs of ISFJs. First, they provide them with quiet time for reading; and second, the preservation of knowledge and traditions con-tained in libraries fits their values. Service clubs provide them with well-defined roles that permit them to offer help to others in a calm, assured manner. In whatever groups they join, they are likely to give quiet, coop-erative service and reserve any accolades for the group itself.

ISFJs are very dependable and frequently help their teachers. They are skilled at organizing material supplies. It is the fortunate teacher who secures their assistance in such things as keeping the art cupboard in order. As a fifth-grade teacher who uses practice centers explains,

> Each year I look for students who can help me keep the practice centers sup-plied. Often the best helpers are ISFJs. They seem to enjoy the sense of being helpful to me and their classmates. Their skills in organization and neatness keep the practice centers in top condition.

Most ISFJs have excellent memories, especially for personal events. They can often repeat entire conversations. Events often seem to replay in their heads, enabling them to see events from many different perspectives. Many of their most important memories deal with security or safe keep-ing. They are frequently the best preservers of past traditions.

ISFJs expect teachers and schools to provide secure learning environ-ments in which each person's property is safe. Together with this need for safety, ISFJs usually have a strong sense of territoriality. ISFJs may some-times complain that they have more than their fair share of work to do. This is often a legitimate complaint, and sometimes it is a signal that they are crying out for help. In other cases, ISFJs may really be asking others for gratitude and they might be devastated if someone else did the work. More than any other type, ISFJs define themselves by what they do for others.

ISFJs like harmonious, smoothly running classrooms that are neat and quiet. They prefer rules to be clearly defined. Like ISTJs, they like to have plenty of time to do their work and dislike being rushed from one activity to another. Also like ISTJs, they like assignments to be narrowly defined with precise instructions about how they should be done. While some types are inspired to greater levels of creativity when they are given ambiguous and open-ended directions, ISFJs and ISTJs usually become anxious about possibly not meeting the teacher's expectations.

Discipline Issues

ISFJs may exhibit periodic streaks of stubbornness that seem out of keeping with their usual quiet, compliant ways. *Solution:* Since ISFJs tend to be stubbornly firm only about those things that are very important to them, teachers should try to make an effort to be more flexible when possible. Issues that may cause them to be stubborn can concern such things as personal property rights and maintaining customary schedules. If the teacher is unable to accommodate ISFJs, they can tell the student in a calm but firm way that as the teacher, they have chosen to do things in a particular way. Most SJs, particularly ISFJs, respond relatively well to statements that in essence say, "Do it because I (the authority figure) said so," provided they are not overused.

Because of their quiet, unassuming manner, ISFJs may become the target of bullying students. This can be disruptive since ISFJs are likely to seek teacher intervention. *Solution:* Teachers can help them become more assertive. To be successful, ISFJ students may need the support of their teachers to encourage their assertive behavior. The teacher can reinforce their new skill of standing up for themselves with appropriate praise.

Academic Orientation Issues

ISFJ students sometimes have difficulty participating in group discussions, especially debates. They may spend more of their time trying to figure out what other people want to hear than focusing on what they really want to say. *Solution:* Sometimes simply affirming that the class really wants to hear what they have to say is enough to get ISFJ students to express themselves. If they participate, teachers should ensure that their efforts receive acceptance so that their participation will be reinforced. Sometimes, it might help to ask ISFJ students to write down their thoughts and have another student read what they have written for them.

Preliterate students can simply whisper their thoughts to another student who can repeat them. This will help them feel that they are not putting themselves on the line so much.

ISFJs sometimes have difficulty with technical and theoretical classes. When they do have difficulties, they can become consumed with worry and be unable to function properly. *Solution:* Teachers can help them plan strategies to learn the material. Because ISFJs tend to be excellent at memorization, they should be encouraged to use this skill to make up for any shortcomings they have in other areas. Planning and implementing the strategy will focus their energy on how to learn the material and alleviate some of their worry.

Interpersonal Behavior Issues

ISFJ students, like ESFJs, frequently take on too much responsibility. In their desire to cooperate with others, they may accept more work than they can comfortably handle. *Solution:* ISFJs need to learn to say no. Teachers can give them opportunities to role-play several different ways of saying no. It may be necessary to give them the assignment of refusing to accept a new responsibility at least once a day.

ISFJs can sometimes be worriers and complainers. *Solution:* Teachers can listen sympathetically to the ISFJ's worries and complaints but retain a sense of detachment. Teachers should listen and respond to the point the ISFJ is making, but they should refocus the conversation if the concerns become repetitive. ISFJs may complain that they are taken for granted and that no one appreciates them. ISFJs are so quietly helpful that they often *are* taken for granted. Teachers should make an effort to acknowledge their work, either publicly or in the form of a note, and encourage other students to show gratitude to the ISFJ as well.

Summary

ISFJ students are motivated by teachers who set clear standards for classroom work and behavior. ISFJs work very hard at meeting the standards of teachers who give them some personal attention. ISFJs work most effectively when they have some quiet time and private space in which to work. They prefer teachers who give real-world examples that involve people over those who emphasize fantasy and imaginary thinking.

Chapter 9

Sensing–Perceiving
Artisan Students

The phrase carpe diem is an apt description of the Sensing–Perceiving (SP) Artisan student's approach to life. They tend to live their lives with a sense of immediacy. They are often the people who teach us to think in terms of "if not now, when?" For SP students, there is no better time than the present. And during the present moment, they enjoy having the freedom to act on their impulses. In doing so, they become energized. Teachers who learn to capitalize on this energy are often favorites of SP students.

SPs make up approximately 38 percent of the general population (Keirsey and Bates, 1984). They enjoy the pleasures life offers them. They do not like to dwell on the past or worry about the future. For them, now is all there is, and now is full of all kinds of wonderful things to do.

SP students like to be active and generally have a high level of physical energy. They like mobility and can become bored or fidgety if they are inactive for very long. They are the most likely of the types to be labeled hyperactive. According to Keirsey (1988) and Johnson (1995), they are sensitive to confinement and prefer assignments that enable them to do something physical. Activities such as giving demonstrations, repairing things with tools, or doing an experiment give them opportunities to experience learning through action.

Teachers will find that SPs enjoy activities that emphasize their personal performance and highlight their ability and flair. For Extraverts, this might include debating or giving oral presentations; for Introverts, it might include drawing or model making. Hands-on manipulation of materials and experimentation with tools can be exciting for SPs. They take great pride in their ability to be effective craftspeople in their work.

SPs generally prefer to read material with an action theme; writing that involves a practical purpose will interest them most. They enjoy telling others about exciting actions or events they've observed or experienced. When they are engaged in art projects, they often vary the assignment or the media. They particularly enjoy games that emphasize competition and sheer fun.

SPs are often more efficient when they work on many things at once. They often take on many activities at once because they enjoy variety and dislike feeling bound by routine. Some SPs can have difficulty completing projects because they allow themselves to become overloaded or because their attention often shifts to a new activity. SPs can sometimes have inconsistent academic performance, often as a result of their shifting focus or interest. They may become absorbed in a topic, only to lose interest altogether at some later point. When they are motivated, they work hard to beat their competition and strive to perform the best.

SP students are often more apt to take risks than are students of other types. In their need to keep their lives exciting and fun, SPs can often become very competitive. They like challenging themselves and others and occasionally will give or accept dares involving considerable danger. They usually bounce back quickly from disappointments and setbacks. They will usually return from a disappointment, ready to try something again and convinced that this time they will win.

SPs want to know how something will benefit them right now. It is hard for SP students to exert themselves for distant goals without any clear short-term payoff. When they are asked to do tasks that hold no obvious immediate payoff, they may become master negotiators who aim for a way out of the work. They seem to instinctively know how they will benefit from something, as well as how others will. They sometimes appear to believe that nearly anything is negotiable if an offer is made that appeals to the self-interests of the parties involved.

SPs typically are highly adaptable to changing circumstances. It is not unusual for them to drop everything at a moment's notice to help a friend or to suddenly go some place where they can find excitement. They usually think well on their feet. They are not as concerned that they do everything the best way but focus more on getting the job done. Their ability to improvise, using whatever materials are available, makes them great tacticians.

With their willingness to take risks, their pragmatic view of the world, and their great adaptability, they are often the best of all types at recognizing and seizing opportunities. These same qualities also make them better than most types at handling emergency situations. In either case, they do not hesitate to take action, are able to calmly assess what needs to be done, and can make do with the available resources.

Having an SP student, particularly an Extraverted SP, on their side can be one of a teacher's most powerful assets. A single SP student can dramatically influence an entire class by easily stirring up enthusiasm for or against a teacher or subject. Fortunately, SPs are generally very accepting.

SPs are likely to have friends in their own age group. They easily accept others who are different than they are, although they may wonder why anyone would not want to be like them. They enjoy and can sometimes exploit these differences. When SPs make friends, they are very likely to be generous with their time and resources. For instance, they might lend their last pencil to a friend, even though they will end up getting in trouble for not having a pencil themselves.

SPs often view themselves as one of a kind. They have a well-developed sense of personal autonomy and want to make an impact on the world. SPs enjoy being complimented on their virtuosity and their sense of timing. To pull off an action with flair and finesse can be personally rewarding for them.

SPs like to be praised for what they do and how they do it. Praise, for them, is most effective if it is delivered with a high level of energy and excitement. SPs like to be complimented for their boldness and willingness to take risks. They like to be praised for their grace, flair, and timing in doing school work, and for their cleverness, adaptability, tolerance, and endurance. SPs view themselves as one of a kind and particularly like to be praised for their special qualities.

To know what is important to SPs, teachers will need to listen to their stories. Their stories, unlike those of SJs, which tend to focus on the "shoulds" and "oughts" of life, usually describe the fun or failure of the moment. Even when an event occurred in the past, SPs may switch to the present tense to give the story a stronger impact. They often use action or colorful words to describe their stories as well as the current colloquial words.

SP students are energetic, exciting, and flexible. They are usually highly competitive and perform well under pressure. They like to make games out of everything and may make up songs or dances to help themselves memorize material. The classroom is seldom dull when it contains SPs. They are usually physically active and well-coordinated. Since they enjoy change, they are generally tolerant of teachers experimenting with new techniques. Assessing moment-by-moment needs and adapting to changing needs is fairly easy for SPs. They are often pragmatic and good at figuring out the bottom line as well as generous with their time and possessions. They tend to be impulsive and sometimes do things without thinking about them, which they later regret. SP students are enjoyable because they are generally fun, cheerful, exciting, and tolerant.

There are two major categories of SP Artisan students: STP Operators and SFP Performers, which are illustrated in table 14.

Table 14 SP Artisan Students	
STP Operators	**SFP Performers**
ESTP Negotiators	ESFP Actors
ISTP Tinkerers	ISFP Artists

STP Operators

STP Operators usually have a sense of boldness about them. They may take command of a situation during a crisis when the action is highly exciting, and later relinquish their lead role. When there is a need for quick decisions, they may choose to give directives to others. They tend to view themselves most positively when they have developed a sense of virtuosity in some skill. Often these skills involve their ability to be particularly observant of the way things vary. This ability also plays a role in their capacity to be adaptable and pragmatic. When their need for adventure and risk taking becomes tied to academic success, they can become highly successful students.

ESTP Negotiators
Basic Characteristics

Adjectives that describe the typical ESTP are active, energetic, and versatile. They are adaptable realists who view each situation from a pragmatic perspective. With their alertness to clues from both the environment and people, they can make quick assessments and take quick actions. These qualities often make them skilled negotiators and dynamic persuaders.

Potential Career Paths

ESTPs often pursue careers in the action arenas of civil service, such as firefighter, paramedic, or detective. They like interaction with others, changing situations, and risk. Some enjoy the field of finance in positions such as stockbroker, insurance salesperson, and banker. Others enjoy positions in the entertainment and sports field such as sportscaster, reporter, promoter, fitness instructor, or athlete. The trades offer them variety and physical activity with jobs such as carpenter, general contractor, and construction worker. In the fields of business, they may become entrepreneurs, land developers, and salespeople.

Preferred Classes

ESTP students typically like history, math, political science, speech and debate, job training programs, and physical education. In a five-field comparison of study areas, their preferred sequence of interest was found to be business, medicine, liberal arts, engineering, and science. They may enjoy social and action events as extracurricular activities. Classes that deal with real events, facts, and observable changes generally appeal to SP students.

Common Behaviors

ESTP students are highly competitive. By incorporating competition into an academic subject, teachers can effectively motivate them, provided the subject is one that involves the use of the ESTP's innate skills. Many ESTPs choose not to compete in purely academic subjects because they do not think that they can win. When ESTPs can associate winning with academic learning, they will generally compete. To help ESTPs make this connection, teachers can encourage them to either compete with a buddy or as a member of a team or to improve on a previous score. Games that require quick reactions, physical skill, and knowledge of a subject can be used to help them make the connection between learning and achievement. Examples of games that generally work well with ESTPs are described in chapter 14. Teachers can try to find areas in which ESTP students have natural ability and encourage them to use their abilities to compete academically.

ESTPs are often popular. They can be charming and even flamboyant. The socially sophisticated skills they may cultivate can make them likely members of the "in" group at school. Others may see ESTPs as empathetic because of their ability to read and respond to body language, even though empathy is not typically a strong suit of this type.

ESTPs, like ISTPs, often like to challenge themselves and others to try something risky. Giving and taking dares occurs more frequently when an ESTP is leading a group. They enjoy testing their physical limit and often make excellent athletes. Team sports often appeal to them more than individual ones.

ESTPs and ESFPs are among the most likely types to volunteer when a teacher asks for a student to demonstrate a new concept. They often do not mind appearing a little silly, as long as they can get a laugh.

ESTP students typically like classrooms that have a high energy level and contain lots of action. They like the noise associated with an exciting atmosphere. This kind of environment also allows them to become involved physically and strategically.

ESTPs and ISTPs are usually able to remember many facts and recall them quickly. The student who knows the names and vital statistics of every professional basketball player is very often an STP. Unlike NTs, who tend to remember systems of information, STPs can memorize facts in virtual isolation.

Although ESTP students can be rebellious, more often they simply ignore authority. When this approach does not work, they tend to do only what will pragmatically solve the immediate problem. For some ESTPs, the ends justify the means. "It is easier to get forgiveness than permission" is a phrase that could have been coined by an ESTP. ESTPs are more likely than other types to exhibit inappropriate behaviors in class because of their tendency to be oblivious to authority. However, once ESTPs see obedience as being in their own best interest, they will usually work hard to follow the rules.

ESTP students may exhibit a boldness in the classroom that commands a teacher's attention. They often volunteer to demonstrate things to the class and like to show off. This behavior can be disruptive unless teachers channel this boldness into positive activities. For example, one ESTP middle school student wanted to get attention any way she could. She knew exactly what to say and do to bother each of her teachers. One teacher saw that this student was bright and regularly commented on her abilities. The student began to come after school because she enjoyed the positive attention. Her behavior and grades subsequently improved in all of her classes.

ESTPs often gravitate toward situations that make use of their tactical abilities—getting the most out of the available resources. They may also gravitate toward areas that utilize their ability to react quickly in a crisis or to expedite timely processes. Teachers who manage to use the abilities of ESTPs in these areas can help them to further develop their skills.

Discipline Issues

ESTP students are the most likely among the types to be labeled hyperactive (Johnson, 1995). *Solution:* Teachers need to recognize that the energy of ESTP students can be an asset rather than a liability. Teachers can take advantage of the ESTP's love of a challenge. For example, they might tell them that they have exactly sixty seconds to get rid of their excess energy by taking a stretch break. Such students could watch a clock that has a second hand, with the goal of being back in their seats at the end of the sixty-second period. Teachers may need to set ground rules regarding noise level and range of movement. They can tell the class that they are looking for the most original way for students to expend extra energy.

ESTPs can often say things that are extremely upsetting to others, including their teachers. *Solution:* In such situations, teachers should make an effort to avoid exhibiting anger or using sarcastic or emotionally charged remarks. ESTPs can often get some enjoyment out of creating such excitement. Let them know succinctly, without lecturing, that they have stepped over the line. If consequences are necessary, simply carry them out. Actions are more effective with them than words.

Academic Orientation Issues

ESTP students can run the risk of dropping out of school due to boredom or lack of impact. *Solution:* When ESTPs who have received high school diplomas or college degrees are asked what motivated them to do so, they will often cite the desire to earn money. Teachers can appeal to this desire by telling them that college graduates earn almost twice as much as high school dropouts. Since delayed gratification is generally not a great motivator for SPs, they will respond better if they have role models who can illustrate the end results of their future goals. The more tangible the benefits of staying in school can be made, the better they will respond. High school job training programs are often effective for ESTPs because they enable them to experience different working situations.

Some ESTPs lose interest in school and view it as irrelevant. *Solution:* Teachers need to encourage these students to become involved in activities that enable them to make an impact, such as joining or starting a club or running for school office.

Interpersonal Behavior Issues

ESTP students often have a good sense of humor. While this is one of their most engaging attributes, they may sometimes find negative outlets for it; for instance, playing practical jokes on others. They can alienate friends who become the brunt of their pranks or they can find themselves taking on the role of bully. *Solution:* Teachers are not likely to stop the tendency to play practical jokes altogether so they should take charge of it. ESTP students should be told firmly when their joke playing has escalated too far.

ESTPs can sometimes take their negotiating skills too far and begin playing con games on others. Usually the con game's objective is to bring about laughter. *Solution:* Providing other opportunities for laughter in the classroom may prevent the problem. If such incidents occur, teachers, using a lighthearted tone, need to inform ESTPs that they see through the game. Teachers can also ask ESTPs to describe a time when they were the victim of a con. This can lead to lively classroom discussions about the difference between a joke that is funny and one that is hurtful.

Summary

ESTP students are motivated by teachers who challenge them to be competitive and risk taking in constructive ways. The greater the excitement and the need for tactical action, the more they enjoy learning. Making some part of classroom time seem like a real-life adventure will almost always motivate ESTPs. Teachers who allow no variety or freedom in their classrooms are not likely to motivate ESTPs to demonstrate their true skills.

ISTP Tinkerers

Basic Characteristics

Adjectives that describe the typical ISTP students are independent, adventurous, and expedient. They tend to be calm observers of life. They like to apply their concrete analytical skills to learn the how and why of things. ISTPs often have abundant physical energy and like to seek out effective and efficient ways to apply their skills.

Potential Career Paths

The tendency of many ISTPs to use tools in achieving practical hands-on results often leads them to positions in the trades, such as computer repair technician, mechanic, commercial artist, or athletic coach. Their technical expertise is also useful in such occupations as chiropractor, computer programmer, or electrical engineer. Some ISTPs pursue action fields and may become race car drivers, pilots, or intelligence agents. Those who enjoy manipulating data may pursue business or finance fields in positions such as securities analyst, economist, purchasing agent, or legal secretary.

Preferred Classes

ISTP students usually like math, auto repair and woodshop, graphic arts, agriculture, science, job training programs, and physical education. In a five-field comparison of study areas, their preferred sequence of interest was found to be business, medicine, liberal arts, science, and engineering. They often enjoy athletic events as extracurricular activities. ISTPs prefer classes that allow them to work with real objects or manipulate data.

Common Behaviors

ISTPs students adapt more readily than other SPs to the typical school environment, and they are often successful in school. Their preference for Introversion and Thinking helps them quietly pursue the observation and manipulation of objective data, such as numbers, facts, or objects.

ISTPs are often the tinkerers of the world. They typically have a compelling need to know *how* things work—from such things as pencil sharpeners to motorcycles. Tools usually attract them. They enjoy taking things apart, then putting them back together. This trait is often first apparent in kindergarten classes. ISTP students spend more time engaged with building blocks and putting together objects than in cooperative play. Their hand-eye dexterity may be more well developed than their peers.

Young ISTPs are sometimes behind their peers in language acquisition. The ISTP world is the world of action, not the world of words. ISTPs like to show who they are by the things they do. They often sit back quietly and watch the world, gathering the information they need. When they decide it is time to take action, they are usually quick, forceful, and accurate. One teacher, realizing that an ISTP student did not want a speaking part in the class play, utilized the student's speed and skill with tools by making him the sound effects person. The student, who previously expressed boredom with school, had such a positive experience in this role that he became a more attentive student.

While ISTPs are generally polite and cooperative, they will sometimes refuse to do a task if they see no point to it. They are more likely to be quietly stubborn than openly defiant. ISTPs tend to be independent loners.

ISTPs and ESTPs often pride themselves on the fact that others cannot figure them out. They like to keep other people guessing about what they are going to do next. When learning about personality type theory, these two types are likely to feel that they break the mold and do not fit into any predefined categories. Consequently, these two types are likely to respond especially well to reverse psychology, provided it is not overused. One teacher who knew her ISTP student was not performing up to his potential used this strategy, saying in a teasing tone: "I just know you're going to get a D this quarter. You got one last quarter, and your work this quarter is not any better. I think you're smart, but you're probably too lazy to bring your grade up." A caveat to teachers trying the reverse psychology strategy is to be aware that, while this strategy can be very motivating for STPs, it can be devastating for students of other types.

ISTPs can be the ultimate minimalists. They believe in conserving energy and do not like to expend more energy than is absolutely necessary. While they generally expend a lot of energy on their favorite activities, they usually put forth a minimum amount of effort with other tasks.

While ISTP students are not afraid of hard work, they just do not like to waste unnecessary effort. Many ISTPs have hobbies that do not require much continuous physical action and often involve solitude, such as reading or playing on the computer. For many ISTPs, life consists of long periods of relaxation punctuated by bursts of activity. ISTPs are likely to enjoy individual sports that require physical endurance and/or ability.

ISTP students like classrooms that provide them with opportunities to use tools—whether it be a calculator or a computer, a table saw or a microscope. They usually appreciate when others ask them to help fix things or explain how to use tools. They especially like to do work that has an immediate application and will often refuse to do what they perceive to be busy work.

ISTPs can be masters of improvisation. Their ability to identify problems, troubleshoot difficulties, and make quick adaptations and variations can make them seem bold and exciting to others. They are most successful when they gain some virtuosity in a given field. Their fields of interest can be as varied as mechanics, computers, construction, and the arts. Teachers can have a great influence on ISTP students by recognizing their abilities and providing them with the resources they need to keep improving.

Discipline Issues

ISTP students will often refuse to do work if they do not see a purpose for it. Teachers may have difficulty convincing students to do the work in such cases. *Solution:* In such situations, teachers will usually find it best to isolate students and let them take the logical consequences of their decision; for example, failing a test. Taking notice of their abilities, and making them aware of how the current material relates to something they care about will often prevent much of the insubordination.

Since ISTPs are risk takers who are often attracted to tools, they are among the most likely of types to become injured. *Solution:* Since teachers will not be able to prevent all accidents, they should make an effort to be aware of this ISTP tendency. Setting up activities so that the ISTP becomes the expert on safety is a useful way to prevent problems. Often these accidents are not as distressing to the student as they are to the teacher.

Academic Orientation Issues

ISTPs students prefer to be efficient and may sometimes put forth too little effort to achieve effective results. *Solution:* Teachers can remind them of the practical results of doing well in school, such as landing a good job and earning a good salary. Setting grade goals for a specific task, discussing *exactly* what they must do to receive the grade, and having them estimate the time needed to accomplish the result will help them improve their planning abilities.

ISTPs, like other SPs, are likely to put off work in a class that they do not like until they fall too far behind to catch up. *Solution:* Prevention of an impossible catch-up situation is the key. Giving them a one-week warning to get their work done when they are a critical point often helps. Some teachers use an alert system to help ISTPs know their status. "Yellow alert" means the students needs to move into action to stay out of a crisis zone; "red alert" signals a crisis. Sometimes, a one-on-one talk early on in the term helps, enabling teachers to express confidence in the student's ability and makes clear to the student that late work will not be accepted.

Interpersonal Behavior Issues

Many ISTP students put up with everything that goes on around them until it overwhelms them, and then they respond in an explosive manner. *Solution:* ISTPs need to learn how to take a private time-out when they feel themselves about to lose control. Teachers should encourage them to address problems when they are calm and to deal with them when they arise rather than letting them build up.

ISTPs tend to have difficulty sharing what is really going on inside of them. *Solution:* ISTPs need to gain practice expressing their thoughts. Teachers can make a game out of this process by asking the ISTP to make two or three statements—one of which is true. The teacher can then see if she or he can guess which statement accurately represents the student's thinking. For ISTPs, though, actions will almost always speak louder than words.

Summary

ISTP students respond to teachers who reinforce their particular skills and allow them to experiment. Teachers who encourage tinkering and troubleshooting will be effective in their efforts to develop the skills of ISTPs. Providing them with a variety of tools for experimentation will also work well. Severely inhibiting their action is a surefire road to disaster for both teacher and student.

SFP Performers

SFP Performers are among the most optimistic of all types. Like SFJ Providers, they have a social bent, but unlike SFJs, who emphasize social standards, SFPs emphasize social fun. Preferring personal freedom, SFPs are among the types least likely to tell others what to do. They need sensory stimulation—such as food, color, clothing, and sound—and the more they are exposed to it, the better. With their people skills, fun-loving attitude, ability to use time freely, and capacity to find sensations that stimulate themselves and others, they often try to make the world a more adventuresome and exciting place for everyone.

ESFP Actors

Basic Characteristics

Adjectives that describe the typical ESFP student are playful, vivacious, and outgoing. They normally accept and tolerate others easily. Their talkative, exciting style enables them to sometimes be very entertaining. ESFPs can also often help others to relax and become more easygoing. They bring a sense of fun to group activities.

Potential Career Paths

ESFPs are found in careers that allow for social participation, action, fun, and variety. They are often found in the entertainment field in jobs such as musician, photographer, and tour guide. Their social skills prepare them for jobs in fields such as health care, social work, and education. Careers such as emergency room nurse, veterinarian, social worker, preschool teacher, or athletic coach often appeal to them. Their practical talents and communication skills are valued in the worlds of business and service. Positions such as salesperson, labor relations mediator, public relations specialist, receptionist, food server, and flight attendant give them opportunities to use these skills.

Preferred Classes

ESFP students usually like classes in drama, history, art, child care, job training programs, and physical education. In a five-field comparison of study areas, their preferred sequence of interest was found to be business, medicine, liberal arts, engineering and science. Their extracurricular activities often center around the social groups to which they belong. They prefer classes that are practical, have lots of variety, and allow them to actively participate.

Common Behaviors

ESFP students are typically cheerful, carefree, and fun loving. These characteristics help to make them one of the most optimistic of all the types. They believe that everything they do will work out for the best and are seldom depressed. When they do feel down, they seldom stay that way for long. Being around an ESFP is often like being around a whirlwind. ESFPs have a combination of speed and stamina that is perhaps matched only by ESTPs.

Other than their optimism, the most obvious feature of ESFPs is their desire to be at the center of attention. ESFPs like to entertain others. They often enjoy acting and telling stories and jokes. They make an effort to please everyone with their performances and seldom use humor that is biting or mean. They are the most likely type to value themselves based on whom they make happy. ESFPs who are allowed to exercise their natural abilities will generally be enthusiastic students. For example, John, an ESFP, loved being on his school's debate team. He went to many competitions and won several awards. He prepared carefully using high quality props and delivered his speeches with flair. When asked why he put so much effort into his presentations, he replied, "I love to see if I can surprise the audience. I don't want anybody bored out there; I want to get them jazzed."

ESFPs usually begin in elementary school as enthusiastic students. They like their teachers, enjoy being around other children, and enjoy art, physical education, music, and other active subjects. By the time they reach the upper elementary grades, however, some ESFPs become frustrated and confused. These ESFPs have had most of their natural instincts systematically discouraged. They have been told to sit still and listen a majority of the time. Although ESFPs are exceptionally adaptable, they can sometimes exhibit problematic behavior if their abilities are consistently undervalued.

ESFPs typically do not like to fight. In response to a challenge, they prefer to joke and not take the situation too seriously. ESFPs tend to be very forgiving and are usually not able to stay angry for long. They generally like just about everyone.

Because of their fun-loving ways, ESFPs often seem younger than they really are. They find it more difficult than any of the other types to plan ahead. Optimism is their hallmark, and they put forth great effort to ensure that things will work out in the end. Because of their flexibility and adaptability, things generally do turn out well—or at least well enough.

ESFPs students are often popular. Others tend to gravitate toward them because they are fun, charming, and entertaining. Like ESTPs, they are usually part of the "in" crowd. ESFPs are especially vulnerable to peer pressure and often take on the characteristics of their friends.

ESFPs and ESTPs are the most likely types to be wearing the latest fashions. Clothing and personal appearance are often very important to them, since they sometimes use their appearance to make a statement.

ESFP students usually like classrooms that provide noisy excitement, action, and lots of hands-on activities. Surprises and changes invigorate them. Classes with a teacher who is willing to share the spotlight with them are an ESFP's dream. ESFPs like group work. If permitted, ESFPs can adjust just about any class to their liking. In math, they like to use manipulatives to touch and see the mathematical concepts in action. In English, they like to act out stories. In science, they often like labwork.

ESFPs are especially likely to do well in internships or on-the-job training. ESFPs who do well in school often report that some person or group repeatedly offered them help. Teachers who appreciate their need for sensory stimulation, excitement, people interaction, and change are likely to be seen as encouraging.

Discipline Issues

ESFPs and ESTPs generally find it more difficult to sit still quietly for long periods of time than other types of students. *Solution:* Teachers at the elementary-school level can try to change activities fairly frequently and exchange desk activities with ones that require movement. Regularly scheduled breaks can also help. Another technique that might work well is "showtime." Students can be given two to five minutes to do whatever they want in front of the class. Some teachers object to giving over class time to nonacademic endeavors, but it is helpful to remember that ESFPs will often become the center of attention anyway. In this way, they will be doing so on the teacher's terms. Teachers can also have their ESFP students teach part of a lesson or give a demonstration.

ESFPs students are usually talkers. They may experience times in which they cannot seem to stop talking or they say things without thinking. *Solution:* Teachers should try not to view their talking as rebelliousness. ESFPs are generally compliant and truly wish to please others. Their behavior results from their extensive energy and strong desire for attention. Showtime can again be used to help curb any inappropriate behavior. Incorporating some form of group work into the classroom will also give the ESFPs an acceptable outlet for their need to talk.

Academic Orientation Issues

ESFP students sometimes have difficulty seeing the value of school. *Solution:* Teachers should concentrate on helping ESFPs see the usefulness of what they are learning and encourage their joyful spirit. Teachers can also try to express an interest in the things they like and not belittle their dreams.

ESFPs sometimes do not like classes that tend to be very theoretical, such as math and science. *Solution:* Teachers can provide concrete examples whenever possible. Since ESFPs like to talk out their problems, encouraging them to join or start a study group often helps. If they are available, internships or other types of training classes can help them to see how theoretical skills are used in the real world. The real world is much more exciting to ESFPs than the theoretical one, and they are likely to learn valuable, transferable work skills in these types of classes.

Interpersonal Behavior Issues

ESFP students often do not appear serious to others. If someone approaches them with a problem, ESFPs are likely to tell a joke or do something to divert attention from the problem, since they dislike conflict. *Solution:* Teachers can emphasize that this type of behavior can be valuable in avoiding unnecessary arguments, but it may cause others to feel they are being ignored. ESFPs sometimes need personal coaching about how to deal with conflicts. Giving them an opportunity to talk about their options is helpful.

ESFPs can sometimes be led astray by others who are misbehaving. They may get caught up in the excitement and not realize that potentially negative consequences will result from their actions. *Solution:* Since friends are so important to ESFPs, it is very important to encourage them to spend time with those who will be a positive influence. Instead of emphasizing the negative qualities of some of their friends, teachers can talk to them about how their friends are cramping their style and taking away their personal freedom. Teachers can help them to find groups that will allow them more freedom to act.

Summary

ESFP students are motivated by teachers who provide them with opportunities to be active and express themselves socially and verbally. They like being assigned tasks that have them running from place to place and keeping up the communication flow. A teacher who has no place for laughter in the classroom will be uninspiring for the ESFP.

ISFP Artists

Basic Characteristics

Adjectives that describe the typical ISFP student are modest, gentle, and trusting. They tend to be observant and understanding of others. They can be very adaptable and become loyal followers unless a leader goes against their values. In their quiet, warm way, they tend to retain the quality of free spirit.

Potential Career Paths

ISFPs enjoy occupations that allow them lots of variety, hands-on participation, and quiet socialization. They are often found in occupations in the medical field, such as visiting nurse, radiology technologist, veterinary assistant, and medical assistant. In the area of crafts and artistry, they may choose occupations such as painter, dancer, designer, jeweler, and fashion designer. Some choose fields that are technical or deal with facts, such as computer operator, surveyor, geologist, and mechanic. Service-oriented jobs such as storekeeper, elementary teacher, beautician, bookkeeper, and legal secretary also appeal to ISFPs.

Preferred Classes

ISFPs students like classes that focus on practical skills, such as art, agriculture, decorating, job training programs, and physical education. In a five-field comparison of study areas, their preferred sequence of interests was found to be medicine, liberal arts, science, engineering, and business. In extracurricular situations, they often enjoy being around the action in social situations. They prefer classes that emphasize variety and cooperation.

Common Behaviors

ISFP students, along with ESFPs, tend to be the most easygoing of the generally easygoing SPs. They cope well with change and get along with most of their classmates. They usually have a positive outlook at school and prefer to have positve relationships with their teachers. ISFPs are usually slow to become angry and forgive easily. Most often, they are able to see the humor in a situation. However, they are quick to defend the character or ideas of those who are important to them.

ISFP students are usually very kind and considerate of their classmates. Like ISFJs, they often help others quietly, with no fanfare. They exhibit little or no desire to change other people's behavior, rather they enjoy observing what others do without making judgment. They like to be around groups that are engaging in exciting behavior, but they may be more of an observer than a participant. They generally do not like to be made the focus of attention in the classroom unless they chose the role themselves.

Among the SPs, ISFPs are the least likely to exhibit inappropriate behavior. Like ESFPs, they want to please their teachers, but, unlike them, ISFPs find it fairly easy to be quiet. In fact, ISFPs often have a quiet and unassuming style. ISFPs are less likely to demand the teacher's attention than some other types; they do, however, want it. Teachers may need to ensure that they give ISFPs adequate attention so that they progress in their work.

ISFPs express themselves through action rather than through words. Their communication with classmates and teachers can sometimes be indirect. It is important that teachers be observant of the activities they seem to enjoy. Since they prefer being involved with activities that are useful in the present and have less patience with conceptual or abstract learning, teachers will be most successful in helping them to learn when they tie their interests to the conceptual learning. As one ISFP student remarked,

> I didn't like science very much until we studied photosynthesis. The pictures were interesting, but the best part was when we experimented with plants to see what happened if they didn't get enough water or sunlight. I'm using what we learned for my vegetable garden at home.

While ISFPs are not naturally drawn to organizing, organization of materials is a part of the classroom experience. The ISFPs style of organization is very concrete and attuned to color, line, texture, and shading. One student, who often had trouble locating her homework assignments, organized each of her classes by color. She gave each of her textbooks a different colored paper cover. She then used corresponding colors on her homework assignments. Even when her papers were mixed up, she could easily find all of her classwork.

ISFPs often have an almost mystic connection to nature. They may have an uncanny ability with animals or they may love to garden. Working with nature is a spiritual experience for them. Many ISFPs enjoy the outdoors. In addition to outdoor activities, ISFPs often like to read. Historical books or novels that tell about how people lived and action/adventure or mystery works often appeal to them. Like other SPs, they generally like books that have a first-person narrator and take place in the present tense. They enjoy the people-related subjects of social studies or history, as long as the courses are taught with a sensibile, humanistic approach.

ISFP students enjoy classrooms that have lots of hands-on activities but are not excessively noisy. Their enjoyment of hands-on activities may lead them to become highly skilled. ISFP students are often gifted in the arts, such as painting, drawing, sculpture, and music. When teachers respond to an ISFP's talents with excitement, their skills will be further stimulated. Since they thrive on variety, their skills and interests may migrate from one area to another.

Discipline Issues

ISFP students are not usually the instigators or the center of the excitement. But they sometimes can get swept up into negative behavior that others have initiated and may need to take their share of the resulting discipline. *Solution:* Young ISFPs may find it hard to predict the consequences of their behavior. It is best to help them learn when the excitement is positive or when it is likely to bring about a high personal cost. Teachers can ask them about their past experiences in terms of how behaviors led to given consequences. They can also help them to recognize when certain behaviors are apt to lead them into trouble. This process will help ISFPs gain experience in making the connection between their behavior in given situations and the resulting consequences.

ISFPs can sometimes get so caught up in observing other people's behavior that they can fail to get their own work done. *Solution:* Reminders, which work with SJs, will come across as nagging to SPs. Teachers can focus their attention back to their own work by making it seem more exciting. One way to do this is by making specific challenges, such as how much work can be done in a set period of time.

Academic Orientation Issues

ISFP students often enjoy reading, but some complain of poor comprehension because their minds can tend to wander. *Solution:* Teachers can help them learn to organize what they are reading into small sections and identify the main topic of a paragraph. ISFPs often respond well to one-on-one tutoring—either by an adult or a peer—which helps to keep their minds focused on a given task.

ISFP students can sometimes have poor study habits. *Solution:* Teachers can help ISFP students learn good study habits by providing them with as many details as possible. For example, instead of telling them to make an outline of a chapter, telling them *how* to outline a chapter will have better results. It is important to provide them with plenty of specifics as well as an ample amount of praise.

Interpersonal Behavior Issues

ISFP students sometimes make commitments that they later need to break. Many times, this is because they often agree to things because they do not like to say no. *Solution:* Teachers can help them learn to ask for time to think things over before committing to things. Teachers can also role-play with the ISFP students to help them learn to decline requests graciously. It is important to talk to them about how they can hurt others when they fail to keep their commitments and encourage them to agree to do things only if they are certain that they can follow through.

ISFPs are typically very kindhearted and do not like to see other students hurt. For this reason, they can get themselves caught up in other people's problems. They can also take on the anger or pain of others. *Solution:* Sometimes teachers can help ISFPs to let go of some of this negative involvement just by listening to them and helping them think about what they are able to do in a situation. If they are able to take some small action in such situations, the impact of the problem often lessens.

Summary

ISFP students are motivated by teachers who take the time to pay attention to them and appreciate their gifts. By appreciating their adaptability, encouraging experimentation, and recognizing what they value, teachers can get in tune with ISFPs. Teachers who allow ISFPs freedom of expression and do not constrain them too much will be beneficial to those students.

Chapter 10

Intuitive–Feeling
Idealist Students

Intuitive–Feeling Idealist (NF) students strive to be authentic, to be who they truly are. This desire often leads them on a search for their own unique identity. Teachers who encourage NF students to develop and express their unique gifts are likely to see them flourish in the classroom.

NFs make up only 12 percent of the general population (Keirsey and Bates, 1984). NFs often speak in globalistic terms, rather than use precisely defined wording to express themselves. Similes and metaphors frequently appear in their speech and writing. Because they dislike excluding or alienating anyone, NFs often use language that is all-inclusive and sometimes imprecise. This is in sharp contrast to NTs, who tend to use language to make distinctions and to categorize. While NTs are generally more accurate, NFs are often more effective communicators, and they are often more accessible to their audience.

Teachers will find that NFs generally prefer small-group discussions and one-on-one interactions because it helps to personalize the learning process. They also enjoy lectures about real people who were able to solve their own problems. History taught from a perspective that focuses primarily on facts and dates is likely to bore them, but when they learn about beliefs and actions of influential people, they are likely to become fascinated.

NF students enjoy learning about ideas and values. For them, learning is a personalized and subjective exercise. They often enjoy reading, especially fiction and fantasy that focuses on people. In older NFs, the ability to understand a work of literature's meaning on several different levels and to explore hidden meanings or secondary themes becomes highly developed. Poetry also often appeals to NFs because of its extensive use of metaphors.

Fantasies, mysteries, and not-too-realistic romances are likely to be popular with NFs. They generally enjoy make-believe and the process of imagining what could be. Some NFs also like science fiction. They generally prefer books that tap into their natural desire to fantasize. However, biographies may also appeal to them because they are always curious about how other people view the meaning of life.

NF students tend to like writing essays because they can add their own personalized spin to things. They can often see so many sides to a question that they often find true/false and multiple-choice questions more difficult than do other types. Essays provide them with more of an opportunity to demonstrate *everything* they know. NFs are often able to see things from multiple perspectives. They enjoy examining questions that surround what it would have been like to be various people, inhabiting various times, and experiencing various events. For instance, they might wonder what it would have been like to have been an Egyptian child when Cleopatra ruled.

NFs, particularly Introverts, are likely to spend time daydreaming. Most see themselves as creative. With their creative bent, it is not surprising to find that NFs often enjoy creative writing, poetry, and art. To criticize an NF's creations is to criticize the NF. Because of their active imagination, some may find ghost and horror stories especially frightening.

NF students tend to want to include everyone and are exceptionally good at fostering affiliation. They like to emphasize what people have in common, the unity of human experience. When other students comment negatively about cultures that are different from their own, an NF is likely to find the similarities. They encourage cooperation and harmony. A lack of harmony can be extremely stressful for most NFs, so they work hard to protect the feelings of everyone. Games that are especially competitive may be difficult for NFs. They generally prefer to compete against themselves rather than against others.

NF students often view their role in a group as that of maintaining good feelings. They like to ensure that everyone's emotional needs are met. They often dislike competition, seeing it as divisive, and prefer that their classmates work together so that no one is left out or chosen last. They tend to be very empathetic toward others.

NF students usually have a strong desire to please their parents and teachers and will sometimes attempt almost anything to try to please them, including changing their temperament. Since they empathize with others, they can become adept at taking on the behaviors and speech patterns of other types. Young NFs, in particular, live in a world of paradox. On the one hand, they desperately want to reach their full potential. On the other hand, they desperately want to please others. Sometimes these two separate desires can create conflict, especially when they want to please are critical of their unique abilities.

NF students desire and appreciate praise. They tend to perform best for teachers who recognize their personal worth. Teachers should praise them for who they are rather than what they do. NFs appreciate praise for their kindness, insightfulness, authenticity, and creativity. They like personalized comments written on their work that address them with the word "you"; for example, "You made a creative use of metaphor here" is more meaningful to them than a note that says "creative metaphor." NF students also value eye contact, since it often suggests that a teacher sees them as an individual. Many NFs like to write poems and stories, which they may ask their teachers to read. When teachers are asked by their NF students to read their personal works, it is a good idea to clarify the reason for this. Sometimes they simply want the teacher to know them better and may be seeking a sense of personal validation.

NFs particularly enjoy being catalysts for others. As catalysts, they often encourage others to achieve their potential. They usually want to see only the best in people since they believe in the general good of all people. This can sometimes cause them to be too credulous. They can sometimes find it difficult to see others as untrustworthy. Some older NFs, however, seem to develop a skill for identifying deception or artificiality. Young NFs benefit from adults who encourage them to tap into their intuitive abilities to help them develop more sophisticated discernment.

Along with their desire to believe in the best of others, NFs tend to be romantic. Of all the temperaments, they are the most likely to idealize someone as "the perfect person" or a "hero." Often this person is someone they can look up to, such as a parent or a teacher. They can easily become crushed if the person they look up to fails or disappoints them.

Friendships are particularly important for NFs. People often think NFs agree with them because of their ability to completely focus on an individual person and his or her concerns. When an NF is with a person, they focus on that individual and desire a relationship that allows them to share their own values and views.

NF students are good at harmonizing and demonstrating sensitivity and caring toward others. They work hard to please teachers and seldom break rules. Group work is often enjoyable for NFs since they enjoy working cooperatively. They help all members of a group get what they need from the process and work hard to protect other people's feelings. NFs are very focused on others. Other people are often attracted to NFs because they listen intently and empathetically. In a group setting, NFs function as catalysts to bring out the best in others. They enjoy metaphors and searching for meanings that are beyond what is apparent on the surface. Creativity is often a theme for NFs, and they tend to have a rich fantasy life. They prefer learning about what *could be* rather than what *is*. NFs can be extremely vulnerable to criticism, especially if it is from a teacher they idolize. NF students are enjoyable because they frequently are creative, empathetic, and want to please others.

There are two major categories of NF Idealist students: NFJ Mentors and NFP Advocates, which are illustrated in table 15.

Table 15   NF Idealist Students

NFJ Mentors	NFP Advocates
ENFJ Teachers	ENFP Boosters
INFJ Writers	INFP Dreamers

NFJ Idealist Mentors

NFJ Mentors are often appreciated by their peers because of their listening skills and willingness to give clear-cut advice on how to solve personal problems. As adults, they often pursue careers that enable them to use their talent at guidance. Like SFJs, they prefer to be cooperative, so their directives to others are likely to be focused on reaching a common good. ENFJs students are often natural leaders who will give selective directives to other students; INFJs are more likely to wait for others to seek them out than to give directives.

ENFJ Teachers

Basic Characteristics

Adjectives that describe the typical ENFJ student are charismatic, congenial, and personable. They are concerned with the welfare of others and are supportive of other people's needs. This sensitivity, along with a tendency toward highly developed verbal skills, enables them to be both tactful and persuasive.

Potential Career Paths

ENFJs typically have a great facility with communication skills. They are often found in such fields as public relations, journalism, communications, and fund-raising. Their sensitivity toward others' values and perceptions makes them good in various counseling occupations, such as psychologist, mediator, career counselor, and religious leader. Many are found in education or human services positions, such as teacher or professor, dean of students, or residential housing director. In business, they may be human resources development trainers, small business executives, recruiters, or sales managers.

Preferred Classes

ENFJ students usually like art, English, music, child development, languages, and speech classes. In a five-field comparison of study areas, their preferred sequence of interest was found to be engineering, liberal arts, medicine, science, and business. One of their favorite extracurricular activities may be watching movies. They prefer classes that allow them to engage in cooperative interactions such as group discussions.

Common Behaviors

ENFJ students may have a history of helping other students or siblings to learn. Unlike ESFJs, who want to help others obey the rules and do things properly, ENFJs want people to develop to their own highest potential. They are very attuned to other people's feelings and values. When they are helping someone, they often adapt their language and technique until they begin talking and behaving very similarly to the person they are helping. This is their way of ensuring that the person truly understands what they are saying.

When helping another person, they like to explain the reasoning behind doing things a particular way and what the benefits of doing things a certain way will be. Whereas an ESFJ might say, "This is the way you're supposed to do it"; an ENFJ would be more likely to say, "If you do it this way, then you will know how to do this" or "Doing it this way will help you to do this." To balance their desire to help others, ENFJs need to be careful about saving enough time to meet their own needs. If they do not, they may become exhausted and feel resentment toward those they have helped.

ENFJ students generally like school and often perform well. They thrive in classrooms that are warmly supportive and harmonious. Cooperative learning techniques generally work well with ENFJs, who enjoy interacting with their peers as they learn. While ENFJs may talk too much in class, they are not apt to create problems or disruptions otherwise. ENFJs can often put their tendency to be talkative to good use in speech or public speaking classes. They generally do better in classes where there is some clearly defined structure than in classes with a looser, less defined structure.

Like other NFs, ENFJs have a desire to understand themselves and to understand others. But they also want others to understand what higher values are important to them. Of all the NFs, ENFJs and INFPs are the most driven by their personal values. They know what they believe in and feel they know what would make the world a better place. It is important to them that others share their desire to make improvements in the world. They look beyond themselves and emphasize themes that promote the common good. A high school senior class experienced disappointment upon learning that the senior quad renovations they had helped raise funds for would not be completed prior to graduation. But an ENFJ senior made the observation that "the students who are complaining are missing the point. What is really important is that we have made a difference for our high school. We have left a tremendous legacy for future classes."

ENFJs seek idealized or meaningful relationships. They are sensitive to values conflicts and rejection from close friends. It is common for them to seek out heroes who embody the values they see as important and to imitate those heroes. Their heroes can be parents, teachers, or friends. This hero-admirer relationship can become very intense and others may see the ENFJ as being favored by the parent or teacher. ENFJs often endow their heroes with idealistic attributes. The heroes may feel uncomfortable and find it impossible to live up to such idealization.

ENFJ students are natural leaders, although they are not commanders like ENTJs or administrators like ESTJs or crisis managers like ESTPs. Instead, they like to lead by communicating a vision that is attractive to others. It is not uncommon for ENFJs to assume an almost spiritual-like leadership over their friends. They work hard to convince their friends that their errors are keeping them from complete happiness. They try to persuade others to do the right thing, rather than command them to do it. Theirs is a benevolent leadership.

ENFJs are typically good communicators. They can play their audience to elicit different emotional responses—from joy to fear to anger to pride. Because of their facility with words, others may criticize them for being glib or insincere. ENFJs may take such criticisms as personal rejection because, like all NFs, they strive for authenticity.

Discipline Issues

Teachers need to be aware that many ENFJ students respond very negatively to any criticism, no matter how well intentioned it may be. They may become upset and overly sensitive. *Solution:* As with most NFs, ENFJs need to receive many positive comments to offset one piece of constructive criticism. They respond well to praise, so teachers should praise them often. Since they tend to be sensitive to criticism, teachers can often correct small misbehaviors with simple body language, such as giving them a small frown. When publicly correcting them, teachers can try to connect the correction with some praise. For instance, when telling them they are being too loud, a teacher might point out that the student's strong voice is perfect when reading aloud but needs to be lowered during study time.

ENFJ students are likely to start working on a project after getting only a global sense of the directions. They do not usually wait for the details before they begin to take action. Later, they may bother the teacher by asking questions that have already been answered. *Solution:* Teachers should tell students that they need to listen to *all* the instructions before beginning a project. Teachers need to ensure that the instructions are easy to follow. Writing instructions down will also help. Teachers can also assign one student, probably an SJ, to answer questions that students might have about the details of a project, leaving the teacher free from interruptions.

Academic Orientation Issues

ENFJs usually perform well as students. However, if they become unsure of their relationship with the teacher or the class seems especially lacking in harmony to them, they may perform poorly. *Solution:* Teachers should make an effort to praise ENFJs and ENFPs as often as possible. INFJs and INFPs will require a little more evidence of a praise giver's sincerity. Teachers should praise these students for who they are: "You are a kind person. I appreciate the way you helped Robert"; "You are very creative. I wouldn't have thought of doing that." If they must be criticized, teachers should do so as gently as possible. They should try to begin and end the criticism with praise. ENFJs, like other NFs, tend to overgeneralize, so teachers should be certain to explain the specific thing that needs correcting. Instead of saying, "This is sloppy reasoning," saying, "Your paper was enjoyable to read. In this paragraph, though, I don't think you clearly expressed yourself; the rest of your argument was well thought out," will have much better results.

Schools encourage students to learn about and select potential career paths. ENFJs may pick an unsuitable career path to please someone they idolize. *Solution:* To help students choose careers that are more suitable for them, teachers could try the following: First, have students research several potential careers. When this is done, have the students discuss the tasks and duties of specific jobs with someone who is already in the field. Finally, students could break into small groups and give each other feedback about whether or not they see those tasks fitting the particular student's style.

Interpersonal Behavior Issues

ENFJ students sometimes take disagreement very personally. If someone disagrees with their ideas, they may feel personally rejected and may carry a grudge. The grudge may escalate into a win-lose situation in which others are forced to take sides, which can deeply divide a group. *Solution:* Teachers can help ENFJs by encouraging them to step back a moment and review what the other person actually said. This may help them look at the objective content of the criticism rather than to see it as a personal attack. Often the ENFJ will find that the other person, in fact, only disagreed with one small part of their idea and had a high regard for the ENFJ.

ENFJ students have such a great need for harmony that they may have some relationships that are not based on honesty. For example, one ENFJ student told two of her friends that they were each her *best* friend because she wanted each friend to feel special. Eventually, the friends found out what the ENFJ said to the other and both felt betrayed. *Solution:* ENFJs need to be encouraged to be honest and to refrain from exaggeration. Exaggeration may damage their reputation. A one-on-one or classroom discussion on misleading others about one's true feelings usually solves this problem quickly.

Summary

ENFJ students are motivated by teachers who recognize and value their skill in helping others reach their highest potential. They quickly and accurately attune to other people's needs, so they appreciate teachers who allow them to fulfill those needs. If their extensive communication skills can be put to use in the classroom, they usually inspire others to do their best. Teachers who give praise generously but who are also fair are appreciated by ENFJs.

INFJ Writers

Basic Characteristics

Adjectives that describe the typical INFJ students are compassionate, empathetic, and intense. They can commit to a goal and pursue it with great determination. In their drive to serve the common good, they can be quietly forceful or they can assume invisibility to empower others. They are often complex and deep.

Potential Career Paths

INFJs typically have a capacity for creative approaches to problems and are tuned into other people's preferences. These abilities may lead them into such fields as counseling, teaching, psychology, or library science. Some INFJs feel a calling to missionary or religious work. Others enter the social services in occupations such as a social scientist, health care administrator, or director of a nonprofit agency. In the arts, INFJs are often playwrights, novelists, or poets. They may also be artists or designers. Those attracted to business may be employee assistance program coordinators or organizational development consultants.

Preferred Classes

INFJ students usually enjoy art, English, music, psychology, and creative writing classes. In a five-field comparison of study areas, their preferred sequence of interest was found to be science, liberal arts, engineering, medicine, and business. Books and movies are frequently their favorite extracurricular activities. They prefer classes that allow them time to understand complex concepts and promote human harmony.

Common Behaviors

INFJ students are likely to achieve good grades and to be considered intelligent by their teachers and peers. They generally prefer classes that discuss theory in relation to people rather than classes that focus primarily on isolated impersonal facts. Some INFJs appear to be very logical and precise. These students may be drawn to the sciences, where they are likely to be as successful as their NT counterparts. Other INFJs focus more on quietly helping other people and gravitate toward service or counseling and teaching fields.

Classrooms in which teachers make efforts to recognize each student's contributions and special qualities will stimulate INFJs. Teachers who recognize the curiosity and creative bent of INFJs are likely to see ample illustrations of their talents. INFJs can see life from multiple perspectives and are likely to have wide-ranging interests. Their desire for affiliation is demonstrated by their tendency to like group work and discussions. INFJs seldom demonstrate behavior problems. They are usually quiet, well behaved, and attentive.

INFJ students enjoy reading. They enjoy reading material that is rich in imagery, fantasy, and metaphors. They are often very good at interpreting the meaning of a literary work, what an author truly meant, including all of its complex layers.

Because of their highly developed imagination, INFJs can become terrified by horror stories. They can imagine exactly what each character felt and may empathize to an excessive degree. When driver's education courses use movies or photos that show many scenes of accidents with bodily injuries, it is not uncommon for INFJs to report recurring nightmares. One INFJ student said she was in no hurry to get her driver's license since she could still see the horrific pictures in her mind months later.

INFJs want affiliation with other people, but their introversion often keeps them from reaching out. People are likely to comment that INFJs seem warm but distant. INFJs do let their guard down, but only when they choose to do so and on their own terms. They usually have a few close friends. As they grow older, they often find more people attracted to them because of their ability to empathize with others.

Many INFJs are natural counselors. Their Introversion helps them to be good listeners, and their Judging preference enables them to give people suggestions about how to solve their problems. INFJs tend to be insightful. They work hard to create rapport between themselves and others. People seeking their counsel generally find that they listen carefully and use the information they are given to establish a common ground. These characteristics often cause people to naturally gravitate to INFJs for advice.

Most INFJs are highly intuitive. Whereas the intuition of INTJs tends to focus on ideas, the intuition of INFJs tends to focus on people. Their intuition helps them to see complex patterns that underlie human relationships; however, because they aren't always consciously aware of how their insights develop, they may have difficulty verbalizing what they see.

INFJs can be very intense and have a vision that they spend much of their time trying to fulfill. This vision usually connects strongly with their personal values. Once INFJs have their vision firmly in mind, it can be nearly impossible for them to let go of or change a part of it in spite of any new information they receive. They work hard to bring other people into line with their vision and will passionately, although usually quietly, defend the values that underlie it.

Like ENFJs, INFJs have persuasive abilities. While ENFJs are more likely to want to persuade others to do what they deem is right, INFJs usually want people to listen to their warnings about potential problems and their vision for improvement. Both ENFJs and INFJs are comfortable giving directives, but both prefer to encourage cooperation rather than lay down the law.

INFJs tend to be very consistent and to value integrity, but they often have convoluted, complex personalities that can sometimes puzzle even them (Keirsey and Bates, 1984). Much of their puzzlement arises from the fact that they pursue authenticity internally rather than externally. Yet they believe they are showing their real and complete selves to the external world. One INFJ student who thought she was an open book to others was quite surprised when a classmate told her that he enjoyed being her friend because she was so deep and complicated.

Discipline Issues

Like ISFJs, INFJ students are generally quietly compliant but can occasionally be stubborn if their values are violated. *Solution:* Rejecting what an INFJ says may be construed as a rejection of their values and, ultimately, of them. When possible, teachers can try to determine what value has been violated and see if they can work around it. When attempting to change a value, telling one or two anecdotes that demonstrate instances when the value is ineffective may help. They generally need time to assimilate this kind of information. Logic is usually unproductive in such instances. It may be best to allow the INFJ to not participate in an activity that is particularly objectionable and do an alternate assignment in its place.

INFJs usually dislike disorder. Disorder may take on an emotional form, such as a game with unclear rules or rules that are not being followed, or a group discussion that has degenerated into name calling. Or the disorder may take on a physical form, such as school papers becoming mixed up and disorganized. Physical disorder is often difficult for

INFJs because Sensing is their least preferred skill and requires a great deal of of energy. If the disorder becomes too overwhelming, the INFJ may lash out at others. *Solution:* Telling INFJs to calm down will make them feel even worse by adding outer conflict to their inner conflict. Teachers should try to fix what they can—clarify rules, bring an end to the name calling, and so on. They can also give INFJs time-outs from class to correct an upsetting situation like having mixed up school papers.

Academic Orientation Issues

INFJ students may be extremely quiet and fail to participate in discussions and debates. If a class grade depends partially on their participation, they will often do poorly. *Solution:* INFJs do have opinions, but they are more apt to share them if they are asked for them. Teachers can give them time to think through their ideas and/or write them down, and then ask them to share them with the class. They need extra time to be sure that they do not say something that is untrue or unclear. INFJs want to express their viewpoint clearly *and* avoid offending anyone unnecessarily.

INFJs generally perform well as students. If they do not, it is generally because they are experiencing some kind of conflict at home or with their friends. They desperately want harmony and to have meaningful relationships. *Solution:* There is no easy solution. If you decide to make up some of the gap by developing a relationship with the student, here are a few guidelines: 1) Be prepared to devote considerable time since some INFJs are very intense, 2) do not directly attack their value system or you will lose their trust, and 3) use criticism very sparingly.

Interpersonal Behavior Issues

INFJs tend to be so insightful that they may interrupt another person because they assume they know what that person is about to say. *Solution:* Teachers can remind them gently that it is impolite to interrupt and that others need to be able to complete their own thoughts. For example, a teacher could suggest that the INFJ make a mental guess at what another person is going to say. The student should be told to listen carefully to find any discrepancies between their guess and what the person actually said. Making a game out of the tendency may help the student to stop pushing for a conclusion.

Some INFJ students are frustrated because they want friends but cannot figure out how to go about making them. INFJs often seem hard to get to know and extremely complex to understand. *Solution:* INFJs need to try to express more of their thoughts. They often approve of others but fail to express their feelings. They usually prefer to have one or two close, intense relationships. However, they are likely to want more than any one or two people can give them. They need to be reminded not to demand too much from a relationship and encouraged to focus on the things they enjoy about their friends rather than the faults they find in them.

Summary

INFJs are motivated by teachers who value the unique gifts of each student. They benefit from teachers who draw them out and encourage them to use their empathy and long-term visions to help others. They particularly appreciate teachers who encourage their creative abilities. Those teachers who demonstrate integrity and some flexibility while avoiding excessive disorder will gain their admiration.

NFP Advocates

NFP Advocates are less likely than NFJs to tell other people what to do. They prefer a sense of personal freedom and are sensitive about intruding on other people's sense of freedom. However, NFPs do want to influence how other people think about social concerns. Information about social issues fascinates them and they enjoy sharing this information. Whereas INFPs can become the solo crusaders when significant social values are threatened, ENFPs act more like cheerleaders who influence group behavior.

ENFP Boosters

Basic Characteristics

Adjectives that describe the typical ENFP student are charming, communicative, and enthusiastic. ENFPs are very people oriented, and their restless, curious nature leads them to be highly informed about many topics. They use their imaginative perception to identify concerns that may go unnoticed by others.

Potential Career Paths

ENFPs typically have an innovative approach to life that enables them to succeed in many occupations. They are often creative and can be found in occupations such as cartoonist, artist, investigative reporter, composer, or columnist. If they are in business, they are often most successful in areas that allow them to be entrepreneurial, such as consultant, inventor, sales representative, or restauranteur. Their long-range thinking is an asset in marketing and planning, where they may be marketing consultants, copywriters, advertising account executives, strategic planners, or publicists. ENFPs naturally have an impact on others and may be found in social service or educational fields in positions such as social scientist, rehabilitation worker, ombudsperson, or art teacher.

Preferred Classes

ENFP students usually enjoy art, English, music, drama, languages, and sociology classes. In a five-field comparison of study areas, their preferred sequence of interest was found to be liberal arts, medicine, science, business, and engineering. Their extracurricular activities center around their social groups. They prefer classes that allow them to work with many people on many projects and to solve problems creatively.

Common Behaviors

ENFP students tend to be enthusiastic and gregarious learners. Many of them enjoy school because they like their peers and teachers. ENFPs enjoy cooperative learning and participating in group discussions. Their avid curiosity leads them to be interested in a variety of activities and knowledge. They especially prize warm, nurturing, and fairly active classrooms with teachers who are affirming and generous with praise.

ENFPs almost always have several things going on at once. They tend to be happiest when they are surrounded by friends and loved ones and have plenty of activities to engage in. ENFPs have the unique gift of taking an ordinary situation and making it a meaningful time of sharing or remembrance. They can skillfully weave together the people and materials that are immediately available to draw out significance.

ENFPs resemble ESFPs in many ways. They are optimistic, outgoing, and usually popular. It can also be as difficult for them to sit still as it is for the ESFPs. The more that is going on, the happier they are. They are bundles of energy, sometimes without direction. With their high energy level, enthusiasm, and trust in the goodness of others, they often seem younger than they are. Some people see them as naive or credulous, but their optimistic attitude tends to attract others and bring positive opportunities to them.

ENFPs are often good actors and enjoy make-believe. It is fairly easy for them to put themselves in the place of the character they are playing and become the part. Most ENFPs enjoy dramas and like performing in them.

Both ENFPs and ESFPs enjoy performing. While ESFPs want the freedom to perform and praise for their flair and grace, ENFPs want praise for who they are. ENFPs are constantly, sometimes frantically, trying to elicit praise from others around them. The less positive the feedback they get, the harder they will try to get praise. They are likely to praise others lavishly to the point that they begin to appear insincere. Lavish praise is actually what they would like to receive. They sometimes work themselves to exhaustion in their search for praise from significant others. ENFPs, like other NFs, strive for authenticity, but their desire to please others can cause them to take on roles that do not reflect who they truly are.

Other people are drawn to ENFPs because of their high visibility and sympathy. Often, so many people crave the unconditional acceptance and empathy that they naturally give that they can become emotionally drained. Despite this, ENFPs enjoy having lots of friends and seldom stay drained for long.

ENFPs tend to be romantic. Giving extravagant gifts or tokens of their affection is normal for them. They believe in the best of everyone. However, reality sometimes disappoints them. In relationships, they hope for a complete unity of values. Each time they discover that this is impossible to achieve, they are disappointed. While some ENFPs can identify falseness in people quickly, others are credulous and insist on believing in the best of others in spite of mounting evidence to the contrary. ENFP students are likely to complain loudly when someone is unkind to them. It is hard for them to understand how others can be hurtful when they have worked so hard at being nice to everyone else.

ENFPs can be excellent diplomats. They tend to have an exceptional awareness of what other people are thinking and can often draw out common viewpoints and help others reach a consensus. Their compassion and insightful nature often brings others to tell them private confidences. They are also excellent conduits of information and are usually up on the latest news. They will gather a great deal of information on subjects that match their values. When opportunities arise, they may dramatically present this information to others in the hope that it will persuade them to adopt their values. ENFPs do not try to force people to do things; they persuade them through an abundance of information. It is no wonder that this type is sometimes seen as the "herald" or "messenger."

ENFPs are excellent at helping people affiliate toward a common objective. They use their natural enthusiasm to energize others. One ENFP student was an excellent team cheerleader. Her classmates always chose her to be on their team. While she was not necessarily the hardest working member, she had skills that made her invaluable: She was the heart of the team, the team spirit. She gave team members constant encouragement to believe in their ability to succeed. Whenever there was disagreement, she helped clarify miscommunications by gathering information and translating it so everyone would understand. In short, she acted as a catalyst, bringing out the best in everyone else.

Discipline Issues

Like SPs, ENFP students may have difficulty sitting still and may be talkative. *Solution:* ENFPs usually enjoy acting. Teachers can include them when they allow SPs to have showtime. Teachers can give ENFPs expressive reading opportunities to do or act in plays or dramas. When they are given opportunities to be the center of attention, they will be more likely to cooperate at times when they are not. ENFPs are usually excellent group members. Group work meets two of their needs simultaneously: It allows them to talk and to help others. To avoid discipline issues with ENFPs, the most important thing is build relationships with them through public praise, written notes, or friendly facial expressions.

ENFPs can sometimes shift from person to person to offer help. This behavior may annoy other students who do not want their help. *Solution:* Teachers should praise ENFPs for being helpful but explain to them that other students need to boost their self-concept by successfully solving some hard problems on their own. Teachers can also encourage ENFPs to do peer tutoring when it is needed. Having them explain material to others can also help ensure that they truly understand it.

Academic Orientation Issues

ENFP students may spend so much of their time helping others that they can fail to complete their own work. *Solution:* Sometimes ENFPs can fail to complete their own work because they do not like to work alone or because they are trying to get positive feedback. Teachers can let them work with a buddy if it is feasible and also praise them often so they can focus their attention on doing their work.

ENFPs may say that they understand something when they only really understand the general outline or concept. *Solution:* One technique teachers can use is to have the student draw a picture or write and perform a play that contains all of the important information they are to learn. This will help them explore the relationships between ideas. When they have explained the illustration or acted out the play, teachers should praise their artistic ability and help the students identify areas in which they may have missed an important idea. Assigning ENFPs to teach the material to another student is another good technique, as they will work hard to justify the teacher's trust in them.

Interpersonal Behavior Issues

ENFP students may become overly involved in helping their friends and can become hurt when the friends tell them to essentially back off. *Solution:* Teachers can explain that others may sometimes misinterpret their good intentions as a desire to be controlling. They can encourage ENFPs to offer help in ways that allow others to accept or refuse the offer.

ENFPs may alienate some of their friends by playing favorites. They may have one best friend one day and another best friend the next, and one or both of the friends may not understand this behavior. *Solution:* Teachers should remind ENFPs that they can hurt other people's feelings by suddenly dropping their friendship without an explanation. They can encourage these students to communicate openly with their friends about any problems in their relationships.

Summary

ENFP students are motivated by teachers who praise them often. They benefit from teachers who recognize and make use of their ability to help others and energize groups. ENFPs enjoy classrooms that include group work and/or time for students to work together. They are sure to appreciate teachers who avoid criticism and value their enthusiastic friendliness.

INFP Dreamers

Basic Characteristics

Adjectives that describe the typical student INFP are devoted, deeply caring, and virtuous. They tend to be the most idealistic of all the types and are often the most individually unique. They may become absorbed in creating wholeness and virtue. INFPs can be reticent until their values are challenged, at which times they stand firm for their beliefs. They also often function as peacekeepers in their drive for unity.

Potential Career Paths

INFPs often are advocates for causes and may be found in religious occupations such as missionary, minister, rabbi, or religious educator. Their cause may be changing business cultures as organizational development specialists, human resources development specialists, or social scientists. In the educational field, they may be college professors, researchers, or speech pathologists. INFPs enjoy expressing themselves in very personal ways in fields that allow them room for freedom and inspiration. They may be attracted to the arts in such positions as writer, journalist, editor, architect, or musician.

Preferred Classes

INFP students usually like art, English, music, sociology, psychology, and drama classes. In a five-field comparison of study areas, their preferred sequence of interest was found to be medicine, science, liberal arts, engineering, and business. They often enjoy movies and individually challenging physical activities such as hiking for extracurricular activities. They prefer classes that allow them to work alone, with occasional interaction with others in a supportive environment.

Common Behaviors

Since INFPs are driven by their own inner values, they tend to be the most individual of all the styles. INFPs are generally quiet, dreamy, and sometimes almost invisible in the classroom. They may appear to take on the features of their surroundings. INFPs can be convincing as NTs, SPs, and, occasionally, even SJs. The key to identifying INFPs is to make note of how they react to messages that identify them as unique. INFPs value uniqueness more than any other type. They appreciate teachers who make great efforts to find their special qualities.

INFPs like classrooms that are nurturing and include some make-believe and fantasy in the lessons. They dislike classrooms that are too regimented in nature, favoring individualized discipline and assistance. They have a deeply personal approach to life and thrive in classrooms that allow them to define their own ethics rather than those that impose external values on them. At the core, they want to be true to themselves.

INFPs enjoy make-believe and fantasy. Mary McCaulley, a colleague of Isabel Briggs Myers, was asked to recount her experiences as an INFP. She recalled once asking her mother why her father, a naturalist, never taught her any facts about nature while they were on family picnics. "She said he tried to, but I was too busy looking for dryads and fairy rings to listen" (Scanlan, 1994). Books help provide INFPs with entry into this special fantasy world, and INFPs often read voraciously.

INFPs are often romantics. They are likely to romanticize any significant others and may feel disillusioned when these individuals fail to live up to their ideals. INFPs strive for authenticity and self-actualization. This search for their unique identity can be a lifelong pursuit.

INFPs typically have a holistic approach to life. In their worldview, everything connects to everything else. They want to encourage the natural harmony of life.

INFP students may alternate between a drive toward perfectionism and a need to be free of externally driven standards. This behavior is often seen in English classes where they may be torn between their desire to meet a teacher's expectations and their need to express personal views that they do not want to submit to outside evaluation. For example, one INFP student, whose essays consistently received high grades, refused to submit any of his poetry because he did not want his self-expression graded. INFPs may begin a course with perfection as the standard. After only a few weeks into the term, when they begin to fail to meet their unrealistic expectations, they may feel like overall failures. At this point, they may swing to the opposite extreme of viewing the class standards as irrelevant and focus exclusively on the expression of their own values. This pattern can cause INFPs to develop avoidance behaviors, which, in extreme cases, can result in school phobia.

INFPs tend to be highly idealistic. They often have heroes who seek higher moral ideals. While they are generally compliant and adaptable, they will not violate their morals and will stand firm if their values are threatened.

INFP students are generally easygoing and quiet. It is not unusual for others to take them for granted. Like most NFs, they work hard to please others and be accepted. As children, they will often sacrifice their own needs in their quest to win approval from significant adults. If their self-sacrifice is not appreciated or is criticized, INFP children may overpersonalize remarks or become sullen and self-critical. Young INFPs who feel unaccepted often spend a good amount of time quietly brooding. Like other NFs, sarcasm can often be crushing for them.

INFP students seldom state what they want directly unless their personal values are violated. They prefer to have their personal freedom and do not like to tell others what to do. They often drop hints instead. If the other person does not pick up on the hints, they are likely to step up their approach by using short, mildly caustic comments. If this approach does not work, they are likely to retreat. One does not win the deep friendship of an INFP too easily. Once won, however, the affiliation is usually long and intense.

The most important thing to remember about INFPs is that the crucial aspects of their personality are all internal. Their abilities and deep feelings are kept locked up inside. Only a few close friends are given the opportunity to get to know them well.

Discipline Issues

INFP students appear to spend much of their time daydreaming. *Solution:* In general, unless it is seriously affecting their performance, teachers can ignore this behavior, as dreaming is an integral part of their intellectual and emotional growth. When they seem to be dreaming, they are often following their own thoughts to wherever they lead them. INFPs are, consequently, very divergent thinkers and often come up with ideas or ways of looking at things that are unique. Daydreaming is at the core of the INFP's phenomenal creative abilities.

INFPs may join a group that encourages unproductive behavior if they do not receive appreciation for their unique abilities. *Solution:* Teachers can spend some one-on-one time with INFP students. Writing notes or talking with them individually and praising them for who they are can be effective. Effective praise might be along the lines of "You're an insightful person. I enjoyed your story." INFPs who feel appreciated for their unique qualities will be less likely to join groups that encourage undesirable behavior. Making judgments about the group or its members may be counterproductive.

Academic Orientation Issues

INFP students are often slow to reveal themselves by participating in class. Younger INFPs, in particular, may be reluctant to speak out in front of an audience. *Solution:* When possible, teachers should let INFPs set their own pace. Forcing them to talk before they are ready or asking them to rush through a presentation can reinforce their reluctance. Teachers who give them adequate time coupled with personalized positive attention usually can help them overcome their hesitancy.

INFPs are sometimes difficult to help with career planning because they are likely to excel in many academic areas. *Solution:* One way to help INFPs plan their careers is to identify what they value rather than just look at their grades. INFPs need a career that allows them to act on their values. Encouraging them to express and define their values will often help them focus on a career path.

Interpersonal Behavior Issues

INFPs have high expectations of others and can easily become crushed if others do not meet their expectations. *Solution:* Class discussions about how to build caring relationships and communicate disappointment and anger to others will often help them. Sample questions might include,

"How do you feel when others talk about you behind your back?"; "Are some people more perceptive of others' feelings?"; and "What can you do to keep relationships happy?"

INFP students can sometimes become irritable and snap at others. A common cause for this behavior is a lack of personal time or space. *Solution:* Teachers at the elementary level usually have some way of giving students private time and space when they are becoming overtired and irritable. In such cases, giving the INFPs time out from the conflict will often eliminate further confrontation. By the time students reach the upper grades, this behavior does not usually occur in the classroom.

Summary

INFP students are motivated by teachers who recognize their uniqueness and encourage them to develop their individuality. They appreciate teachers who allow them to develop at their own pace but also expect good things from them. They may swing between perfectionistic standards and freedom from standards. Teachers who help INFPs find an effective balance between these two will help them in their quest to achieve personal wholeness.

Chapter 11

Intuitive–Thinking Rational Students

Intuitive–Thinkers (NTs) live in the world of ideas and are constantly seeking knowledge. They want to control themselves and the world around them by learning everything they can about the things that interest them. Their ultimate goal is to understand why the world works the way it does so they can change and control it. Teachers who understand that these students are seeking the overview, the big picture of how the world operates can tap into their visionary abilities. Teachers who focus on the depth of knowledge and ingenious solutions to problems that NT Rational students bring forth will be a great asset to them.

NTs make up only 12 percent of the general population (Keirsey and Bates, 1984). Since there are usually only one or two NTs in a typical American classroom, not all teachers recognize the temperament and/or know how to effectively work with these students. Their unusualness may contribute to their being identified as highly intelligent or as lacking in basic abilities.

Although NTs make up a small portion of the total population, they comprise almost half of National Merit Finalists. NTs often excel in science and math, although they can master nearly any subject. They can become scientists, inventors, and philosophers. They are natural systems thinkers who enjoy unraveling complex information and interrelationships. This love of complexity can affect their relationship with others and can sometimes cause difficulties in communication. They often want others to be able to follow their reasoning and can have difficulty simplifying it for others. Not all types enjoy dealing with the many levels of complexity that fascinate NTs and may become impatient with the detailed explanations of NT students. Teachers can help NT students learn to customize their explanations to their audience.

In school settings, NT students like Socratic questioning, independent study, and complex projects. They enjoy exercises that encourage creative problem solving, such as puzzles, brain teasers, and strategy board games. They also enjoy doing science projects for the intellectual challenge they present. For example, one sixth-grade NT student won a science fair award for his project on the accuracy of weather forecasters. He thoroughly enjoyed learning about probability. The information he discovered fascinated him, and he was more interested in the knowledge he gained than in receiving the award.

Teachers find that NTs generally enjoy logically presented lectures about abstract and intellectual subjects. They want stimulation in the world of ideas. The topic of future trends can trigger an exhilarating debate for these students. When they become attracted to a particular subject, they may spend hours reading about it and researching it. Their reading tends to be in areas that they find self-challenging. They often read to satisfy their curiosity. On the other hand, they especially dislike busywork because spending time on topics they do not find interesting may not make sense to them.

Competency is a major issue for NT students—both their own and that of others. NTs will work very hard for teachers whom they perceive as competent. Their primary focus of competency is on intellectual capability. In order to achieve competence in a subject, they seek rules and principles from which they develop a structure for their cognitive world. When NT students become fascinated with an area, they believe they *should* be able to know everything about that subject. Once they are satisfied with their level of understanding, they may move on to a new topic.

The NT's drive for competency is attached to their inner standards for improvement. NT students will often pressure themselves to meet ever-escalating standards; the high point of last week becomes the expected level for this week. Because NTs frequently succeed at reaching these escalating standards, some teachers may develop similar expectations of their NT students. When the standards reach an unrealistic level and the performance cannot be sustained, NT students, and possibly their teachers, are likely to feel a sense of failure. This kind of situation is generally resolved when NTs learn effective ways of prioritizing their efforts. Teachers can help their NT students come to terms with the realization that they cannot be competent in all areas by helping them with developing priorities and realistic expectations.

As NT students mature and define their areas of competence more narrowly, they may spend most of their time focused on those areas and ignore or reject other areas of learning. The benefit of this approach is that they become very knowledgeable in a few select areas. However, they can also give up and perform below standard in certain subjects if they decide that those subjects are unnecessary or not worth their time. Since NT students are so self-defined and self-driven, teacher feedback may have limited impact on them. Teachers can have a positive influence if they convince NTs that a subject gives them an opportunity to express the coherence and effectiveness of their ideas. However, such efforts may be undone if teachers focus on the below standard performance and convince their NT students that they are seen as incompetent. Any message of incompetence feeds the self-doubting behavior of NTs and may further encourage avoidance behavior.

As very young children, NTs may become frustrated until they develop enough vocabulary and signals to express their desires to others. Extraverted NTs may develop an idiosyncratic vocabulary in their rush to communicate with others. Introverted NTs may not use words until they see themselves as very competent in their ability to communicate. Vocabulary development is often important for NTs, as they typically strive for exactitude in their thoughts and communications. Long sentences that express their ideas and views with many conditional or qualified statements are common among NTs. They do this to try to fully describe all of the truths and exceptions of a subject succinctly. Providing them with enough time to express their ideas is very effective in helping their development.

From an early age, most NTs get along better with adults than with their peers. They often have a well-developed vocabulary that they use very precisely. NTs enjoy talking to adults who take their ideas seriously. They often ask thoughtful questions and can have a dry sense of humor.

NTs can be the most difficult type to successfully praise. They commonly view praise with suspicion and can only accept praise from those they view as competent in a given area. To counter these skeptical tendencies, teachers should be very specific in their praise. NTs like receiving praise for their ideas or their reasoning ability. They tend to view praise for a well-done routine task as insincere. NTs also like praise for their creativity, perseverance, or for having done an exceptional (not just above average) job.

NTs approach learning from a skeptical and pragmatic viewpoint. Rarely do they accept information at face value, and they will question something until it has proven its worth before adding it to their storehouse of knowledge. This approach often influences their drive to learn and may cause different reactions in those who are trying to teach them.

NT students are good at logical thinking, solving puzzles, and understanding theories. They are often intelligent and witty, with a boundless curiosity about how things work. NTs enjoy learning for the sake of learning and want to understand and control their world. They typically believe that the mind can accomplish anything. As a result, when they want to master some piece of knowledge, NTs usually become extremely focused. Young NTs sometimes seem mature beyond their years because of their thoughtful, insightful views. NTs like work that requires analysis of an overall picture or a unifying theme. They tend to use language precisely and accurately. With a strong sense of their own individuality and confidence in their ability to control their world, their behavior can often cause others to see them as arrogant. NT students are often enjoyable because they tend to be insightful, quick learners and critical thinkers.

There are two major categories of NT Rational students: NTJ Organizers and NTP Inventors, which are illustrated in table 16.

Table 16 NT Rational Students	
NTJ Organizers	NTP Inventors
ENTJ Commanders	ENTP Improvisors
INTJ Scientists	INTP Theorists

NTJ Organizers

NTJ Organizers, along with STJs, are often blunt and to the point. They can easily give classmates directives on what to do, making them natural group leaders. This is especially true for ENTJs, who have a penchant for achieving objectives and propelling a group in a particular direction. Unlike NTPs, who like to generate new ideas, NTJs have an inner drive to create solutions to systems problems. They envision outcomes, the actions required to bring them about, and gather the resources to put the plan into action. NTJ Organizers are very conscious of time constraints. Natural strategists who hate to duplicate effort, they seek out the most efficient ways of doing things.

ENTJ Commanders

Basic Characteristics

Adjectives that describe the typical ENTJ student are dynamic, controlled, challenging, frank, and decisive. ENTJs are natural leaders who think strategically and futuristically. With their determination to turn their ideas into reality, they often convince others to assist them in accomplishing their objectives. They move toward their goals in a straightforward manner, guided by an underpinning of logical principles.

Potential Career Paths

ENTJs often exhibit leadership qualities and are drawn to situations that give them opportunities to lead and to create their own visions. They are often found in management positions in business, particularly in upper management. Positions in the world of finance that allow them to forecast trends and develop effective financial plans often attract them. In the consulting arena, they express their vision to others and influence business strategies. Professions with higher status or leadership potential, such as judge, psychologist, or scientist, also attract them.

Preferred Classes

ENTJ students usually like math, science, public speaking, English, political science, and logic classes. In a five-field comparison of study areas, their preferred sequence of interest was found to be engineering, science, liberal arts, medicine, and business. They may enjoy athletic events as extracurricular activities. Classes that engage their analytical and goal-oriented strategical skills strongly appeal to them.

Common Behaviors

ENTJ students are generally cheerful, confident, optimistic, and natural leaders. Often popular, they are likely to run successfully for class office or club positions. These visionary leaders are likely to lead the group into some new area or endeavor. Business as usual is not their strength. A challenge or project that needs developmental work will bring out their best leadership skills.

ENTJs have forceful but optimistic personalities. They often have very decided opinions, will often share their views quite readily, and do not typically back down easily. They are also likely to dominate class discussions. Once ENTJs have focused on a particular goal, they will often discard any ideas that do not bring them closer to their set objective. This focused, logical behavior often makes them very dynamic and persuasive.

ENTJs often become leaders, even when it is not their intention. Alan Brownsword (1987) tells of one ENTJ who went to watch the building of a homecoming float. He ended up taking charge, and the float won first prize. Later, he became convinced that the teachers in his country were underpaid. His county had a high per capita income but ranked 127th in the nation in teacher salaries. He quickly organized a group that he called Students for Teachers and arranged for both students and parents to make a presentation to the school board. When ENTJs perceive a problem, they often immediately organize the people and resources necessary to solve the problem.

ENTJs want to control their outer world, as opposed to INTJs, who want to control their inner world. Like INTJs and, to a lesser extent, the other NTs, ENTJs will not allow anyone else to control them. This is not to suggest that they are disobedient or uncooperative; it simply means that they need to believe that they are making a choice to obey others. One ENTJ first grader had misbehaved at home. As a result, his parents told him that he could not play on his computer or watch television. At first, he was very upset. He finally regained control by making a sign for the computer that read "No Playing" and a sign for the TV that read "No Watching." By creating these signs, he put himself in control of obeying the limits his parents set.

The energy of ENTJs is usually harnessed to goals and objectives. Just knowing the next step to be taken is generally not enough information for ENTJs. They prefer the teacher to talk about the major objective and milestones that must be met to reach the objective. Since they are strategic thinkers, they like to have some room to test their own strategies. They may offer teachers alternative methods or milestones that can be used to meet the same goal. ENTJs need opportunities to test their own strategies, and it is useful if teachers allow them some opportunity to do so. When their ideas are not appropriate, it is sometimes useful for teachers to explain the reasons that they need to follow the teacher's method. However, teachers need to be careful about getting into a debating situation with ENTJs.

ENTJs usually work on one project at a time until they reach a clearly defined goal. They can often work on multiple aspects of a given project simultaneously. Adult ENTJs are usually able to manage very complex projects. ENTJs can develop the ability to break projects into smaller steps and tasks so that they can work on multiple aspects of a project at once. The desire of ENTJs to achieve objectives can cause them to become highly gifted in several areas.

ENTJs seldom take criticism personally and do not expect others to take their criticism personally. They are very straightforward in their communications when they think someone else should change the way they are doing something. ENTJs prefer that others express themselves in the same clear-cut manner. Anything that will hinder them from achieving a particular goal is worth questioning and critiquing.

Discipline Issues

ENTJ students are often commanding and focused and may try to direct classroom activities. *Solution:* Since ENTJs have a need to lead, teachers should try to find areas where they can lead. For example, a teacher could ask them to help organize a school activity, such as a field trip. They can utilize their excellent planning skills to help reach a decision about where to go on the trip. The fewer parameters they are given, the better they will like it, since they dislike being micromanaged.

An escalating power struggle is a danger with ENTJ students. When they have focused their attention on something they want, they will often not accept no for an answer. For example, a student who wants to work on a computer might argue with *each reason* a teacher gives for why the computer is off limits. *Solution:* Teachers need to let the ENTJ know that they are not willing to argue their position, but if appropriate, they may explain their position. If the teacher's position is not negotiable, he or she must make clear that the decision is final. If the ENTJ continues to press the issue, he or she may need to be isolated from classroom attention.

Academic Orientation Issues

Although ENTJs usually perform well as students, having their leadership abilities and their ideas rejected may cause them to reject school. *Solution:* ENTJs can be encouraged to take on positive leadership roles, such as running for class officer or starting a new club.

ENTJs may have problems working in groups. They generally have strong personalities and may alienate themselves from their peers, especially if they take on an attitude of superiority. Some students may resent their desire to take charge. *Solution:* ENTJs can benefit from discussions, readings, and examples on leadership. Teachers may hold class discussions on the qualities that make good leaders and on effective leadership within teams. Today schools are giving more time to team projects, as teaming skills are becoming more essential in the world of work.

Interpersonal Behavior Issues

Some ENTJ students have developed social skills while others have not. When their social skills are undeveloped, ENTJs may become so focused on achieving their goals and presenting their ideas that others may see them as overpowering and intimidating. *Solution:* ENTJs need training in listening to and affirming others' ideas and in expressing their opinions more tactfully. Role-playing can be beneficial as can feedback from others. Having them analyze things they have said and how others might misinterpret them is also a good technique to use with ENTJs. Sometimes, ENTJs say that they cannot understand how anyone could take the things they have said personally. They need to understand that other people often *will* take their statements personally, and that if they do not modify what they are going to say to account for the responses of others, they will not get what they want from others.

ENTJs typically believe that anyone can do anything they set their mind to. They tend to demand that others conform to their own high expectations. *Solution:* It is helpful to remind ENTJs that while everyone has valuable skills, no one can do everything equally well. Teachers can encourage them to analyze each person's skills and weaknesses, then formulate a plan to maximize group effectiveness.

Summary

Teachers who show that they value the leadership skills of ENTJ students can powerfully motivate them. ENTJs appreciate teachers who challenge them by giving them complex problems to solve and allowing them free reign in solving them. They like teachers who provide overall goals along with interim goals and limit the number of rules that they must follow.

INTJ Scientists

Basic Characteristics

Adjectives that describe the typical INTJ students are autonomous, high achieving, and intricate thinking. They are often visionaries who use their single-minded concentration to develop complex systems. The pursuit of truth and excellence is such a strong drive for INTJs that it can cause them to act demanding, critical, firm, and tenacious.

Potential Career Paths

INTJs use their vision to create new systems. They excel at long-term planning and intellectual challenges. Technical fields that involve complex problems make use of their ability to analyze and develop new systems. These abilities can also lead them to the field of medicine. Like ENTJs, INTJs gravitate toward the professions, especially those that allow them to act independently. Many INTJs seek positions in higher education, where they often become known as experts. Their visionary abilities may also lead them to enter creative fields where they have the opportunity to do original work.

Preferred Classes

INTJ students generally like math, science, computer, engineering, and theory classes. In a five-field comparison of study areas, their preferred sequence of interest was found to be science, engineering, liberal arts, medicine, and business. They may enjoy lectures, drama, or music as extracurricular activities. Generally, classes that help them to understand complex systems will fascinate them.

Common Behaviors

The most individualistic and independent of all types, INTJ students are generally intellectual, persistent, logical, and self-confident—sometimes to the point of arrogance. Like ENTJs, INTJ students are drawn to ideas and theories that they can apply; however, they generally spend some time gaining a well-developed understanding of an idea before they act upon it. Often self-critical and self-driven, they work hard at maintaining a minimum level of personal competence that meets their constantly escalating standards.

INTJ students like to see their ideas worked out, accepted and applied. When their inner drive is harnessed to a goal, they become focused and seldom are swayed by outside input. They often take on ambitious projects they see as having a pragmatic application to develop their competence at strategically reaching their goals. And they can demonstrate a surprising level of persistence. For a unit on safety, one INTJ sixth grader chose to write and direct a movie illustrating safety tips. Although normally reticent, his enthusiasm for the project helped him enlist the help of all his classmates. As the project evolved, the teacher thought it was becoming too complex for one student to manage, but the INTJ insisted upon staying in control. The final product, a one-hour film, was quite a hit.

INTJs are often drawn to math, science, and computers because of the complexity of these fields. They can retain and manipulate in their minds vast amounts of abstract material. INTJ students develop their ability to generalize, classify, summarize, and present evidence. They are constantly comparing new data they receive to what is already in their minds and are usually able to quickly identify logical inconsistencies.

INTJs students are often original thinkers. They strive to develop their own internal vision. For them, reality can be malleable. What is most important to them is the power of ideas. When they take a global or big picture approach to a subject, they often make intuitive leaps about what is possible. When they approach a problem at a detailed level, they try to connect their ideas in a linear way and often appear to be using computerlike logic.

The need for personal space is associated with their ability to concentrate on complex systems. Concentration usually requires some protection from interruptions. Teachers who can help INTJs find some personal space will enable them to work more effectively. The single-minded concentration possessed by INTJ students may be a mixed blessing. On the one hand, they can maintain a focus on a topic that allows them to attain a greater depth of knowledge than most students. On the other hand, they may miss out on activities that are happening in the classroom because they are minimizing their external focus.

INTJs can sometimes be very intense. When they develop an interest, they can become deeply interested in it. They can be passionate about their ideas and can see strong criticism of their ideas as a direct attack on themselves.

In conversations, INTJs are likely to want to expand upon or define more precisely topics that interest them, even if the topic of conversation has shifted. They will often drop out of conversation to clarify their own thinking and may become oblivious to changes in topic. Some INTJ students ignore the views and feelings of those who don't agree with them; others may learn to skillfully reframe, then weave other students' points into their own persuasive arguments.

Discipline Issues

INTJ students can sometimes become so focused that they have difficulty changing activities. They may at times refuse to stop what they are doing. *Solution:* Giving INTJs a warning signal that time is nearly up will help them avoid becoming locked in to a particular activity. Teachers can give younger children five-minute, two-minute, and one-minute warnings before announcing that an activity is over. Older students may want to use a timer to help signal when they must quit working on a particular activity.

If an INTJ experiences a loss of competence in an academic or personal area, they may begin to obsess about the problem. The problem can become globalized, affecting all areas of their lives. When this occurs, they may become extremely uncooperative because they sense that they have nothing to lose. *Solution:* Teachers can make use of INTJ students' tendency to globalize by focusing on areas in which they are competent and helping them to globalize the competence to other areas. Encouraging them to set reasonable goals in areas in which they feel incompetent can also help. Since they have a habit of escalating their standards, they may need help determining what standards are reasonable.

Academic Orientation Issues

INTJ students are often labeled as either superior or poor-performing students. Negative labels will likely cause them to do poorly in school if they begin to believe the labels. *Solution:* Since INTJs need adequate time to develop their strengths, teachers should avoid letting the escalating standards set by the INTJ students outpace their level of development. Through giving positive feedback and providing opportunities for INTJs to engage in areas where they see themselves as competent, teachers can help them build self-confidence. Building their confidence in one area is likely to translate into success in other areas.

INTJs may do very well in their favorite subjects while doing poorly in others. *Solution:* Teachers can discuss with INTJs the connection between least favorite and favorite subjects. Talking about systems and strategy and linking competency in one subject to competency in another will be helpful. If they are generally self-confident, teachers can challenge them to increase their competency in their less-preferred subjects. Giving them distant goals will work, since they learn for the long- as well as the short-term.

Interpersonal Behavior Issues

INTJ students may have poor social skills because such things are relatively unimportant to them. *Solution:* One technique that may help is offering to teach INTJs the "technology of social interaction." INTJs may respond well if they treat the issue as though they were doing a scientific experiment. One teacher had his INTJ student make a conscious effort to smile five times each day for a week and then report back to him with his findings. The student expressed amazement at the effect that a few smiles had on others. INTJs can also be encouraged to join groups with interests similar to their own to prevent them from becoming completely isolated.

INTJs are often so inner driven that it is hard for them to understand that others need praise. For INTJs, praise means listening intelligently to others' ideas. *Solution:* INTJs need to learn how to recognize when things are worth praising and how to give unconditional praise. Learning temperament and type theory can be helpful to them. Once they are familiar with these theories, teachers can ask them to predict what kind of compliment a person of each personality type would most value and help them craft unconditional compliments. Developing this skill will enable them to establish better relationships with others.

Summary

INTJ students respond well to teachers who encourage their interests and listen to their ideas. They respect teachers who know a lot about a subject and can recommend good resource materials. Teachers who are interested in what INTJs have to say and can discuss ideas rationally will stimulate them to higher academic achievement. INTJs flourish when they are given a fair amount of autonomy in which to pursue their own interests.

NTP Inventors

NTP Inventors are among the most naturally curious of all types. ENTPs want to know as much as possible about everything and INTPs want to know everything about a particular area. Both types apply themselves to originating new ideas or designing new systems that are focused on processes. They like to look for novel and pragmatic ways to put things together and explore the possibilities of their ideas. The ability to inject innovation into almost any area is a natural gift for NTPs. In order to pursue new thoughts, NTPs require a sense of personal freedom and may resist conforming to the expectations of others. Because freedom is important to them, they are not likely to give directives to others; they prefer to give new information.

ENTP Improvisors

Basic Characteristics

Adjectives that describe the typical ENTP student are clever, ingenious, and resourceful. Their natural curiosity and questioning style often leads them into enterprising pursuits. They can be stimulating company and are able to argue both sides of an issue. These creative thinkers can unwind systems problems and can be outspoken.

Potential Career Paths

ENTPs are found in many different occupations. They do best in situations where they are given many stimulating and challenging projects. Fluent and persuasive speakers, they may be lawyers, politicians, or political analysts. They often enjoy fast-paced, highly charged environments. Entrepreneurial positions such as photographers, journalists, public relations specialists, marketing professionals, or musicians offer the kind of challenge that many ENTPs seek. Those who prefer longer-term systemic views may become regional planners, systems analysts, or computer network administrators. In any profession, they tend to focus on innovative solutions to problems.

Preferred Classes

ENTP students usually like math, science, engineering, computer, politics, and art classes. In a five-field comparison, their preferred sequence of interest was found to be science, liberal arts, engineering, business, and medicine. They are often attracted to extracurricular activities involving social groups and athletic events. They enjoy classes that allow them to play with concepts and see the movements in complex systems.

Common Behaviors

ENTP students are often generalists. Their typically insatiable curiosity causes them to become enthralled by many different subjects. Young ENTPs may delve into areas that others see as beyond their age. They may become equally captivated by a toy that others think is too juvenile for them. ENTPs, along with ENFPs, often behave outside age boundaries that others define as normal.

ENTPs may become fascinated with history if it is presented with an emphasis on systems and patterns. They do not like to memorize dates. History for them can seem like a series of power plays and influential ideas. They are generally interested in knowing what was happening in terms of music, art, politics, science, food production, and cultural norms during a particular time in a particular country. They are likely to become captivated by the influences within the system. They like to understand such things as the forces that sustained the Renaissance movement or the factors that contributed to the development of atomic energy.

The ENTP preference for extraversion is apparent in the ability to spontaneously talk about almost anything. To keep conversations going, they can use their remarkable ability to argue both sides of a issue. Their extraversion is also expressed in their preference to be around others. One first-grade ENTP was put in an advanced reading group by herself, since she was reading at a fourth-grade level. Instead of progressing further, however, she decided to stop reading, since she did not want to be isolated from her peers. The teacher then moved her to a regular reading group.

ENTPs naturally gather information. One ENTP student read an entire volume of an encyclopedia in one sitting in her quest for intellectual stimulation and breadth of interest. Since ENTPs do not normally prefer such introverted activities, they are likely to do this kind of activity while surrounded by others who are talking or while a TV or radio is playing. Many say they are happiest when they are surrounded by lots of stimulation.

ENTP students do best when they have some degree of autonomy. They may frustrate teachers by ignoring authority and standards. They have an open attitude in life and are constantly seeking new possibilities in the world of people and things. They do best when they are given some combination of restraint and freedom. One high school ENTP taking Spanish did well on his tests but failed to turn in his homework. The teacher knew that he wanted to become an engineer and realized that in this field his creative ideas would be welcome but that he would also be expected to meet certain standards. During a meeting with the student, the teacher explained her concerns about his behavior. She talked about the need for both creativity and meeting standards in the field of engineering. They discussed the implications of his current performance in the Spanish class. His exams and participation were at a high level, but his low submission of homework brought his grade down to an average level. By talking about the systems, influences, and consequences rather than the rules, the teacher presented a view that made sense to him. He realized that he needed to meet defined minimum standards to be seen as competent.

ENTPs can be influential in the area of human relationships and human systems. They can create environments that are stimulating to others and have a naturally upbeat attitude. They enjoy enlivening discussions by coming up with unique approaches to a problem, and it is not uncommon to hear them debate both sides of an issue to explore the relative merits of different approaches.

When working on group projects, ENTP students are likely to be the innovators. For them, development of the initial concept will be exciting and fun, but they may leave the completion of the project to the others. If they are working alone, teachers may want to have them describe how they will finish a project. One teacher never used the word "finish" with an ENTP student. She talked about what else the student could do to "Wow them," which kept the student excited through the project's completion.

Discipline Issues

Because of their insatiable curiosity and their tendency to scan their environment for multiple inputs, ENTP students may sometimes find it difficult to stay on task. They are able to see many possibilities and often want to explore them all. They can have difficulty completing tasks. *Solution:* Teachers need to encourage ENTPs to balance their ability to multitask with the benefits of satisfactorily completing one specific project. Repeatedly demanding that they finish a project usually will not work. ENTPs need to learn how to achieve completion, but if teachers try to force them to do only one task at a time, the likely result will be an ineffective stalemate. One way to persuade ENTPs to complete a task is to convince them that lack of completion is preventing them from exploring a new idea. ENTPs do not like to have their options closed off. Sometimes, they simply need to learn the consequences of not completing a task on time. The consequence needs to be something that diminishes their ability to explore other things.

ENTPs may frustrate teachers by finding materials too simple and becoming bored. *Solution:* Teachers should encourage ENTPs to work with the specified materials and be inventive about what else can be done with them. Letting them create new possibilities will foster their natural inventive abilities.

Academic Orientation Issues

ENTP students sometimes have difficulty with memorization. The problem stems from their ability to find alternative ways of perceiving things. *Solution:* Teachers can encourage these students to come up with innovative ways to memorize things, such as rhyming or drawing rebus puzzles. By having the opportunity to add their own twist to things, ENTPs can often learn to memorize.

ENTPs tend to reinvent everything. If they are not allowed to use this inventive ability, their performance level may drop. *Solution:* ENTPs will usually perform well as students if their ability to invent and enhance things is encouraged. Teachers can also encourage them to come up with creative reasons for why learning a particular subject is valuable and challenge them to develop their own inventive way to learn the material.

Interpersonal Behavior Issues

Since ENTP students like to see the world from a positive perspective, they often hide their negative feelings. When negative things build up, ENTPs may withdraw. *Solution:* If the withdrawal behavior is mild, teachers may not need to do anything. It may be a part of the normal ebb and flow for the ENTP, which may lead to renewed energy. If the withdrawal behavior is more longlasting, however, it may be necessary to talk to the ENTP about problems in the system. Talking about their personal problems causes them to be defensive, and an impersonal discussion about a "system" will increase the likelihood that they will be able to devise an inventive, workable solution.

ENTPs tend to have lofty goals, which can sometimes be unrealistic. *Solution:* Teachers can help ENTPs to engage in reality checks, where they can ask themselves about the risks and skills that will be necessary to complete a given goal. Learning to use risk assessment and cost-benefit analysis will be very helpful to them.

Summary

ENTP students respond to teachers who encourage them to engage in innovative projects. They like difficult problems that have many different parts to solve. Teachers who can unobtrusively encourage them to complete projects without stifling their creativity will be a great benefit to them. It is beneficial for ENTPs to have teachers who can explain the rules of whatever system currently holds their interest.

INTP Theorists

Basic Characteristics

Adjectives that describe the typical INTP student are detached, precise, cognitive, reserved, and impersonal. INTPs live in a world of ideas emphasizing logical analysis. Using their speculative abilities, they construct new theories that they subject to critical thinking. They can be skeptical and self-determined and have strongly defined interests.

Potential Career Paths

INTPs typically have a complex internal logical system that allows them to analyze long-term complex problems with great insight. They may spend years collecting information on one subject. They often enjoy analyzing problems and proposing innovative solutions. Their analytical and innovative thinking equips them to pursue careers in medical, technical, and research fields. They may become pathologists, pharmacists, scientists, technical support engineers, or researchers. To fulfill their need to work on the cutting edge of ideas, they often seek positions at high levels of academia or in professions that demand complex thinking. They may use their innovative talents in the creative fields.

Preferred Classes

INTP students like math, science, logic, language, philosophy, and art. In a five-field comparison of study areas, their preferred sequence of interest was found to be science, medicine, engineering, liberal arts, and business. They may enjoy lectures, drama, or music as extracurricular activities. Classes that allow them to analyze concepts in depth and to question other people's thinking particularly intrigue INTPs.

Common Behaviors

INTP students want to know a great deal about everything. They also are likely to gain such a depth of knowledge about a field that others regard them as specialists. Their level of understanding about a subject generally arises from their ability to formulate and test a series of hypotheses. The amount of knowledge they accumulate is often very thorough and complex. When a classmate asks for a complete explanation of a topic, INTPs may find the task daunting. The depth of their knowledge may make it very difficult for them to give a succinct explanation.

Many teachers choose to tap their INTP students' desire to absorb knowledge by granting them time for independent study. Allowing time in the school library can give INTP students the opportunity to consult a greater range of resources. Like all introverted intuitives, INTP students need some time to be preoccupied with their own thoughts. Teachers can sometimes observe this behavior and believe the INTPs are not working, and reprimand them for not paying attention. However, INTP students see themselves as productively working when they are quietly thinking. If they are engaged in approved independent study, teachers should allow them time to think.

INTPs tend to be extremely precise with their use of language. Word choice is very important to them, and they will often search for the perfect way to express what they want to say. They often use long but grammatically correct sentences. They can apply precise logic and often see distinctions that are unapparent to others. INTP student's love of words and meanings is often evident in their sense of humor. All NTs seem to enjoy word puns, but INTPs are the masters. Using alternate definitions of words can be highly amusing to them.

INTP students are often excellent writers who have well-developed vocabularies. Some INTPs find writing to be a useful way of clarifying their thoughts. However, because they are constantly revising their thinking, another person may need to tell when they need to see a work as finished. Incisive reasoners, INTPs are often able to notice logical inconsistencies in what other people say or write, even if months have passed between the statements. INTPs will win most arguments that they make an effort to win.

INTPs, like INTJs, need to understand the why of things before they can learn the how. Many types prefer to learn the rules first, then apply the rules using a process they have learned by rote, and, finally, try to understand the reasoning behind the rules. INTPs, like INTJs, reverse this process: They want to first understand why the rules are true, after which they try to make reasonable guesses about rational extensions of the rules. They often do not memorize formulas, but instead derive them each time they need to use them.

INTPs, like INTJs, tend to be very independent. They seldom respond to social pressures. They are more likely to reject the person or group that is pressuring them than they are to change. However, if they can be convinced that it would be logical to change their behavior, they will often change.

INTP students are likely to consider a project complete once they have worked it all out mentally. They may sometimes experience difficulty producing tangible products. One INTP student did a great deal of research for an English paper. She had the logic of the paper completely designed in her head. When the teacher reminded the class that the paper was due the next day, the student realized she had more of the paper in her head than was written on paper. The student stayed up most of the night in order to finish her paper. Although she did receive a good grade on the paper and enjoyed the excitement of the last minute rush, she also was somewhat dissatisfied that she lacked time to include all the points she wanted to make. INTP students can benefit from discussions on estimations of time and effort.

Discipline Issues

INTPs can become sarcastic and may complain if they think that a rule or procedure is illogical. *Solution:* It is extremely important for INTPs to believe that the teacher understands their position. Teachers should restate the student's point of view and praise them for their logical reasoning when possible. Then the teacher can explain their own point of view.

INTPs can sometimes become lost in an ongoing, flowing thought process and fail to put their thoughts into action. If they do not achieve a balance between thinking and acting, they may have difficulty in the world of work, where they may be seen as too unproductive. *Solution:* While internal thinking time must be allowed for INTPs to function effectively, teachers also need to encourage INTPs to put their thoughts into action. Since making an effective connection between the complex inner world and the outer world is very important for INTPs, teachers need to design activities that allow this connection to take place. For instance, the teacher can provide a time for INTP students to share their thoughts with at least one other person.

Academic Orientation Issues

INTP students may become lost in the process and not complete their work on time. The work may not seem perfect or complete enough to them, and they may feel there is another aspect that still needs developing. *Solution:* Sometimes teachers need to tell INTPs that they are finished with their work and that any additions, corrections, and improvements may be made in subsequent drafts for extra credit. It is important to allow INTPs to have some open-ended projects while at the same time insisting that they meet the deadlines of other projects.

INTPs may use their knowledge of the multiple definitions of words in a sarcastic or demeaning way. This behavior may alienate some of their teachers or peers. *Solution:* Teachers should encourage their development of words and definitions but help them to determine when this type of behavior is effective and when it is annoying or hurtful to others. It is important that teachers avoid giving instructions about how to make judgments. Instead, teachers should guide them in judging their own behavior.

Interpersonal Behavior Issues

INTP students sometimes have trouble developing social skills. They can become so entranced with their own internal thinking that they do not pick up on behavioral clues from other people. *Solution:* Discussions and opportunities to practice social interactions can be helpful to INTPs. Providing them with a theory about how people differ normally is very useful for INTPs, who are fascinated by theories. They can also benefit from discussions and readings about body language, and from analyzing physical behaviors and assigning names to them.

INTPs may appear to drift off when they are talking with other people. Unlike INTJs, who usually marshal their own arguments, INTPs may disengage themselves from the conversation and go off exploring all of the logical connections. *Solution:* INTPs may need help developing their skills of listening and responding to others. Paraphrasing in varied language what other people have said will be very helpful for them.

Summary

INTP students are motivated by teachers who value their incisive reasoning skills. They like teachers who explain the why of doing things as well as the how. Teachers who are sensitive to their need to begin acting on their thinking will be very beneficial for them. INTPs enjoy teachers who can use words skillfully.

PART FOUR

Making the Personality Connection

Schools were established to teach students the skills they need to become productive citizens. Curriculum is designed to emphasize the knowledge and behaviors deemed necessary for successful participation in society. This section discusses common teaching techniques and illustrates and explains their appeal to students of particular types.

Teachers are aware that while some techniques are very effective with some students, they have little impact on others. Some teachers stick to tried-and-true methods; others experiment until they find methods that reach every student. What are these differences between students? How can a teacher know what methods are likely to meet which type of student? How can the teacher tap the student's motivation to learn?

Human beings are born learning machines. As small children, they learn to walk and talk. When they become students, they are expected to learn to read, write, and do arithmetic. By school age, we see more distinct differences in learning behavior. *What* students want to learn and *how* they want to learn can vary widely.

SJ Guardians want to learn so that they can obtain a job and begin supporting themselves and serving others. As employees, they can serve both their employers and their families. Guardians are more interested in learning things that have been proven to work rather than things that are vanguard or experimental, and they generally want jobs that are valued as contributing to a group or society as a whole. Young Guardians generally want to learn what the teacher prescribes because the social structure that they are a part of, the school, tells them that they *should* learn these things.

SP Artisans are more interested in learning material that can be applied in the present rather than material that is theoretical. Learning for future needs does little to motivate them. Learning that gives them quick benefits is exciting and fun. They want a job that gives them the ability to make an impact. Young Artisans learn because learning is fun, or challenging, or because it helps them make an impact.

For NF Idealists, the acquisition of academic skills can help them reach their potential as human beings. They also want to learn to help others reach their dreams. For them, learning is personalized and subjective. Idealists are more interested in learning about ideas and values than in learning that is strictly factual and omits the human factor. They want to have a job that allows for personal growth or enables them to help humankind as a whole. Young Idealists want to learn to please their parents, teachers, or other loved ones.

Of all the temperaments, NT Rationals have the most insatiable need to *know*. Gaining academic skills is imperative to Rationals because they *must* learn. This applies to Rationals of any age. They want to learn the underlying system that comprehensively connects ideas and facts. Systems must withstand the testing and critiquing of the Rational's mind to be accepted. They usually choose a job that encourages or at least permits continual learning. Young Rationals want to learn because they are driven to understand the world.

Different students want different things. The Artisan student might not be very happy in the classroom that the Guardian describes as ideal and vice versa. The Idealist in a Rational-style classroom might be starved for warmth; the Rational in an Idealist-style classroom might be starved for intellectual challenge. Teachers must be familiar with a variety of teaching techniques in order to meet the needs of the various styles of students in their classrooms.

Some teachers may read the sixteen descriptions in chapters eight through eleven and think that they must learn fifteen new ways of communicating. That is not true. In fact, each teacher has something in common with fifteen out of the sixteen types. For example, ESFJ teachers have at least one polarity in common with every student except an INTP. In this case they might want to spend extra time reviewing the INTP student description.

Most teachers probably already have some acquaintance with techniques for students preferring Extraversion, Sensing, Feeling, and Judging. (Ninety-eight percent of American students will have at least one of those preferences.) Experienced teachers may only need to add a few strategies to better reach the students preferring Introversion, Intuition, Thinking, and Perceiving. The most valuable skills any teacher can add are that of tolerance of differences and recognizing and valuing abilities different from one's own.

The following chapters explain various teaching techniques, including suggestions for using books, homework, tests, games, and computers, and give teachers a formula that they can use to help them use the personality connection to effectively teach the various students in their classroom.

Chapter 12

Classroom Techniques

In this chapter, we will discuss the effectiveness of various well-known classroom techniques as they relate to temperament and personality type. Different styles need different techniques to engage their natural talents. Obviously, none of the techniques will work well for all students. By including a variety of techniques, teachers are more likely to be successful with all of their students. Teachers with an understanding of temperament and type can intelligently vary their teaching techniques to target specific students who are having difficulty. The descriptions below provide *generalized* likes and dislikes of student styles as applied to classroom style and techniques, keeping in mind the range variation for each student's specific needs and motivations.

Student Styles

SJ Guardians like structured, traditional classrooms. They are inclined to be quick to notice deviations from the norm and can easily become uncomfortable with them. They tend to like standard assignments with specific instructions and clear-cut deadlines. Guardians enjoy knowing the rules and having a sense of belonging. They feel more respected when they know their performance is up to a norm. Guardians who believe that the teacher has clear academic and behavioral expectations and is fair will usually be conscientious hard workers.

SP Artisan students like exciting, accepting classrooms. They enjoy variety and like change for the sake of change. They have incredible amounts of energy waiting for direction. SP Artisans usually like nontraditional assignments best, especially those that allow them to use their bodies. They also enjoy competition and games. Teachers should use humor and challenges liberally with these students. SP Artisans who believe that the teacher values *their* special qualities will work hard to impress the teacher and their classmates.

NF Idealist students tend to like harmonious, nurturing classrooms. They usually want to please and need lots of praise. They want to be acknowledged as human beings, not just as good workers. Introverted Idealists are content to quietly help an accepting teacher, while Extraverted Idealists usually want to help more actively. They particularly enjoy group work and creative assignments and do not usually like competition. NF Idealists who believe that the teacher appreciates each student's special qualities will generally be supportive and produce excellent work.

NT Rational students like serious, knowledgeable classrooms. They want to learn in order to make sense out of their world. They want their classes to stimulate them intellectually. NT Rationals appreciate opportunities to show their depth of understanding about technical or logical systems. They enjoy being asked about their ideas. If they are given the opportunity to work through difficult problems, they are likely to perform well. NT Rationals who believe that the teacher values their ideas and sees them as competent will usually be superior students.

Classroom Teaching Techniques

In the following sections about classroom teaching techniques, we have limited our discussion to those temperaments and types that are affected strongly—either positively or negatively—by using the particular technique mentioned. In addition, we do not explain the teaching techniques because we assume they are familiar to most teachers.

Workbooks

Workbooks are most popular with SJ Guardians because they typically require answers that are specific and either right or wrong. The other types and temperaments often find them boring, although they will generally be more popular with the Judging types of any temperament than with the Perceiving types. While SP Artisans may benefit from workbooks, it is usually hard to get them to do the work. Intuitive types may also find that workbooks generally do little to stimulate their creative thinking and may find them too easy. Teachers can try to find workbooks that are more interesting and fun to stimulate these students. Creative Publications, for example, puts out many books that are filled with fun worksheets. One of these books uses sports to teach general math. Others are in the form of puzzles. Among these are *Pre-Algebra and Algebra With Pizzazz* and *Handy Math: Focus on Sports*.

Lectures

Lecturing is a good teaching technique for SJ Guardians and NT Rationals. Some teachers think, especially after attending many motivational presentations, that lecturing is not a good way to teach. While it's true that lectures, particularly noninteractive ones, may leave SP Artisans cold, SJ Guardians and NT Rationals often enjoy them. SJ Guardians like learning about the past. NT Rationals like acquiring knowledge. As long as lecture is not used exclusively, it can be a valuable tool in the hands of a teacher who enjoys it.

Course Outlines

Even elementary school SJ Guardians appreciate having a course outline. It makes them feel secure when they know approximately what will happen in class at any given time. Course outlines that give deadlines can be useful for both Judgers and Perceivers. Judging types will work steadily toward the deadline and may finish before the deadline, while Perceiving students will work backward from the deadline to decide when to begin an assignment. They usually rely on a burst of energy to do their best work right before the deadline.

Memorization

Memorization is what SJ Guardians usually do best. Most of the temperaments can memorize well, but SJ Guardians often use this skill as their primary way of earning good grades. Some types find memorization difficult. ENTPs, for instance, only memorize when they have to and then only for the short term. Since their minds are so inventive, some ENTPs find it almost impossible to memorize. In general, Perceiving types sometimes become bored with memorization because it lacks variety. Intuitives want connections, not isolated facts, and will use memorization if they see that it enhances their abilities to make connections.

Rhetorical Questions

Rhetorical questions are popular with SJ Guardians. These are questions that review a lesson that has just been taught. For example, after a lesson on early American history, a teacher might ask the following questions: "Name one tribe of Native Americans who met the European settlers," "Who bought Manhattan?" "From whom?" "For how much?" NT Rationals have one of two responses to rhetorical questions: Either they wish to dominate and prove their expertise, or they feel that they understand the big picture and do not need the details.

Contracts

Some teachers use written contracts with students that specify what assignments a student will do by a specified date. Judging types and SJ Guardians, in particular, like contracts because they know exactly what they have to do to earn a particular grade. Contracts with SP Artisans need to be designed very carefully. If there is too long a time frame or too many projects, they may fail to meet their obligations. Intuitives can take or leave contracts. NT Rationals or SP Artisans may sometimes be tempted to use a contract as an excuse to perform only at the minimum level, so teachers need to ensure that the minimum performance is acceptable.

Complete Sentences

Many teachers insist that students do all of their work in complete sentences, which appeals to Judging types. This is a variation on the workbook-style repetition. Insisting on complete sentences can be good for all styles when they are still in the learning process; however, it could excessively frustrate students who simply want to get their thoughts on paper. It may be detrimental to insist that students who have proven a thorough understanding of complete sentences always follow this rule. NT Rationals, in particular, despise busywork and will often rebel against slavishly following this rule. Teachers may want to relax the requirement of doing all work in complete sentences—except in English and writing classes—once students have proven their competency.

Showing Work

Showing work, a term used by math teachers, applies when students are required to show all the steps they took to reach the answer to a problem. It's a good idea to have students show work for several reasons: (1) half the answers may be available in the back of their textbooks, (2) they might copy their work from a friend, and (3) showing work will help students remember how to do particular problems. SJ Guardians find it easy to unnderstand why they should show work. Some students, especially NT Rationals and SP Artisans, may insist that they can do the problems without showing work. In these cases, teachers can ask the students to do a problem that is similar to the most difficult problem in the chapter in their heads. They are seldom able to do so. If they can do it, they probably understand the concepts so well that they will not gain any learning by having to show work. This challenge method is a good way to prove that showing work is not simply busywork.

Audiovisuals

Audiovisual techniques such as filmstrips, movies, and slide shows usually appeal most to SJ Guardians and SP Artisans because these students tend to need pictures to go along with words. Since audiovisuals are invaluable for giving students experiences they cannot have otherwise—from watching exploding volcanoes to touring India—all types of students can benefit from them. Teachers may wish to follow audiovisuals with discussions, questions, or some other technique to increase learning by all styles. Introverted Intuitives may be tempted to let their attention wander during audiovisuals and may get lost in their own thoughts unless the subject is especially appealing to them.

Manipulatives

Manipulatives, which are counters and other objects students can handle and are used most often in math, appeal especially to Sensing types. They are especially valuable for teaching math skills to the primary grades. The hands-on experience helps Sensing students understand the whys of addition and subtraction. These students do not generally like to work in the abstract and learn best when they can actually touch objects and move them around and can literally see results. Intuitive students on the other hand, may be offended by what they consider "baby games," as working in the abstract is where they excel.

Dioramas

SP Artisans will usually enjoy dioramas. SJ Guardians normally enjoy them as well, but can be stressed if they do not know exactly how the teacher will grade them. NT Rationals will not see much point in them and may perceive them as busywork. This can be overcome if their creativity and imagination are encouraged. The teacher can say, "I'm sure that there are things you can put in your diorama that most students would overlook," or "Feel free to express your view of the scene." NF Idealists can enjoy dioramas if they are allowed to be imaginative and put animals or people in the scenes. Since they are attuned to relationships, they will likely personalize the creatures and tell stories about them. Requiring too much accuracy of detail, however, may cause them stress.

Show-and-Tell

Extraverts, especially SPs, enjoy show-and-tell because it gives them the chance to be the center of attention and to feel special. While most elementary-level students like to be a part of show-and-tell, Introverts may find the experience excruciating. A little sensitivity goes a long way—the teacher should try to give the Introverts, particularly the Introverted Judging types, advanced warning for show-and-tell exercises.

Drama

Drama appeals to SP Artisans and NF Idealists. SJ Guardians will enjoy watching and participating in dramas unless they feel that it is interfering with what they view as the "real" purpose of school. NT Rationals usually will not have much use for drama unless they can be in charge or feel that they can learn something from the experience. An ENTJ first grader told his principal about a play he was in about trains. When asked what he liked about the play, he focused on what he had learned about trains and on what he was able to teach his parents about trains.

Oral Book Reports

Extraverts will generally like to give oral reports while Introverts generally will not. SJ Guardians will often like them if they have an outline telling them exactly what is expected—how long the report should be and what questions need to be answered. For example, what is the main plot? Who are the main characters? Would you recommend this book? Which character did you like best/least? Extraverted SP Artisans would probably enjoy dramatizing part of the book and explaining why they chose to dramatize that part of the work.

Alternative Assignments

SP Artisans learn by doing. In general, they will enjoy many kinds of alternative assignments, such as making models, teaching other students, or making up a rhyme/song/dance to help them learn rote facts. When assigning these types of projects to SP Artisans, teachers need to be clear about due dates because Artisans may procrastinate.

SJ Guardians will usually feel uncomfortable with nonstandard assignments. They may feel very stressed by being asked to do something out of the ordinary. When giving these kinds of assignments to Guardians, teachers can help them by giving concrete suggestions for topics and samples of completed work so they feel they know the rules. NF Idealists will often like alternative assignments that enable them to express their creativity.

Teacher Notes to Students

Writing personal notes to students is most effective with Introverted Feeling types. Introverts do not usually want to be the center of attention, so they enjoy being recognized in a more private way. Most Feeling types really like positive notes from their teacher. NT Rationals, on the other hand, would probably appreciate the note only if it focused on their ideas and thinking ability.

Cooperative Learning

Organizing students into cooperative learning groups is effective for many students, but it is not designed for all types. Extraverts usually enjoy it much more than Introverts, and Introverted NT Rationals generally dislike it. SJ Guardians and NF Idealists frequently enjoy working with others in cooperative groups. However, they become disillusioned if they end up doing most of the work. Introverted Guardians may view cooperative learning as chaotic, partly because of the noise level that can arise during such activities.

The question will probably arise of how best to group students for cooperative learning. Mixing students of varying ability in the same group is usually very effective, but how can one address temperament and personality type? One college teacher found that when she grouped students together by the same temperaments, they finished their work quickly with little arguing. Unfortunately, the finished product was usually unbalanced and relatively predictable. When she mixed temperaments in the same group, each group spent a lot of initial time in discussion trying to hash out their differences, but the finished product was well-balanced and creative.

Group Projects

Group projects, such as drawing a mural or putting together a report, are most popular with Feeling types and Extraverts. Although all types can benefit from participation in group projects, Thinking types usually prefer to concentrate on individual achievement. Extraverts like group projects because they enjoy opportunities to talk and work with others. Group projects give Feelers a chance to work cooperatively and to give and receive praise.

Peer Tutoring

Feeling types, especially NF Idealists, generally enjoy peer tutoring because they like to help others. Extraverts often like the peer interaction. NT Rationals tend to dislike peer tutoring, especially Introverted NT Rationals, since it takes time away from the thinking they really want to do. Forcing an NT Rational to offer or receive peer tutoring may result in bad feelings between the students. This is particularly true if the NT Rational is the one being tutored, since they may feel they are being viewed as incompetent.

Journals

NF Idealists will probably be the best at writing journals; however, most other Feeling types will also enjoy writing journals. SFs usually like to write about what has happened to them. NT Rationals will often use a journal to record their ideas and theories. STPs usually will not want to be bothered with such things; they operate so much in the present that they do not like to pause and reflect on what they have done.

Discussions

NF Idealists usually like discussions since they enjoy democratic class-rooms. NT Rationals can enjoy expressing their own ideas but may not show the same consideration to other students. Since NT Rationals are generally good at defending their ideas, they may try to turn a discussion into a debate so they can state their point of view more forcefully. Sometimes NF Idealists will interrupt a good exchange if the discussion starts turning into a heated debate. They prefer harmony, wanting every-one to affirm everyone else. SJ Guardians like discussing the facts. Extraverted SP Artisans like discussions, especially if the topic is exciting to them.

Even if Introverts never say a word, they may be intensely interested in discussions and may thoroughly enjoy listening to the other students and the teacher. They often feel that they are participating, even if they do not actually say anything. In her book *The Developing Child*, Elizabeth Murphy (1992) gives an excellent suggestion for getting all students to participate in discussions. Murphy suggests that each student in a group be given several tokens. Each time a student speaks, she or he gives one token to the group leader. Once students have used all of their tokens, they cannot speak again until everyone else has used all their tokens. This ensures that Introverts participate and encourages Extraverts to think before blurting out whatever comes to mind. Also, Introverts may have something they want to say but are unable to break into a conversation dominated by Extraverts. The use of tokens gives them an orderly way to get their turn.

Creative Writing

NF Idealists are usually the best creative writers. NT Rationals can also use creative writing as a way to explore their ideas. Creative writing often does not come as naturally to Sensing types, but, once they are taught the necessary skills, they can do very well. One technique that works well with Sensors is to have them draw a picture and write a story about it. Teachers can help by asking questions about the picture, such as, Who are the people in the picture? How old are they? What are their names? Are they related to each other? What are they doing? What happened before what is shown in this picture? What will happen after the events shown in the picture? Once Sensors become familiar with this technique they can generate stories without assistance.

Divergent Thinking

Intuitives are best at divergent thinking and brainstorming. Sensing–Thinking types generally want to come to one conclusion. Perceiving types have an advantage in this area because they naturally look at alternatives. A classic example of a divergent thinking technique is asking students to write down as many uses of paper clips as they can. Students will usually come up with simple answers, such as "to hold paper." Then they will be more creative with answers such as "to make a necklace," or "as a weight for the front of a paper airplane."

Debates

NT Rationals usually enjoy a good debate. STPs are also often good debaters. Extraverts are more likely to enjoy debates than Introverts. Thinking types enjoy expressing and challenging ideas, while Feeling types may find the climate too warm for their liking in a good debate. It is important to remind these students that they can disagree with someone's views and still respect and like the person.

Socratic Questioning

Socratic questioning is most popular with NT Rationals, who truly believe that the mind can accomplish anything if it works hard enough. Thinkers like the logical format of the questions. Sensing types will sometimes become irritated with Socratic questioning and ask the teacher to simply give them the information. However, they will often do well if questions are fairly concrete. Although, as a rule, teachers using Socratic questioning should not give a definite answer to a question, it may be necessary to do so to help Sensing students know that they are on the right track.

Independent Study

NT Rationals are likely to get the most out of independent study. They are motivated to learn for learning's sake. Introverts are generally more comfortable working on their own. Perceiving types often enjoy the freedom that goes with independent study. SJ Guardians tend to get uncomfortable if they do not know exactly what the standards for success are. With most types, it is best to establish clear deadlines. For Judging types, clear deadlines help them to know how to pace themselves. Perceiving types may need occasional reminders to help them meet the objectives by the deadline. This technique helps all temperaments and types with time estimation skills that are very valuable in the world of work.

Teacher Readings

Introverts, in particular, enjoy having others read to them. NF Idealists enjoy letting their imagination go while listening to the story. Extraverted SJ Guardians usually enjoy readings, also. Other Extraverts may enjoy being read to if they have the opportunity to discuss the material afterward. Chapter 13 gives examples of books with near universal appeal that are most suitable for reading to a class. Some Extraverts, especially SP Artisans, enjoy being read to if they are also permitted to *do* something, such as drawing a picture illustrating the story.

Summary

Table 17 provides a quick reference summary of the classroom teaching techniques discussed in this chapter. Teachers can use the information to analyze the techniques they currently use or to choose techniques to reach a particular style of student. We are assuming that a high-quality version of each technique is used. For example, no student, no matter what learning style, would enjoy working with poor quality workbooks or audiovisuals.

The table makes comparisons by temperaments (SJ = Guardian, SP = Artisan, NF = Idealist, NT = Rational) or by preference pairs (E–I, S–N, T–F, J–P). The number ratings by temperament and type preference for the techniques are based primarily on our classroom experiences, although a few values have been extrapolated. To describe the ratings in more detail:

"3" means that, barring a particular student's problems interfering, most students of that temperament or type will enjoy the technique.

"2" means that while most students of that temperament or type will enjoy the technique, some will not or that the technique may need to be amended slightly for a particular style for those students to truly enjoy it.

"1" means that the particular type of student will especially like only applications of the technique designed for their temperament or type. For example, most workbooks leave SP Artisans cold, but work books that include pictures and puzzles and appear more like games will usually be popular with them.

"C" means Caution. Some subgroups of this temperament or preference may respond negatively to this strategy, Refer to the specific chapter for further details.

A blank space means that there are too many variables that must be considered before determining that the techniques would be effective for that particular temperament or type preference. For example, on workbooks, it is not useful to score T and F, since ISTJs and ISFJs will usually like workbooks, but ENTPs and ENFPs usually will not.

Table 17 Teaching Techniques and Ratings by Temperament and Type Preference

Classroom Techniques	SJ	SP	NF	NT	E	I	S	N	T	F	J	P
Workbooks	3	1		1		2	2				2	
Lectures	3	1	2	3	1	2					2	1
Course Outlines	3					2					3	
Memorization	3		2								1	
Rhetorical Questions	3	1	1	2	2	1	2				2	1
Contracts	3	1	1	1							3	
Complete Sentences	2		2	1		1					2	
Showing Work	2			C			1				1	
Audiovisuals	3	3	1	1		2	3	C				
Manipulatives	2	3					2	C				2
Dioramas	2	2	1	1		2	2			1		2
Show-and-Tell	1	2	1	1	3	C						
Drama	1	3	2		3					3		2
Oral Book Reports		2	2		2	C						
Alternative Assignments		3	2									2
Teacher Notes to Students	2		3			2				3		
Cooperative Learning	2		2	C	2					3		
Group Projects		1	2		2				C	3		1
Peer Tutoring	2		3	C						3		
Journals	1	C	2			1				3		
Discussions	2	1	3	1	3					2		
Creative Writing			3	2		2		2				
Divergent Thinking	C	1	3	3				3				2
Debates		3	3	3	3				3	C		
Socratic Questioning		1	3				C	2	2			
Independent Study	1	1	1	3		2		2				2
Teacher Readings	2	1	2	1	2	3						

SJ = Guardian; SP = Artisan; NF = Idealist; and NT = Rational.
3 = Really Likes; 2 = Often Likes; 1 = Likes Certain Applications; and C = Caution; and Blank = Too Many Variables.

Chapter 13

Books, Homework, and Tests

Recommended Books for Teachers

This section lists a few books available to teachers that we have tested and found to be useful resources when exploring methods appropriate to particular learning styles. They provide teachers with a variety of activities, puzzles, and discussion materials that can be used to reach students of different types.

Bet You Can't by Vicki Cobb and Kathy Darling (1980) is a science book that is full of activities that seem like they should be easy but are nearly impossible to do. Sensing types, especially SP Artisans, enjoy physical challenges. NT Rationals like to discover why the activities are impossible. Extraverts are likely to want the attention that comes with trying to beat the challenge.

Think About It! by Marcy Cook (1982) is a book of mathematics problems for upper elementary and middle school students. It includes enough problems to take up 180 school days. Most of the problems appeal more to Intuitives than to Sensing types. Both Introverts and Thinking types enjoy taking the time to solve the book's puzzles.

The Book of Think (1976) and *The I Hate Mathematics Book* (1975) by Marilyn Burns are aimed at upper elementary and middle school students. These two books offer specific techniques that are especially effective in helping Sensing students learn some Intuitive-type thinking. Intuitive types may naturally be better at these kinds of tasks than Sensing types.

Everyday Law for Young Citizens by Greta Barclay Lipson, and Eric Barcley Lipson (1988) is a social studies book targeted at grades five through nine. This book is excellent for Sensing types. Each section opens with a realistic scenario, asks for the students' opinions of whether a law was broken in the scenario, and then tells readers what the law says (often as interpreted by the courts). It also has suggested classroom activities, most of which would appeal to Sensing types and Extraverted NF Idealists. The book teaches legal terms as well. If students really disagree with what the law says, teachers may wish to teach them how to change unfair laws and have them write letters to their local and national representatives. SJ Guardians, in particular, like learning about laws, especially when they deal with people their own age. SP Artisans like learning about laws as they are, rather than previous laws or possible future legal changes.

Recommended Books for Students

As teachers, we all want to encourage students to read. The benefits of reading include learning new vocabulary, new information, and gaining insight into different cultures. We have found that students must first learn to read what they love before they will be able to love what they read. Students will only learn to love reading if they enjoy what they read. The more they read, the more they will learn to enjoy different kinds of books. It is important to determine what each student likes to read and encourage him or her to read similar things. We have found that the principles of temperament and type theory can be useful in helping teachers decide what books to recommend to each student, as some types are more likely to enjoy certain books than others. We have attempted to give teachers a guideline for recommending books on this basis. We have also included the grade range to indicate the reading level each book requires. Few books designed for first to third graders are preference or temperament specific, since preferences at this level may be unclear, and their limited reading vocabulary restricts the kinds of books they can read. Some books for older students are not temperament/preference specific because the stories appeal to a diverse readership. Some good examples are *The Chronicles of Narnia* by C. S. Lewis, *Charley and the Chocolate Factory* by Roald Dahl, *Charlotte's Web* by E. B. White, and *Mary Poppins* by P. L. Travers. The C. S. Lewis series has action for the SP Artisans, fantasy, allegory for the NF Idealists, and science fiction for the NT Rationals, and a moral lesson for the SJ Guardians. Such books are the best kind to read aloud to the class as a whole.

When recommending reading material to students, do not forget magazines, newspapers, comic books, and short stories. Also include nonfiction works that seem appropriate, such as history, reference works, fact books, trivia books, and almanacs.

Books for Each Temperament and Type

In the next four sections, we will give examples of the kinds of reading material most likely preferred by each temperament.

SJ Guardians

SJ Guardians tend to like books that are grounded in reality and have little fantasy. They often like historical novels and stories that tell how people lived in other places or times. Many SJ Guardians like biographies. They also like reading material that can be read in small bits at a time, such as magazines and newspapers. They often like books that give lists of things, such as the top ten sports or highest-grossing movies. Some books that generally appeal to these students include:

For grades 4 to 6,

- *The Little House on the Prairie* series by Laura Ingalls Wilder. SJ Guardians enjoy learning about what life was like in the late 1800s in America.

- *The Incredible Journey* by Sheila Burnford. This book is set in Canada and vividly describes Canadian scenery.

- Books by Beverly Cleary, such as *Ramona the Pest* and *Runaway Ralph*. Her books tend to be popular with most Sensing types, but especially SFJs. Her books talk about common children's issues.

For grades 7 to 12,

- *Swiss Family Robinson* by Johann Wyss. This story about a shipwrecked family captures SJ Guardians' imaginations.
- *Extraordinary Origins of Everyday Things* by Charles Panati. This book tells where and when many of our customs originated.
- Readers Digests' *Strange Stories, Amazing Facts of America's Past.* This fascinating book appeals to most Sensing types, with short excerpts presented in an attention-grabbing style.
- Books by Charles Dickens such as *Oliver Twist* or *Great Expectations.* SJ Guardians enjoy reading about what life was like for the under-privileged people in nineteenth-century England.
- *The Outsiders* by S. E. Hinton. Although the main character appears to be an Intuitive, this book appeals more to Sensing types because of its gritty reality-based nature. SJ Guardians enjoy taking in the social commentary the book makes.

SP Artisans

Like the SJ Guardians, SP Artisans like books that are grounded in reality and have little fantasy. They like action books that are not bogged down in excessive description. Artisans often enjoy horror stories, such as books by Edgar Allan Poe. Sensors are likely to enjoy crime and detective stories. They often prefer books that have many bits of information rather than a continuous storyline. They like fact books on such things as sports, world records, and history. Younger SP Artisans are often drawn to comics and *Choose Your Own Adventure* books. Some books that generally appeal to these students include:

For grades 4 to 6,

- *How to Eat Fried Worms* by Thomas Rockwell. Many young Artisans enjoy stories that are humorous with a seemingly "gross" theme, like this one.
- Comic books. Comic books include lots of action and color in an easy-to-read format.
- The *Choose Your Own Adventure* series. These books have multiple endings, depending on what option the reader picks. Artisans enjoy trying to outwit the author and avoid getting "killed."

- *The Guiness Book of World Records.* This famous book of records grabs SP Artisans' interest, as they try to find the most peculiar information in it. SJ Guardians often like it, also.

For grades 7 to 12,

- Horror stories. Some examples are the *Flowers in the Attic* series, books by Stephen King, and stories by Edgar Allan Poe, such as "The Tell-Tale Heart."

- *Hiroshima* by John Hershey. This book describes in detail what happened when the atomic bomb was dropped on Hiroshima. Although the author is American, he tells this story from the viewpoint of the Japanese survivors. It is full of graphic descriptions given in a dispassionate format.

- *Reader's Digest Book of Facts.* This book is full of fascinating information on a variety of topics that SP Artisans will enjoy. SJ Guardians often like this book, also.

NF Idealists

NF Idealists like books that have fantasy (possibility thinking) and/or discussion of human relationships and personal growth in them. Books that have both are the most enticing to these students. Most Idealists enjoy myths and legends because they discuss underlying human themes and archetypes. In general, NF Idealists do not like horror stories or books that show the gritty detail of the seamier side of life. Many of them enjoy poetry and romances. Some books that generally appeal to these students include:

For grades 4 to 6,

- *The Wizard of Oz* series by Frank L. Baum. These books describe a fantasy world from a child's point of view.

- Books by Lloyd Alexander, such as *The Book of Three.* One in his series tells how Taran, a pigkeeper in a fantasy magical land called Prydain, grows up.

- *The Chronicles of Narnia* by C. S. Lewis. Although this series has universal appeal, NF Idealists especially enjoy the rich imagery and use of allegory.

For grades 6 to 8,

- Books by Madeleine L'Engle. She has written many books, including a trilogy that begins with *A Wrinkle in Time*. In this trilogy, the main characters travel to other planets in order to save someone.
- *The Earthsea Trilogy* by Ursula K. LeGuin. This series traces the adolescence and young adulthood of Ged, a sorcerer. The books are set in a magical land.

For grades 9 to 12,

- Books by Anne MacCaffrey, such as *Dragonriders of Pern*. Her Pern series combines fantasy and science fiction in stories about the human condition.
- Books by Elizabeth Peters, such as *The Lion in the Valley*. Her books usually have strong female characters. She uses language cleverly, and each book contains a mystery. These books have a softer touch to them than books more likely to be favored by NT Rationals.
- Books by the Brontë sisters—*Jane Eyre* by Charlotte Brontë and *Wuthering Heights* by Emily Brontë. These classic romance/mysteries often appeal to NF Idealists.

NT Rationals

NT Rationals like many of the same books that appeal to NF Idealists, except that they are not as interested in people themes. They are likely to enjoy hard-core science fiction because many of them identify with their existential themes. They also like science fiction because it focuses on what *might* be. NT Rationals enjoy predicting the changes to a cultural system when certain rules change. They enjoy comparing what they think would happen with what the author thinks would happen. They like books that challenge them to think and to predict. Because of this, they often like mystery and puzzle books. Rationals like books that make clever and precise use of language. Some books that generally appeal to these students include:

For grades 4 to 6,

- The *Encyclopedia Brown* series by Donald Sobol. This series uses a lot of advanced vocabulary. NT Rationals like the series because each short story is a puzzle that the reader needs to solve. Answers are contained at the back of the books.

- The *Danny Dunn* series by Williams and Abrashkin. This series combines the use of many scientific and technical terms with mysteries. NT Rationals enjoy solving the mystery before the book ends.
- Books by E. L. Konigsberg, such as *From the Mixed-up Files of Mrs. Basil E. Frankweiler.* This author's books arc full of difficult vocabulary and complicated sentence structure, which NT Rationals tend to like. Her stories are fascinating to most NF Idealists as well, but frustrating for most Sensing types.

For grades 7 to 12,

- *The Hobbit* by J. R. R. Tolkien. This book is a science fiction/fantasy classic. NT Rationals usually like Tolkien's books. Most of the other temperaments find this book slow moving and not particularly engaging.
- Books by John Christopher, such as *The White Mountains.* These are science fiction books specifically for children. Some of his books are enjoyed by NT Rationals as young as third grade. NF Idealists often enjoy his books, but they usually prefer books that have a less harsh (less existential) tone.
- *Flowers for Algernon* by Daniel Keyes. This book discusses what might happen if someone who was severely mentally retarded became a super genius. Books that discuss the role of intelligence in personality are fascinating to NT Rationals.

As a general rule, Introverts enjoy reading more than Extraverts. Even many Introverted SP Artisans consider reading a hobby. But Extraverts certainly enjoy reading as well. Sensing types tend to prefer reality-based books, while Intuitives like fantasy and make-believe. Thinking types prefer expository works that provide or explain information in a logical way, while Feeling types prefer narrative works that have a storylike quality. Since the Sensing–Intuitive dimension seems to be the more important of the four type dimensions that impact reading, we have concentrated on this dimension. In tables 18 and 19, we have listed books that are most likely to appeal to each of these types. Books are arranged in approximate order of reading level, beginning with the easiest-to-read books. Table 20 contains books and interest rating levels for temperament and type preferences.

Table 18 Books That Appeal to Sensing Types	
The Berenstain Bears	*B Is for Betsy*
Books by Laura Ingalls Wilder	Books by Beverly Cleary
Little Women	*Swiss Family Robinson*
Sarah, Plain and Tall	*Black Beauty*
Heidi	*Sounder*
Pippi Longstocking	Books by Lucille Clifton
Books by Marguerite Henry	*Harriet the Spy*
The Taste of Blackberries	The *Nancy Drew* stories
The *Hardy Boys* stories	*Trixie Belden* series
The Adventures of Tom Sawyer	Books by Scott O'Dell
The Incredible Journey	*Incident at Hawk's Hill*
Books by Elizabeth George Speare	*Treasure Island*
Call of the Wild	Books by John Steinbeck
Books by Charles Dickens	Books by Ernest Hemingway
Books by Herman Melville	*Kon-Tiki*
The Red Badge of Courage	

Recommended Homework and Test Strategies

Students of each learning style find it easier to demonstrate their knowledge and understanding with certain kinds of questions and assignments. Students will benefit most from assignments or tests that include questions designed to give students of each temperament and personality type an opportunity to demonstrate their abilities.

Homework and Tests for Each Temperament and Type

When making up questions for each type of student, teachers should try, whenever possible, to run the questions by someone (perhaps another teacher) of that same temperament. Sometimes a change of only one or two words can make a big difference. In general, teachers will get better work from students if students are permitted to choose questions or tasks according to their temperament and type.

Table 19   Books That Appeal to Intuitive Types

The Trumpet of the Swan	*The Borrowers*
Wonderful Flight to the Mushroom Planet	*Ludo and the Star Horse*
	Escape to Witch Mountain
Mrs. Coverlet's Magicians	*Miss Pickerell* series
Books by Ruth Chew	Books by Ursula K. LeGuin
Books by Zilpha Keatly Snyder	*The Wizard of Oz* series
Homer Price	*The Phantom Tollbooth*
Books by Lewis Carroll	*The Sword in the Stone*
Books by E. L. Konigsberg	Books by John Christopher
Chitty-Chitty Bang-Bang	*Freaky Friday*
Books by Madeleine L'Engle	*I Heard the Owl Call My Name*
Books by Lloyd Alexander	Books by Chaim Potok
Watership Down	*The Legend of Sleepy Hollow*
Books by Sir Arthur Conan Doyle	Books by J. R. R. Tolkien
Books by Isaac Asimov	Books by James Thurber
Books by the Brönte sisters	Works by Shakespeare
Star Trek stories	

- SJ Guardians tend to like true/false questions, short-answer questions, and matching tests.
- SP Artisans tend to like true/false questions and essay questions that ask for facts.
- NF Idealists usually like short-answer or essay questions that ask for opinions and interpretations.
- NT Rationals tend to prefer multiple-choice questions and questions that require insight into what they've been taught.

In this section, we have chosen three subjects—spelling, history, and English literature—and designed questions or assignments for these subjects that would appeal to each of the four temperaments. We hope that these examples will clarify the concept of individual differences related to temperament and stimulate teachers to design their own homework assignments and test questions keeping these differences in mind.

Spelling Words

At the elementary level, spelling is a weekly event. Here are some sample tasks to assign to students that will help with spelling:

1. Copy the words in cursive ten times each.
2. Break each word into syllables and write the dictionary definition.
3. Write one sentence for each word.
4. Write a story using all of the spelling words.
5. Make a word-find puzzle using all the words.
6. Make a crossword puzzle complete with clues.
7. Practice spelling words with a parent for ten minutes and have the parent confirm in a note that they did so.
8. Make up a short skit or song using all of the words.
9. Write each word along with one antonym and one synonym.
10. Draw a picture of each word and label it or draw a picture using the letters of each word.

SJ Guardians will like tasks 1, 2, 3, and perhaps 5 because these are familiar activities that they know how to do. SP Artisans will like 5 and 10 because of their gamelike feel. They will also like 7 and 8 because these allow them to be active. NF Idealists and NT Rationals will like 4 and 9 because of the thinking and creativity needed. NTs will be the mostly likely to take up the challenge of 6, which requires strategic thinking abilities.

History

Here are some questions on the American Civil War that are likely to appeal to each temperament.

- *Facts and Comparisons for SJ Guardians:* (1) List the major battles from 1863 through 1865 and tell which side won. (2) Who was the better leader, Lincoln or Davis, and why?

- *Action for SP Artisans:* (1) Describe the tactics used in the Battle of Gettysburg. What would you have done differently on either side, and why? (2) Pretend you're a confederate soldier. Tell your story. Include at least one major battle.

- *The World of People and Possibilities for NF Idealists:* (1) Could the Civil War have been prevented? Support your view. (2) Discuss the relationship between *Uncle Tom's Cabin* and the Civil War.

- *Systems and Strategies for NT Rationals:* (1) How did the Civil War affect the American economy? (2) If you were Davis, how would you have run the war?

English Literature

Romeo and Juliet is a play that is commonly read in the ninth grade. Here are some sample questions about the play designed to appeal to various temperaments:

- *Facts and Comparisons for SJ Guardians:* (1) Make a timeline of the significant events of the play. (2) Compare the social customs of Romeo and Juliet's day with those of today. (3) How did each person in the play contribute to the ultimate outcome?

- *Action and Pragmatism for SP Artisans:* (1) Was what happened to Romeo and Juliet inevitable, caused by fate, as Shakespeare claims, or did *they* cause what happened to them? (2) Should fourteen-year-olds be allowed to get married? Support your answer with information from the play. (3) How is feuding the same and/or different now as compared to Romeo and Juliet's day? (4) If you were Romeo, what would you have done differently in the scene where Mercutio and Tybalt get killed?

- *The Personal and Metaphorical for NF Idealists:* (1) Discuss the use of imagery in the balcony scene. How was it effective? (2) Why did Friar Lawrence agree to marry Romeo and Juliet? Do you think he should have?

- *Systems and Strategy for NT Rationals:* (1) Identify the themes in *Romeo and Juliet* and outline their development through the play. (2) If you were the prince, what would you have done to stop the feuding?

Table 20   Books and Ratings By Temperament and Type Preference

Books	SJ	SP	NF	NT	E	I	S	N	T	F	J	P
Action/Adventure	2	3					2		2			3
Biographies	2	1					1			2	1	
Choose Your Own Adventure		3		2					2			2
Comic Books	2	3					2					2
Crime/Detective	1	2					2					2
Documentaries	2	2		1			2		2		1	
Fantasy			3	2				2		2		
Guiness Book of World Records	2	3		2	2		2		2			
Historical Fiction	3		2						2			
Horror		3							2			
"How-To" Books	2	2		1			2		2			
Magazines	2	2	1	1	2		2					
Myth and Legends	1		3	1				2				
Poetry			2							2		
Reference Works				2					2			
Romance			2							2		
Science Fiction			2	3				2	2			
Novels						2				2		
Short Stories		2			2							

SJ = Guardian; SP = Artisan; NF = Idealist; and NT = Rational.
3 = Really Likes; 2 = Often Likes; 1 = Likes Certain Applications; and Blank = Too Many Variables.

Chapter 14

Games and Computers

Classroom Games and Other Activities

Most teachers enjoy using games and computers in their classrooms, primarily because their students enjoy them. Because of the simple fact that students who like what they are doing are better learners, such activities offer teachers opportunities to introduce materials and concepts to receptive learners. Most teachers generally prefer that these activities have educational objectives in order to capitalize on student interest. The techniques given in this chapter provide effective ways for teachers to teach all students content, to arouse their curiosity, and to review material using games and computers. But teachers should keep in mind that each student will react to them differently. For instance, SP Artisans are the most fond of games because they view life as a game. Some introverted NT Rationals may dislike games because they prefer to work independently on what interests them. Some of the more specific temperament- and type-based differences will be discussed in this chapter.

Spelling Bees

SP Artisans, particularly Extraverted ones, are the most likely to enjoy spelling bees. Perceiving types, in general, like the spontaneity of spelling bees. SJ Guardians may also enjoy demonstrating how well they have memorized the words, but they usually prefer written tests. Introverted Intuitives are the ones most likely to dislike these contests.

Timed Tests

SP Artisans often enjoy timed tests that enable them to compete against a previous score or another student's score. Perceiving types usually like to have the opportunity to "beat the clock."

SJ Guardians often have difficulty with timed tests. They are likely to read each question several times so that they are certain they understand the question. They also want to be sure that they have the right answer *before* they write it down. On timed tests, SJ Guardians need to be encouraged to write down the first answer that comes into their heads. They can then go back later if there is time to check their work.

Review Statements

An easy but fun classroom game that appeals especially to Sensing types and NT Rationals is writing on the board two or three review statements with something wrong in each. The students enjoy catching the teacher's mistake, especially if the teacher pretends to be oblivious (What? You mean that isn't right?). This game works well with math (e.g., $12.8 - 4 = 12.4$) and with grammar (e.g., This information is just between you and I). Extraverts will likely enjoy this more than Introverts. Thinkers enjoy the challenge of catching another's error.

Mad Libs

Mad Libs is a wonderful game to help students remember the basic parts of speech, and it can be purchased relatively cheaply at almost any bookstore. This is a game in which the teacher, according to the Mad Lib, asks the students for a word that is a particular part of speech. Usually the story the teacher reads back with the words the students have supplied is hilarious. Almost all styles of students enjoy this activity, but it especially appeals to the sense of humor of SP Artisans and NT Rationals. Both Extraverts and Introverts can become involved, although Extraverts tend to enjoy it more because they have the opportunity to show off by coming up with a particularly good word. Sometimes Introverts would rather watch the others, and this is still a good way to learn the parts of speech. Intuitives often come up with the most creative words.

Parts of Speech

This game is also good for reviewing parts of speech. It can be made much more advanced than Mad Libs. This is a game that students play in teams, which appeals to Feeling types, both SFs and NF Idealists. Each student receives a piece of paper with a part of speech on it—a noun, adjective, verb, adverb, preposition, or conjunction—and comes up with a word that is that part of speech. Other students on the team continue until they form a complete sentence. Sensing types, both SJ Guardians and SP Artisans, like to physically become a part of a sentence.

Logic Puzzles and Games

Logic puzzles and puzzles in general appeal to Intuitives, especially NT Rationals. Puzzles help develop critical thinking skills, which Thinkers enjoy. A multitude of puzzle books are available.

Intuitives enjoy one-minute or two-minute mysteries in which the reader (or class) must find the logical inconsistencies in order to determine who is guilty. Donald J. Sobol has written many of these kinds of books. He has a series of *Encyclopedia Brown* books that are suitable for upper elementary-age students. There is also a series of books called *One-Minute* or *Two-Minute Mysteries* by Austin Ripley or Donald J. Sobol that is appropriate for the high school level.

A logic game that requires no materials is called, "Mr. Green likes...." Students are given words or phrases or sentences describing things Mr. Green likes and does not like and are challenged to find the common rule behind them. For example, "Mr. Green likes green but he does not like red. Mr. Green likes the moon but he does not like the sun. Mr. Green likes beets but he does not like carrots. Mr. Green likes poodles but he does not like dogs." The rule in this example is that Mr. Green likes anything with a double vowel. Mr. Green could also like only three-syllable words or only words or phrases that are also titles of books or movies, or words that have p's in them or words made up of letters from the first half of the alphabet. NT Rationals enjoy this game because it requires them to discover the underlying system. They especially enjoy it if they can push the system toward an illogical statement. SP Artisans enjoy the game because they like to beat the competition.

"Who Am I?"

Another good game, especially for Intuitives, is "Who Am I?" Sensing types also enjoy the game, but may not be as strategic in their sequence of questioning. In this game, the teacher mentally picks a well-known person or character whom the students will attempt to identify by asking yes/no questions, such as, Was this person famous? Is the person living? Is this person male/female, over 40? This game can be used to review historical names or literary characters and it can be simplified by using animals for younger students. By helping students formulate a strategy for asking questions, teachers can help them move from generalities to specifics. NTJs, in particular, enjoy learning about effective strategies.

Mind Reader

This game has two objectives. The first is to challenge students' critical thinking skills to discover the rule; the second is to increase rapport between the teacher and one student who is the mind reader. The teacher first picks a student to be the mind reader and explains the rule. The rule is that the tens digit of the first number given by the teacher tells the student which number will be the correct one. For example, if the teacher says, "Is the number 47?" the student knows that the fourth number the teacher says will be the correct one. Next, the student stands in the back of the class facing the rear. The teacher will probably want to say something like, "Jimmy and I can read each other's minds. Would you like us to prove it?" The other students then pick a number between 10 and 100. The teacher asks the mind reader, "Is the number __?" The students will be amazed when the mind reader says yes for the right number. NTs and other Thinkers will usually work hard to try and break the code and will come up with theories that the teacher and mind reader can prove or disprove. Extraverted SPs are the most likely to enjoy being the mind reader. To establish further rapport, the teacher can ask the mind reader to explain the rule if no one has discovered it.

Students can be encouraged to design their own "secret code" in order to play mind reader with the teacher. Usually, a student comes up with the idea of using the ones digit as the clue, so that if the teacher says, "Is the number 47?" the student would know that the seventh number would be the correct one. They could choose formulas that are two more so that 47 would now mean $(7 + 2 = 9)$ that the ninth number would be the correct one.

Trivia

Another game many students enjoy is trivia. SP Artisans enjoy trivia related to physical things (e.g., the fastest runner, the most doughnuts eaten in a half-hour period). NT Rationals enjoy science trivia (e.g., it takes 75,000 pine trees to make a million copies of the *New York Times* Sunday edition, scallops have 34 blue eyes). NF Idealists enjoy learning about people (e.g., ancient Egyptians used black eyeliner, green eyeshadow, and black lipstick to decorate their faces). SJ Guardians like comparisons (e.g., the tallest building, the smallest adult, the longest-lived person). Good sources for trivia are *The Guiness Book of World Records* and history trivia books.

Computer Logic

An excellent technique for teaching Sensing children how computers work comes from Pam Clute, education faculty member at the University of California at Riverside. Thinking types find logic sequencing challenging and fun. Perceiving types enjoy the chaos that occurs during this process.

In this game, the teacher pretends to be a computer, and the student attempts to give the computer instructions for doing something, for example, making a peanut butter and jelly sandwich. (The teacher will need sandwich-making supplies on hand.)

For example, the student might say, "Put peanut butter on the bread." The teacher, as the computer, would say, "But I do not know how to do that." Next, the student might say, "Open the bag of bread. Pull out two pieces of bread." Then the teacher might rip the bag open (instead of taking the twist tie off the top) and pull out the bread. Next, the student might say, "Use the knife to put peanut butter on one slice of the bread." So the teacher might stab with the knife at the top of the unopened peanut butter jar. This goes on until the sandwich is made. Then the teacher has the student write a recipe for making a peanut butter and jelly sandwich using the new kind of logic they have learned. All types and temperaments can benefit from learning to break down their thinking into distinct steps.

Bluff

Another game coming from Pam Clute is called "Bluff." In this game, the teacher divides the class into two teams, A and B. Team A is asked a question. Within a specified time limit, everyone who has the answer written down or is bluffing stands up. The number of students standing represents the number of points that team will receive if the first person gets the answer right. Some students choose to bluff in hopes of getting more points. Then the teacher picks one person from Team B to pick one of the students who is standing. If the person from Team A who is picked has the correct answer, Team A receives the full number of points. If the person picked gets the answer wrong, however, the student who picked the respondent can win all the points for his or her team by giving the correct answer.

This game, which can be used for many subjects, is enjoyed by all types and especially by Extraverts and SP Artisans. NT Rationals like to be the respondent in subjects they know well. Students who are very Introverted may have difficulties, although they can still participate without risking that they will receive too much attention.

Easy Review

This review game uses questions designed by the teacher to review material that has recently been learned. Thinking types will do best with factual and mathematical reviews, and Feeling types will do best with people-oriented subjects. It is best to use questions of both types so students have a good chance of getting a question that suits them. SJ Guardians like to demonstrate that they know the work they are expected to know. SP Artisans and NT Rationals like the competition this process involves. Extraverts usually like being called on.

The game is very simple. Each student puts his or her name on one piece of paper and puts it in a hat. The teacher asks a question and then chooses a name out of the hat, giving the student five seconds to answer the question.

Since Introverts may need a longer response time, teachers should allow enough time for students to come up with the answer *before* they draw a name. Teachers can also help Introverted students by asking them if they know the answer first and moving on to the next student if they do not. This will take the attention off Introverts, who may feel like everyone's eyes are on them, regardless of whether it is true or not.

Jeopardy

This game is patterned loosely after the television game show *Jeopardy*. In this game, students are divided into three to five groups and the teacher makes up a list of questions, assigning values of 10, 20, 30, or 40 points to them, according to their level of difficulty. Breaking up the questions into categories is optional.

The first group can pick how many points they want to try to earn, remembering that the higher the point value, the harder the question. The teacher then gives them the question (a time limit is optional). If they get the question right, they get the points. If they get it wrong, the teacher either gives the correct answer and goes on or allows the next group the opportunity to earn the points. In either case, the next group will then pick their own question, whether or not the first group got theirs right.

NT Rationals enjoy the intellectual challenge of this game, SP Artisans like the competition, and SJ Guardians and NF Idealists enjoy the familiarity of the game. Introverts will usually like this game because they are not personally put on the spot to provide the answers. The group response will normally be given by an Extravert who likes the chance to shine. The change of pace in the game appeals to Perceiving types.

Computers

Computers are here to stay in the classroom even though, according to the *Los Angeles Times* (Weber, 1994), "there is little evidence that computers in themselves lead to sustained improvement in educational performance." Computers *can* help students, but teachers need to be properly trained in what software programs to use, how to use them, and what programs are likely to appeal to which kind of student.

We cannot possibly discuss all the various educational software programs that are available, as there are far too many programs available and technology is changing so rapidly. Instead, we will discuss some general principles about what kinds of programs will appeal to different temperaments and preferences.

In general, Introverts like working on computers more than will Extraverts, and Thinking types more than Feeling types.

SJ Guardians like programs that value accuracy over speed. A current example of this is the game Where in the World Is Carmen San Diego? In order to win this game, students must use reference materials such as the *World Almanac.* SP Artisans would rather randomly guess than spend time researching, which can make the game frustrating for them. Intuitives also like this game because of its puzzle-solving aspect.

SP Artisans prefer fast-paced, arcade-style programs. They want to beat their previous time or score (or beat the best student in the class). They often also like computer art projects.

NF Idealists like to do creative projects on the computer, such as writing a creative story or designing a banner.

NT Rationals are usually very attracted to computers because of their logic-based operation. They like problem-solving programs. A program called *Archetype* is based on a game in which students dig in a sandbox for objects and then analyze them. NT Rationals would like this program, while SP Artisans would rather actually go dig in the sand.

All students need to learn word processing in order to function in the world of work. Feeling types can be motivated to learn word processing if they can use the computer to write letters to friends, for example. Thinking types can be motivated if they can write papers on the computer and use the spelling and grammar checkers (a pragmatic approach to raising one's grade).

Table 21   Games and Activities and Ratings By Temperament and Type Preference

Strategy	SJ	SP	NF	NT	E	I	S	N	T	F	J	P
Games and Activities												
Spelling Bees	2	3			2	C	2					2
Timed Tests	C	2										2
Review Statements	2	2		2	2		2		2			
Mad Libs	2	3	2	3	3	2						
Parts of Speech	2	3	2	1	3		2			3		
Logic Puzzles and Games		1	2	3				2	3			
"Who Am I?"	1	2	2	3	3	2		3				
Trivia	2	2	2	2								
Mind Reader		3	2	2					2			
Computer Logic	2	3	1	1			2		2			2
Bluff	1	3	1	2	3	1						2
Easy Review	2	1	1	2	2	C						
Jeopardy	1	2	1	3	2	1						2
Computer Games												
Arcade	1	3		2	1	2	2		2			3
Art and Graphics	1	2	3	1		2			1	2		2
Mystery Adventure		2		3				1	2			2
Strategy/Problem Solving		2		3		2		2	3		2	1

SJ = Guardian; SP = Artisan; NF = Idealist; and NT = Rational.
3 = Really Likes; 2 = Often Likes; 1 = Likes Certain Applications; C = Caution; and Blank = Too Many Variables.

Intuitives often find that word processing programs help them to develop and refine their ideas. Some SJ Guardians like to type as much of their work as possible, simply because they find typing to be so neat.

Table 21 summarizes the games and activities discussed in this chapter and ranks their level of appeal to students with different temperaments and type preferences.

Chapter 15

Teaching and Learning Styles in Action

Students tend to learn best under teachers who are the same type as themselves. While this should probably come as no surprise, it does *not* mean that students should be grouped in classes so that their type matches other students' and that of the teacher. This would not be serving their needs, as students need to see many types around them so they can best develop their own type without being prematurely labeled. They need to have the opportunity to experiment without being told something along the lines of, "You are an SJ Guardian, so that means you should be responsible, punctual, and a lover of routine."

Even if they are SJ Guardians, they will not necessarily be responsible, punctual, and lovers of routine. *All* people need to learn to operate effectively in *all* of the preferences. Children are unlikely to learn to use preferences that are not natural for them if those preferences are not modeled by the people around them, including by their parents, teachers, and classmates.

Let's imagine that we could create a classroom in which every person in the class was only one temperament—say all SJ Guardians. While a lot of academic learning would take place, the students would not be learning how to accept and appreciate differences. Each member of the class would probably exhibit more and more SJ Guardian qualities and find it increasingly difficult to operate in the Intuitive and Perceiving modes. The class would be likely to be highly routinized with little creativity and excitement. They would probably become more closeminded and more intolerant of differences in others. The same type of argument would apply for each of the other styles. The point is, children will only learn to appreciate diversity if they come into contact with it. All of the types need each other.

Because people are truly different from each other, we sometimes find it difficult to communicate with others at times. In the following sections, we will discuss two processes that may help teachers bridge the gap between their personal teaching style and the needs of their students. The first process helps teachers evaluate their teaching techniques and the impact of these techniques. If there are still students who are having difficulties, teachers should move on to the next process, which is to personalize a program for the individual student.

Evaluating Teaching Techniques and Their Impact

It is best if teachers begin by evaluating the impact of teaching techniques that they currently use. The teacher needs to be competent and feel comfortable in the technique's use.

- *Self-identification.* Reviewing chapters 2 and 3 on temperament and type and chapters 4 through 7 on teaching styles will help teachers to pinpoint their styles with more accuracy. Taking the MBTI inventory from a school counselor is the most accurate way to identify type.

- *Favored teaching techniques and their predicted impact.* Identifying teaching techniques that are commonly used by the styles described in chapters 4 through 7 will help teachers identify which teaching techniques that they prefer. Teachers can then choose one technique to research. Table 17 in chapter 12 on teaching techniques will help teachers identify which styles of student this technique usually reaches.

- *Student observation.* Once they have decided on a technique, teachers should observe which students have difficulty learning from this technique. What kinds of behavioral patterns are these students exhibiting? What kinds of difficulties are they having? For example, do they need more guidelines? Are they unable to sit still? Are they daydreaming? Do they question the exercise itself?

- *Research on students experiencing difficulty.* Teachers can then use chapters 8 through 11 to identify the probable styles of students who are having difficulty. Are the students who are having difficulty of a different style from those who are predicted to enjoy this teaching technique? Which kinds of teaching techniques are effective for these students?

- *Adapting or changing teaching techniques.* Is there some way the current technique could be adapted to reach the students who are having difficulty? After adapting the technique, teachers should again observe student behavior to see how effective they have been. If some students are still having problems, teachers should move on to Process B.

The following example will illustrate how the steps in this process can be used in an actual teaching situation.

Lola teaches high school biology and assigns independent projects for her students. She has always believed that students are best challenged by independent study. Now she wants to test her hypothesis by using this process. Using self-identification, Lola takes the MBTI inventory and is identified as an INTP. She verifies this by reviewing chapters 2 and 3 on temperament and type preferences. She sees herself as an NT Rational and agrees that she is probably an Introvert. She's not sure about the J–P preference. Then she turns to chapter 7 and reads the description of INTP and INTJ. She identifies herself as most like an INTP (Inventor/Definer).

Looking at favored teaching techniques and their predicted impact, Lola finds it interesting that INTPs like independent study as a teaching technique. She looks at table 17 in chapter 12 and sees that independent study is most favored by NT Rationals, like herself. The table also indicates that independent study works at some level for all styles but is more favored by Introverts.

Observing her students, Lola watches carefully to see how students are responding to her technique. She notices that the students she sees as generally quiet are concentrating on the project and showing good progress. She also notices that the students experiencing difficulty with the project seem restless and want to draw her into conversations about it. She has observed that these students usually are outgoing.

Considering research on students who experience difficulty, Lola suspects that these students may be Extraverts and reviews the description of Extraverts in chapter 3. The description fits her perceptions of the students. She looks up independent study in table 17 in chapter 12. She sees that Extraverts are not rated as favoring this technique. She decides to concentrate on meeting the needs of her Extraverted students.

Taking into account adapting or changing her technique a week into the four-week assignment, Lola allows students time to discuss their projects with each other. She observes that the Extraverts begin to complain less about the project. A few students ask her if they can work together on a project. She carefully sets up boundaries to allow her teaching technique to be adapted in this way.

As a result of using the process of evaluating teaching techniques and their impact, Lola has made some variations in the assignment to meet differing student needs. At the end of the project, she compares the results to those of last semester. The students' report of enjoyment is much higher than last semester, and Lola believes that the quality of the work has also improved.

Personalizing a Program for Students Experiencing Difficulty

There are always a few students in each classroom who the teacher has difficulty reaching. Many times, these difficulties result from the student having diverging needs from the teacher due to style differences. The following process will help teachers strike a balance between their own style needs and those of their student's. It provides a way to experiment with techniques that are more likely to meet the student's needs.

- *Self-identification.* Teachers should perform the self-identification step by using the same process described in the previous section, if they have not already done so.

- *Identifying the student's probable style.* Chapters 2 and 3 will help teachers identify students' probable type preferences and temperament. It is rare that a student having difficulty is the exact same style as the teacher. Chapters 8 through 11 will help teachers identify the style(s) most similar to the student's behavior.

- *Identifying effective teaching techniques for this style.* Table 17 in chapter 12 will help teachers identify which techniques might reach the styles that appear to be most like the student. Teachers need to determine whether these teaching techniques are commonly favored by their own style. If not, this may be an opportunity for teachers to expand their teaching abilities.

- *Choosing two techniques to test.* Teachers should select two techniques they would like to try and note the results of using them. Has some improvement occurred? Often the technique will need to be used a few times before real growth will be apparent. The two techniques need an adequate test.

- *Choosing additional techniques to test.* If the techniques work, teachers can gradually add more techniques that are targeted for this style of student. They should emphasize the student's competencies in the techniques aimed at their style. Students' feelings of success will usually help them improve their performance in techniques aimed at other styles. The student will also probably respond to the teacher's efforts by adapting better to techniques that the teacher favors.

- *Reassessing personal style.* If several techniques do not work, teachers need to reassess the student's style by repeating the previous steps.

The following example will illustrate how the steps in this process can be used in an actual teaching situation.

Carlos teaches math to seventh graders. Previously, he taught students on the upper track in a different school district. His new school does not track students into differing levels of ability. He is finding more disruption in the classroom and is feeling very frustrated. One student named Mark is creating particular problems. Mark seems bright, but spends more time being the class clown and acting disruptively than he does doing his work. Carlos has two objectives: to find a technique that will improve Mark's performance and to cut down on the amount of Mark's classroom disruptive behavior.

After undertaking self-identification, Carlos was identified as an ISTJ on the MBTI inventory. He verifies this by reviewing chapter 3 on type preferences. Referring to chapter 2, he identifies himself as an SJ Guardian. He checks chapter 3 on type preferences and identifies himself as an ESTJ or ISTJ. Then he reads the descriptions for ESTJ and ISTJ in chapter 4 and decides that he is most like an ISTJ (Monitor/Inspector).

Considering Mark's probable style, Carlos uses chapter 3 to identify the E and P preferences as most like Mark, but he is not sure on the S–N and T–F dimensions. He consults chapter 2 and finds the SP Artisan is most like Mark and the SJ Guardian is least like him. He then reads the ESTP and ESFP descriptions in chapter 9. They both have elements that seem to fit Mark. He also consults chapters 10 and 11 to read the ENFP and ENTP descriptions. Neither of these descriptions appears to fit Mark as well. Carlos decides that Mark is behaving most like either an ESFP (Performer/Actor) or an ESTP (Operator/Negotiator).

Considering the effective teaching techniques for Mark's probable style, Carlos checks table 17 in chapter 12 to see what techniques might reach an Extraverted SP Artisan. He discovers that Mark might enjoy teaching techniques that he does not commonly use. Carlos decides to expand his teaching abilities.

From table 21, Carlos has selected Bluff and Mind Reader as two techniques that might be effective for Mark. He also notes that Bluff might be fun for SP Artisan and NT Rational students and for Extraverted students. Carlos believes that Mind Reader would give Mark the attention he desires. He experiments with these techniques and notes the results.

Carlos doesn't want to give Mark the Mind Reader role until there has been some improvement in his behavior, so he begins with Bluff. All of the students have fun challenging each other to solve math problems. The Extraverts have a specific time when it is okay for them to talk and Carlos still feels in control of his classroom. Mark begins to pay more attention in class because he wants to be able to win at Bluff. His performance begins to improve.

Carlos takes Mark aside and talks about the fun they could have challenging the class with a new game. Mark responds to the positive attention. Carlos teaches him how to be the mind reader. Because Mark enjoys the attention he gets as the mind reader, he helps Carlos with keeping the class in line. His classroom and academic performance improve. Both Mark and Carlos are winners.

By choosing additional techniques, Carlos decides to see what other techniques he could use to keep Mark's performance at this new level. He decides to try some ideas from the book *Bet You Can't* by V. Cobb and K. Darling. Carlos had found that when he added more play and a chance for the Extraverts to talk in his math class, the students enjoyed the class more. The resistance to math has been reduced and several students, as well as Mark, are showing improved performance.

Carlos has been successful with Mark, so he does not need to reassess Mark's personal style. However, he decides to choose another student who is having difficulty and repeat this process. Carlos has found it highly gratifying to achieve success with a challenging student like Mark and wants to repeat his success.

Some Final Thoughts

There is no perfect classroom in which all students are engaged in learning all of the time. This is partly because students are all different. A strategy designed to motivate SP Artisans often leaves NF Idealists cold because Artisans love competition but Idealists are likely to view competition as unharmonious. Activities designed for Extraverts may seem too loud to Introverts and may feel like a violation of their type. Puzzles designed to challenge NT Rationals will often not connect with other students. As long as teachers reach most of the students they are attempting to reach with a particular strategy, they can consider that strategy to be a success. Of course, they may decide that they need to offer alternate tasks for the other types. Again, no one strategy can possibly reach all students all of the time.

It is impossible for teachers to apply all of the suggestions in this book. In the first place, they do not have enough time to do them all. In the second place, none of the ideas provided in this book will work for all teachers. When selecting techniques to try, it is usually best for teachers to pick something that naturally appeals to them and not necessarily the things they feel they need to work on most. When trying some of the specific strategies outlined in this book, it is probably best to use only one or two ideas, for a short period of time, say, two weeks. After becoming comfortable with these new techniques, some new approaches may be added. The suggested strategy for applying this book given in chapter 15 should help teachers evaluate each technique's value. Again, it is best to give each technique a chance to have an effect before deciding to move on to another one.

It is important to find a balance between standardization and customization of teaching techniques. Too much standardization puts some types at a disadvantage if none of the techniques offered are appropriate for their style. Overcustomization to meet each student's needs may lead to classroom confusion and exhaustion for the teacher. It is important for teachers to find the appropriate balance for their own style and teaching experience.

Teachers can use type to help them recognize their students' strengths. Teachers' attitudes toward students they find particularly difficult will change as they come to understand more about the particular student's learning style, needs, and motivations—instead of labeling a student as irresponsible, they could be seen as flexible and exciting. As the student becomes convinced that the teacher values him or her, the student's behavior will often become more positive.

A recognition of type can also help teachers develop a more productive classroom environment. SJ Guardians are happiest in classrooms that are organized and have clear and consistent standards for behavior and academic achievement. SP Artisans enjoy classrooms that allow for some "wiggle room" and sometimes have surprises and breaks from the routine. NF Idealists prefer harmonious classrooms in which each student is valued as an individual. NT Rationals perform best in classrooms in which their ideas are heard and respected and which allow for some autonomy in learning.

Extraverted students will function best when there is some interaction among students, such as group work, class discussion, and games. Introverted students will function best when they are allowed some quiet time to think and reflect. Sensing students like lessons that are concretely based with step-by-step instruction. Sensing students do not typically see hidden meanings as quickly as Intuitives. Intuitive students like lessons in which they must look beneath the surface to find answers, but Intuitive students are not as practical and aware as Sensing types. Feeling students need a harmonious environment, while Thinking students need a logical one. Perceiving students produce their best work when there are not too many rules and they are occasionally allowed to be spontaneous. Judging students produce their best work when there is closure—projects get finished and grade standards are clear.

Where to Go From Here

You may decide that your students could benefit from learning about their own learning style. There are two books that are available to help teachers teach type and temperament to their students. Both are excellent resources and are well written. *Type Tales: Teaching Type to Children* (Farris, 1991) consists of stories designed to be read by teachers to their elementary students. The book has questions at the back for teachers to discuss with their students after they have read the stories. Each chapter illustrates one of the four sets of preferences. *Are You My Type? or Why Aren't You More Like Me?* (Wirths and Bowman-Kruhm, 1992) is for middle school and high school students. It is written in a friendly, easy-to-read style that appeals to adolescents. Each chapter describes one of the four temperaments.

Even if you do not introduce these ideas to your students, it is good to help instill in them the idea that people are different from each other. Tell them that, while they may enjoy a particular activity, another student may completely dislike it and vice versa. Remind them that it is impossible for a person to be good at everything. Explain to them that something that is very easy for them may be very difficult for another student and vice versa. Telling students these things accomplishes two purposes: It helps students not to get too upset over activities in which they are not able to perform well, and it helps them to be tolerant of your attempts to reach students whose learning styles are different from their own.

If you do choose to teach type, ensure that you are first very comfortable with the theory. The most important thing to teach students is of *all* learning styles appreciation. Emphasize that *all* types have strengths and that all have weaknesses. Your natural prejudices for and against particular student types will be apparent, so take care to present the positive portrait that each student type deserves of each type. Teach your students that we each need the other types' strengths, and that we each have strengths to offer others.

Discuss with your entire class or cooperative learning groups the attributes of each learning style. What are its strengths? How does each type of students create conflict with others? Can you name a person you know who is a particular type (Why do you think they are that type?)? After teaching your students about the different learning styles and types of students and preferences, you will almost certainly find that they will be much more tolerant of each other and of you.

Remember that wonderful teachers and wonderful students are of *all* types. There is no better place than the classroom to experience the power and potential of the personality connection. All teachers have a unique opportunity to make that connection and to achieve truly effective teaching and effective learning.

Afterword

We would enjoy hearing from you. Please send us your stories about using temperament and type in education. Since there is little available research on the application of temperament and type in education, shared testimony and experience will help us to reach consensus about what is optimal for each teacher/student style. Your personal experiences and observations regarding temperament and type can help other teachers.

Tell us how this understanding helped you or someone else. Please give us plenty of details about your experiences, along with the types/temperaments of the people involved, if you know them. Remember that "failures" can give other teachers as much insight as "successes." We would especially appreciate stories including multicultural and diverse students.

Please send us your stories in care of Davies-Black Publishing, 3803 E. Bayshore Road, Palo Alto, CA 94303. Thank you.

Temperament Needs, Roles, and Archetypes

This appendix contains two tables that provide a quick summary of what major theorists have perceived as the main needs, roles, and archetypes of the four temperaments and their major subsets. The first organizes the four temperaments to illustrate their comparative names from other works that describe similar personality traits.

The second breaks the four temperaments into the eight subsets that are used in the chapters of parts 2 and 3 of this book. Using various titles for these groupings, other writers have focused on these eight themes. The descriptive names can help teachers see what types of roles different students are likely to play in the classroom.

This appendix is mainly included for those who wish to get a greater background in the theoretical underpinnings of this work. Readers are encouraged to refer to the Resources and References section in the back of this book for materials written by the theorists mentioned to gain a greater understanding of the similarities in themes in the writings.

Table A.1 The Four Temperaments and Their Core Needs and Archetypes

Theorists Keirsey and Myers	NF Idealists	SJ Guardians
Core Needs and Wants	Identity and Self-Actualization Meaning and Significance	Membership and Belonging Responsibility and Duty
Keirsey and Bates	Appolonian	Epimethean
Hippocrates	Choleric	Melancholic
Paracelsus	Nymph/Water	Gnome/Earth
Kretchmer	Hyperaesthetic	Depressive
Spranger	Religious	Economic
Golay	Conceptual-Global Learner	Actual-Routine Learner
	Animal Metaphors	*Animal Metaphors*
Keirsey and Berens	Unicorn/Dolphin	Beaver
Niednagle	Stork	Bee
Golay	Dolphin	Bear

Keirsey and Myers	NT Rationals	SP Artisans
Core Needs and Wants	Knowledge and Competence Power and Mastery	Freedom and Action Excitation and Variation
Keirsey and Bates	Promethean	Dionisian
Hippocrates	Phlegmatic	Sanguine
Paracelsus	Sylph/Air	Salamander/Fire
Kretchmer	Anaesthetic	Hypomanic
Spranger	Theoretic	Aesthetic
Golay	Conceptual-Specific Learner	Actual-Spontaneous Learner
	Animal Metaphors	*Animal Metaphors*
Keirsey and Berens	Owl	Fox
Niednagle	Owl	Hummingbird
Golay	Owl	Ape

Note: From the names used by Keirsey (1988) and Myers (1980, 1985), we use the names for the temperament subsets that we believe are most useful in the teaching profession.

Adapted from the works of *Physique and Character* (Kretschmer, 1925), *Types of Men* (Spranger, 1966), *Gifts Differing* (Myers and Myers, 1980, 1995), *Learning Patterns and Temperament Styles* (Golay, 1982), *Please Understand Me* (Keirsey and Bates, 1984), *Portraits of Temperaments* (Keirsey, 1988), *Temperament Report Form* (Berens, 1988), and *How to Choose Your Best Sport and Play It* (Niednagel, 1992).

Table A.2   Temperament Subsets, Archetypes, and Roles

Theorists	Directive	Informative	Directive	Informative
	NF Idealist **Guidance/Advocacy**		**SJ Guardian** **Logistics/Facilitation**	
	NFJ Mentor	*NFP Advocate*	*STJ Monitor*	*SFJ Provider*
Keirsey	Mentor	Advocate	Monitor	Conservator
Berens	Foreseer	Proponent	Overseer	Provider
Roach	People-Developer	Culture-Builder	Castle-Operator	People-Manager
Symbolic Animal Keirsey	Horse Unicorn	Deer Unicorn	Beaver	Squirrel
Prototypic Archetype Rytting	Medium	Companion	Father	Mother
	NT Rational **Strategy/Design**		**SP Artisan** **Tactics/Performance**	
	NTJ Organizer	*NTP Inventor*	*STP Operator*	*SFP Performer*
Keirsey	Organizer	Engineer	Operator	Player
Berens	Director	Inventor	Maneuverer	Performer
Roach	Castle-Builder	Castle-Designer	Efficiency-Expert	People-Catalyst
Symbolic Animal Keirsey	Eagle	Owl	Fox/Wolf	Hound/Puppy
Prototypic Archetype Rytting	Amazon	Sage	Warrior	Youth

Note: From the names used by Keirsey (1988) and Berens (1988), we use the names for the temperament subsets that we believe are most useful in the teaching profession.

Directive: Comfortable with giving directives to others; focused on task plus effort and time to achieve completion; often seen as "tough" or having a male characteristic. *Informative:* Comfortable with giving information, focused on being persuasive and allowing others freedom of choice; often seen as "friendly" or having a female characteristic.

Adapted from the works of David Keirsey (1988), *Portraits of Temperament;* Linda V. Berens (1988), *Temperament Report Form;* and Ben Roach (1987); *Strategy Styles and Management Types,* and Marvin Rytting (1990), "Androgynous Archetypes."

Temperament/Type Representations in Specific U.S. Populations

The following statistics have been gathered from *Gifts Differing* by Isabel Briggs Myers (1980, 1995) and *Please Understand Me* by David Kiersey and Marilyn Bates (1984). It is interesting to note that of the 8,072 high school juniors and seniors, only 27 percent were SP Artisans. This is below the number that would be expected. Either the SP Artisans had dropped out of the system, or they may have tested as a different type. These figures provide some indication of how representative the different temperaments are in educational populations.

Table B.1 The Four Temperaments and Their Representation in Educational Population Groups in Percentages

Population Group (size of sample)	SJ Guardian	SP Artisan	NF Idealist	NT Rational
General U.S. population	38	38	12	12
11th and 12th graders (8,072)	44	27	16	13
College prep. (4,758)	36	24	21	18
Noncollege prep. (3,314)	56	31	8	5
National Merit Finalists (1,001)	11	6	36	46
Engineering majors (2,188)	27	8	22	43
Finance and commerce majors (488)	43	28	10	18
Science majors (705)	10	7	26	57
Counselor education majors (118)	10	5	76	8
Law students (1,874)	30	11	16	43
Urban police (280)	56	24	8	12
Elementary Teachers	50	13	27	10
Middle and Junior High School Teachers	45	11	30	15
High School Teachers	42	7	34	16
Community College Teachers	35	7	34	23
University Teachers	30	6	33	31
Administrators (124)	55	7	34	23

Table information adapted from Isabel Briggs Myers with Peter B. Myers, *Gifts Differing: Understanding Personality Type* (Palo Alto, Calif.: Davies-Black Publishing, 1980, 1995), pp. 31–51, p. 134; and D. Keirsey and M. Bates, *Please Understand Me: Character and Temperament Types*, 5th ed. (Del Mar, Calif.: Prometheus Nemesis, 1984), p. 155.

Appendix C

Grade and Age Equivalence in the United States

The information in the following table on grade and age equivalence and other aspects of the educational system in the United States is intended to assist readers who may wish to apply the information in this book to educational systems in other countries.

Table C.1   Grade and Approximate Student Age in U.S. Education

Grade Level	Approximate Student Ages
Kindergarten (K)	4 1/2 to 6 Years Old
First	6 to 7 Years Old
Second	7 to 8 Years Old
Third	8 to 9 Years Old
Fourth	9 to 10 Years Old
Fifth	10 to 11 Years Old
Sixth	11 to 12 Years Old
Seventh	12 to 13 Years Old
Eighth	13 to 14 Years Old
Ninth (Freshman)	14 to 15 Years Old
Tenth (Sophomore)	15 to 16 Years Old
Eleventh (Junior)	16 to 17 Years Old
Twelfth (Senior)	17 to 18 Years Old
College/University	18 Years Old and Older

Grade Group Names	Grade Equivalents
Primary grades	K–3
Elementary school	K–6 (occasionally K–8)
Middle school	6–8
Junior high school	7–8 or 7–9
Senior high school or high school	9–12 or 10–12
Junior college or community college	Two-year college
University or college	Four-year college

Resources and References

Bals, J. "Type, APT's Mission and Ethics." *Bulletin of Psychological Type* 18 (1995): 1, 5–8.

Barrette, L. "The Relationship of Observable Teaching Effectiveness Behaviors to MBTI Personality Types." *Meeting the Challenge, Psychological Type for the 90s Conference Proceedings,* Richmond, Va.: Association for Psychological Type, 1991.

Battle, P. "Masks That We Wear: The Practitioner's Interpretation of Type in Different Cultures." Working paper, International Type Users Organization Conference, Montreal, Quebec, Canada, August 1994.

Berens, L. V. "A Comparison of Jungian Function Theory and Keirseyan Temperament Theory in the Use of the Myers-Briggs Type Indicator." Ph.D. diss., United States International University, 1985.

Berens, L. V. *Temperament Report Form.* Huntington Beach, Calif.: Telos Publications, 1988.

Berens, L. V., and A. M. Fairhurst. *Temperament Targets.* Huntington Beach, Calif.: Telos Publications, 1989.

Bissell, R. "Lend Me Your EARs (Expanded Analysis Reports)." Paper presented at the annual meeting of the Southern California Chapter of APT, Anaheim, Calif., May 1995.

Bridges, W. *Job Shift: How to Prosper in a Workplace Without Jobs.* New York: Addison-Wesley Publishing Company, 1994.

Bridges, W. *The Character of Organizations: Using Jungian Type in Organizational Development.* Palo Alto, Calif.: Davies-Black Publishing, 1992.

Briggs, K. C., and I. B. Myers. *Myers-Briggs Type Indicator, Form G.* Palo Alto, Calif.: Consulting Psychologists Press, 1987.

Brownsword, A. W. *It Takes All Types!* San Anselmo, Calif.: Baytree Publications, 1987.

Burns, M. *The Book of Think.* Boston: Little, Brown, 1976.

Burns, M. *The I Hate Mathematics Book.* Boston: Little, Brown, 1975.

Carskadon, T. G., and D. D. Cook. "Validity of MBTI Type Descriptions as Perceived by Recipients Unfamiliar With Type." *Research in Psychological Type* 5 (1982): 89–94.

Casas, E. "The Development of the French Version of the MBTI in Canada and in France." *Journal of Psychological Type* 20 (1990): 3–15.

Choiniere, R., and D. Keirsey. *Presidential Temperament: The Unfolding Character in Forty Presidents of the United States.* Del Mar, Calif.: Prometheus Nemesis, 1992.

Cima, R. L. *The ACTS Model Handbook: An Approach to Providing Treatment to Children in Residential Care Facilities.* Colton, Calif.: R. L. Cima, 1989.

Cobb, V., and K. Darling. *Bet You Can't!: Science Impossibilities to Fool You.* New York: Lothrop, Lee & Shepard, 1980.

Cook, M. *Think About It!: Mathematics Problems of the Day.* Palo Alto, Calif.: Creative Publications, 1982.

Delunas, E. *Survival Games Personalities Play.* Carmel, Calif.: Sunflower, 1992.

DiTiberio, J. K., and G. H. Jensen. *Writing and Personality: Finding Your Voice, Your Style, Your Way.* Palo Alto, Calif.: Davies-Black Publishing, 1995.

Fairhurst, A. M., and L. V. Berens. *Temperament Assessment Card Sort.* Huntington Beach, Calif.: Telos Publications, 1990.

Farris, D. *Type Tales: Teaching Type to Children.* Palo Alto, Calif.: Davies-Black Publishing, 1991.

Fourqurean, J., C. Meisgeier, P. Swank, and E. Murphy. "Investigating the Relationship Between Academic Ability and Type Preference in Children." *Journal of Psychological Type* 16 (1988): 38–41.

Gardner, H. *Frames of Mind: The Theory of Multiple Intelligences.* New York: Basic Books, 1983.

Germane, J. *Balancing Spontaneity and Structure Across the JP Dimension.* Gladwyne, Penn.: Type and Temperament, Inc., 1988.

Germane, J. "JP Holds the Key: Applications and Implications of the JP Index." *APT Bulletin of Psychological Type* 13 (1990): 34–38.

Giovannoni, L. C., L. V. Berens, and S. A. Cooper. *Introduction to Temperament,* 3d ed. Huntington Beach, Calif.: Telos Publications, 1988.

Golay, K. *Learning Patterns and Temperament Styles: A Systematic Guide to Maximizing Student Achievement.* Fullerton, Calif.: Manas-Systems, 1982.

Hammer, A. L. *Introduction to Type and Careers.* Palo Alto, Calif.: Consulting Psychologists Press, 1993.

Hart, H. "Psychological Types of Students Attending a High School Credit Remediation Program for Students at Risk of Not Graduating." *Journal of Psychological Type* 22 (1991). 48–51.

Hirsch, E. D. Jr. *Cultural Literacy: What Every American Needs to Know.* Boston: Houghton Mifflin, 1987.

Hirsh, S., and J. Kummerow. *Life Types: Understand Yourself and Make the Most of Who You Are....* New York: Warner Books, 1989.

Huitt, W. G. "Problem Solving and Decision Making: Consideration of Individual Differences Using the Myers-Briggs Type Indicator." *Journal of Psychological Type* 24 (1992): 33–44.

Inclan, A. F. "The Development of the Spanish Version of the Myers-Briggs Type Indicator, Form G." *Journal of Psychological Type* 11 (1986): 35–46.

Isachsen, O., and L. V. Berens. *Working Together: A Personality-Centered Approach to Management.* Coronado, Calif.: Neworld Management Press, 1988.

Johnson, T. B. "Type: An Alternative to ADD/ADHD Diagnosis." *Bulletin of Psychological Type* 18 (1995): 35–37.

Keirsey, D. *Drugged Obedience in the School: Experimental Narcotherapy Versus Logical Consequences for Chronic Mischief in the Classrooms.* Del Mar, Calif.: Prometheus Nemesis, 1988.

Keirsey, D., and M. Bates. *Please Understand Me: Character and Temperament Types,* 5th ed. Del Mar, Calif.: Prometheus Nemesis, 1984.

Keirsey, D., and M. Bates. *Please Understand Me: The Video.* Del Mar, Calif.: Prometheus Nemesis, 1994.

Keirsey, D. *Abuse It—Lose It.* Del Mar, Calif.: Prometheus Nemesis, 1989.

Keirsey, D. *Portraits of Temperament,* 2d ed. Del Mar, Calif.: Prometheus Nemesis, 1988.

Kennedy, J. F. *Profiles of Courage,* mem. ed. New York: Harper & Row, 1964.

Kretschmer, E. *Physique and Character.* London: Harcourt Brace, 1925.

Kroeger, O., and J. M. Thuesen. *Type Talk.* New York: Dell, 1988.

Lathey, J. W. "Temperament Style as a Predictor of Academic Achievement in Early Adolescence." *Journal of Psychological Type* 22 (1991): 52–58.

Lawrence, C. M., A. W. Galloway, and G. Lawrence. *The Practice Centers Approach to Seatwork: A Handbook.* New York: McKenzie, 1988.

Lawrence, G. D. *People Types and Tiger Stripes: A Practical Guide to Learning Styles,* 2d ed. Gainesville, Fla.: Center for Applications of Psychological Type, 1989.

Lipson, G. B., and E. B. Lipson. *Everyday Law for Young Citizens.* Carthage, Ill.: Good Apple, 1988.

McCarley, N. G., and T. G. Carskadon. "The Perceived Accuracy of Elements of the Descriptions of Myers and Keirsey Among Men and Women: Which Elements Are Most Accurate, Should the Type Descriptions Be Different for Men and Women, and Do the Type Descriptions Stereotype Sensing Types?" *Journal of Psychological Type* 11 (1986): 2–29.

McCaulley, M. H. "Orchestrating Educational Change in the 90s." *Bulletin of Psycholological Type* 17 (1994): 26–28.

McCaulley, M. H., G. P. Macdaid, and R. I. Kainz. "Estimated Frequencies of the MBTI Types." *Journal of Psychological Type* 9 (1985): 3–9.

McCaulley, M. H. *The Myers-Briggs Type Indicator and the Teaching-Learning Process.* Gainesville, Fla.: Center for Applications of Psychological Type,1976.

Mclear, C. T., and F. Pitchford. "African-American Science Student Learning Style." *APT IX Meeting the Challenge, Psychological Type for the 90s Conference Proceedings,* Halifax County, N.C. (1991): 4c–9c.

Meisgeier, C., and C. Meisgeier with M. Meisgeier. *A Parent's Guide to Type: Individual Differences at Home and in School.* Palo Alto, Calif.: Consulting Psychologists Press, 1989.

Meisgeier, C., E. Murphy, and C. Meisgeier. *A Teacher's Guide to Type: A New Perspective on Individual Differences in the Classroom.* Palo Alto, Calif.: Consulting Psychologists Press, 1989.

Meisgeier, C., and E. Murphy. *Murphy-Meisgeier Type Indicator for Children Manual.* Palo Alto, Calif.: Consulting Psychologists Press, 1987.

Minton, L. "Fresh Voices." *Parade* (15 May 1994): 10–11.

Murphy, E. "Education." *APT Bulletin of Psychological Type* 13 (1991): 26–27.

Murphy, E. "Education." *APT Bulletin of Psychological Type* 14 (1991): 30–31.

Murphy, E. *I Am a Good Teacher.* Gainesville, Fla.: Center for Applications of Psychological Type, 1987.

Murphy, E. "Following the APT Ethical Guidelines." *Bulletin of Psychological Type* (1995): 12, 14.

Murphy, E. *Questions Children May Have About Type Differences.* Gainesville, Fla.: Center for Applications of Psychological Type, 1987.

Murphy, E. *The Developing Child: Using Jungian Type to Understand Children.* Palo Alto, Calif.: Davies-Black Publishing, 1992.

Murphy, E., and C. Meisgeier. *Murphy-Meisgeier Type Indicator for Children.* Palo Alto, Calif.: Consulting Psychologists Press, 1987.

Myers, I. B., with P. B. Myers. *Gifts Differing: Understanding Personality Type.* Palo Alto, Calif.: Davies-Black Publishing, 1980, 1995.

Myers, I. B. *Introduction to Type.* Palo Alto, Calif.: Consulting Psychologists Press, 1993.

Myers, I. B., and M. H. McCaulley. *Manual: A Guide to the Development and Use of the Myers-Briggs Type Indicator.* Palo Alto, Calif.: Consulting Psychologists Press, 1985.

Niednagel, J. P. *How to Choose Your Best Sport and Play It.* Laguna Niguel, Calif.: Laguna Press, 1992.

Pearman, R. R. "Ethics of Type." *Bulletin of Psychological Type* 18 (1995): 9–10.

Petersen, P. A. "Personality Type of Adolescents and Their Imaged Personal Heroes." *Journal of Psychological Type* 27 (1993): 17–26.

Provost, J. A., and S. Anchors. *Applications of the Myers-Briggs Type Indicator in Higher Education.* Palo Alto, Calif.: Davies-Black Publishing, 1987.

Provost, J. A. *Procrastination: Using Psychological Type Concepts to Help Students.* Gainesville, Fla.: Center for Applications of Psychological Type, 1988.

Provost, J. A. *Work, Play, and Type: Achieving Balance in Your Life.* Palo Alto, Calif.: Davies-Black Publishing, 1990.

Quenk, N. L. *Beside Ourselves: Our Hidden Personality in Everyday Life.* Palo Alto, Calif.: Davies-Black Publishing, 1993.

Reich, R. *The Work of Nations: Preparing Ourselves for 21st-Century Capitalism.* New York: Knopf, 1991.

Roach, B. *Strategy Styles and Management Types.* Proactive Management Association, Notre Dame, Ind.: 1987.

Rogers, C. *Counseling and Psychotherapy.* Boston: Houghton Mifflin, 1942.

Rowse, A. L., ed. *The Annotated Shakespeare.* New York: Greenwich House, 1978.

Ruhl, D. L., and R. F. Rodgers. "The Perceived Accuracy of the 16 Type Descriptions of Myers and Keirsey: A Replication of McCarley and Carskadon." *Journal of Psychological Type* 23 (1992): 22–26.

Rytting, M. "Androgynous Archetypes: Clarifying the Relationship Between Type and Archetype." *Journal of Psychological Type* 20 (1990): 16–24.

Saunders, F. W. *Katharine and Isabel: Mother's Light, Daughter's Journey.* Palo Alto, Calif.: Davies-Black Publishing, 1991.

Scanlan, S., ed. "Gestures: What Your Hands Reveal About You." *The Type Reporter* 8 (1989): 1–4.

Scanlan, S., ed. "Kidtypes, Parts 1–4." *The Type Reporter* 5 (1992): 47–50.

Scanlan, S., ed. "Relax Mom, You're Doing a Great Job, Parts 1–4." *The Type Reporter* (1991): 40–43.

Scanlan, S., ed. "Older and Wiser, Part 1." *The Type Reporter* 55 (1994): 2.

Scanlan, S., ed. "Teaching and Learning." *The Type Reporter* 2:2 (fall 1985): 1–20.

Scanlan, S., ed. "Type and the Brain, Parts 1–6." *The Type Reporter* 3 (1987–1988): 1–6.

Schurr, K. T., and L. W. Henriksen. "Tests and Psychological Types for Nurses and Teachers: Classroom Achievement and Standardized Test Scores Measuring Specific Training Objectives and General Ability." *Journal of Psychological Type* 23 (1992): 38–44.

Schurr, K. T., L. W. Henricksen, D. E. Moore, and A. F. Witting. "A Comparison of Teaching Effectiveness and NTE Core Battery Scores for SJ and a Combined Group of NJ, NP, and SP First-Year Teachers." *Journal of Psychological Type* 25 (1993): 24–30.

Silver, H. F., and J. R. Hanson. *Learning Styles and Strategies.* Moorestown, N.J.: Hanson Silver & Associates, 1986.

Silver, H. F., and J. R. Hanson. *Teaching Styles and Strategies: Techniques for Meeting the Diverse Needs and Styles of Learners.* Moorestown, N.J.: Hanson Silver & Associates, 1986.

Sim, H., and J. Sim. "The Development and Validation of the Korean Version of the MBTI." *Journal of Psychological Type* 26 (1993): 18–27.

Singer, M. "Cognitive Style and Reading Comprehension." *Journal of Psychological Type* 17 (1989): 31–35.

Smith, J. B. "Teachers' Grading Styles: The Languages of Feeling and Thinking." *Journal of Psychological Type* 26(1993): 37–41.

Spranger, E. *Types of Men.* New York: Johnson Reprint Company, 1966.

Thorne, A., and H. Gough. *Portraits of Type: An MBTI Research Compendium.* Palo Alto, Calif.: Davies-Black Publishing, 1991.

Tieger, P. D., and B. Barron-Tieger. *Do What You Are: Discover the Perfect Career for You Through the Secrets of Personality Type.* Boston: Little Brown, 1992.

Twigg, C. A. "The Need for a National Learning Infrastructure." *Educom Review* 29 (1994): 4–6.

Ware, R., and C. Yokomoto. "Perceived Accuracy of Myers-Briggs Type Indicator Descriptions Using Keirsey Profiles." *Journal of Psychological Type* 10 (1985): 27–31.

Weber, J. "Learning a Costly Lesson on Computers." *Los Angeles Times* (14 May 1994): A1, A20.

Williams, M. Q., T. F. Williams, X Qisheng, and L. Xuemei. "A Glimpse of the Psychological Types of Mainland Chinese Undergraduates." *Journal of Psychological Type* 23 (1992): 3–9.

Wirths, C. G., and M. Bowman-Kruhm. *Are You My Type? or Why Aren't You More Like Me?* Palo Alto, Calif.: Davies-Black Publishing, 1992.

Wirths, C. G., and M. Bowman-Kruhm. *Choosing Is Confusing: How to Make Good Choices, Not Bad Guesses.* Palo Alto, Calif.: Davies-Black Publishing, 1994.

Wirths, C. G., and M. Bowman-Kruhm. *Upgrade: The High-Tech Road to School Success.* Palo Alto, Calif.: Davies-Black Publishing, 1995.

Wynn, M. *Empowering African-American Males to Succeed: A Ten-Step Approach for Parents and Teachers.* South Pasadena, Calif.: Rising Sun Publishing, 1992.

Zeisset, C. "Adapting Teaching Styles to the Four Quadrants." *Meeting the Challenge, Psychological Type for the 90s Conference Proceedings,* Richmond, Va.: Association for Psychological Type, 1991.

Zigler, Z. *Goals.* Niles, Ill.: Nightingale-Conant Corporation, 1992.

About the Authors

Alice M. Fairhurst has been active in teaching and training for more than thirty years. Her interest in teaching and learning has led to work at and observation of behavior in elementary, high school, and college levels, as well as in youth organizations and corporate settings. She has made presentations on the subject of education and dropout prevention for various groups, including the Los Angeles County School District. The author of computer training manuals and various training workbooks, she is currently The Career Development and Monitoring Coordinator at the Jet Propulsion Laboratory, California Institute of Technology.

Lisa L. Fairhurst has been teaching or tutoring for more than a decade. A specialist in applied math, she has taught middle school students, tutored high school and college students, and is currently a home teacher for students in grades one through twelve. Most of her students have been minority students and/or students from disadvantaged backgrounds. The University of California at Riverside recognized her for her Outstanding Contribution to the Educational and Personal Growth of High School Students.

Index